SEEKING TRUTH IN AMERICA

Mark S. Singel

Mechanicsburg, PA USA

Published by Sunbury Press, Inc.
Mechanicsburg, PA USA

www.sunburypress.com

Copyright © 2023 by Mark S. Singel.
Cover Copyright © 2023 by Sunbury Press, Inc.

Sunbury Press supports copyright. Copyright fuels creativity, encourages diverse voices, promotes free speech, and creates a vibrant culture. Thank you for buying an authorized edition of this book and for complying with copyright laws. Except for the quotation of short passages for the purpose of criticism and review, no part of this publication may be reproduced, scanned, or distributed in any form without permission. You are supporting writers and allowing Sunbury Press to continue to publish books for every reader. For information contact Sunbury Press, Inc., Subsidiary Rights Dept., PO Box 548, Boiling Springs, PA 17007 USA or legal@sunburypress.com.

For information about special discounts for bulk purchases, please contact Sunbury Press Orders Dept. at (855) 338-8359 or orders@sunburypress.com.

To request one of our authors for speaking engagements or book signings, please contact Sunbury Press Publicity Dept. at publicity@sunburypress.com.

FIRST SUNBURY PRESS EDITION: October 2023

Set in Adobe Garamond Pro | Interior design by Crystal Devine | Cover by Lawrence Knorr | Edited by Lawrence Knorr.

Publisher's Cataloging-in-Publication Data
Names: Singel, Mark S., author.
Title: Seeking truth in American / Mark S. Singel.
Description: First trade paperback edition. | Mechanicsburg, PA : Sunbury Press, 2023.
Summary: Mark S. Singel, the former Lieutenant Governor of Pennsylvania, provides insight and wisdom from his various recent op-eds that appeared in local newspapers.
Identifiers: ISBN : 979-8-88819-144-6 (paperback) | ISBN : 979-8-88819-145-3 (ePub).
Subjects: POLITICAL SCIENCE / Commentary & Opinion | POLITICAL SCIENCE / American Government / General | HISTORY / United States / 21st Century.

Product of the United States of America
0 1 1 2 3 5 8 13 21 34 55

For the Love of Books!

CONTENTS

Author's Note and Introduction   v

PART ONE: Early OP-EDs   1

PART TWO: 2020 OP-EDs   33

PART THREE: 2021 OP-EDs   97

PART FOUR: 2022 Articles   155

PART FIVE: 2023 Articles   241

Selected Bibliography   283

About the Author   290

AUTHOR'S NOTE AND INTRODUCTION

When the folks at *PennLive* asked me to write a weekly op-ed column, I welcomed the opportunity. I had been in and around government for the past forty-five years and believed that I had developed a unique perspective on politics and politicians that might be of some value as we all lived through the chaos of recent years.

My service on congressional staff in Washington, as a Pennsylvania senator, and as lieutenant governor and acting governor of Pennsylvania taught me about the merit and practicality of moderation in dealing with public policy. Public service was a high calling for me. I was determined to get beyond partisan bickering to achieve consensus wherever possible for the good of my commonwealth and country. By putting pen to paper every week during recent tumultuous times in Washington and throughout the pandemic, I collected my thoughts and offered readers a level-headed analysis of what was happening around us. I didn't hesitate to express my outrage when offensive policies and pronouncements spewed from some of our leaders. Much of my angst derived from the destruction of our democratic traditions, and I found it shameful when fear and hatred became commonplace in the rhetoric of political leaders. It was shocking when the peaceful transition of power gave way to riotous mobs at the Capitol and throughout the country. The ability to speak out through these columns was not just a task for me; it seemed like my duty.

Some of the pieces reflect on things that were very personal to me. The loss of a close friend in the prime of his life (On Human Suffering), the monstrous invasion of Ukraine (We Are Ukraine), and the occasional glimmer of true statesmanship (Bipartisanship) aroused in me a sense of compassion that I tried to convey.

David Crosby passed away recently. He was the artist who brought complex harmonies to classic songs like "Guinevere," "Suite: Judy Blue Eyes," and "Déjà vu." Together with Stephen Stills, Graham Nash, and Neil Young, Crosby brought music that was pitch-perfect into troubled times. In his protest song "Almost Cut My Hair," he explained why he was willing to address the madness. He said he felt like he owed it to someone.

The articles I present to you in this volume are meant to provoke some thought and, perhaps, some action at the time. My inspiration for them was always the desire to make this country and this state a better place. As citizens of this great nation, we have an obligation to pursue what the Founding Fathers called "a more perfect union."

I feel like we all owe it to them.

I would like to acknowledge the continued support for this and all my endeavors from my wife, Jackie. My thanks also go out to the folks at Sunbury Press who handled their editing chores with professionalism. Special recognition goes to Ms. Felicity Aldous who provided valuable research assistance. I have no doubt that she and her siblings will write their own success stories in the coming years.

PART ONE

EARLY OP-EDS

OF POWER, POETRY, AND POSTURING

NOVEMBER 23, 2015

John Fitzgerald Kennedy visited Amherst College to dedicate the Robert Frost Library in October 1963. He was returning a favor posthumously to the poet who had recited "The Gift Outright" at JFK's inauguration less than one hundred days before. He said, "When power leads men towards arrogance, poetry reminds him of his limitations. When power narrows the areas of man's concern, poetry reminds him of the richness and diversity of existence. When power corrupts, poetry cleanses."

The rest of the speech was more than a paean to the great poet; it appealed to us all to rise above the mundane aspects of our lives and choose, in Frost's words, "something like a star."

Words matter.

When leaders use them correctly, they can take us, as Lincoln did, toward the "better angels of our nature." Abraham Lincoln's second inaugural sought to staunch the still-bleeding wounds of the Civil War. He called for "malice toward none and charity toward all."

Most presidents shared similar moments of inspiration at critical times in our history. They subjugated their prominence to the human spirit of the citizens from whom their power derived. Most of them understood that America was not good because of her greatness.

America was great because of her goodness.

> *You will ever remember that all the end of study is to make you a good man and a useful citizen.*
> —John Adams

> *Older men declare war. But it is youth that must fight and die. And it is youth who must inherit the tribulation, the sorrow, and the triumphs that are the aftermath of war.*
> —*Herbert Hoover*

> *No problem of human making is too great to be overcome by human ingenuity, human energy, and the untiring hope of the human spirit.*
> —*George H.W. Bush*

When leaders misuse words, they dampen human potential, and they can incite people to the mayhem of bad choices. We should expect thoughtfulness and compassion from candidates who seek the presidency.

Instead, listen to the words of Trump:

> *I will build a great wall—and nobody builds walls better than me, believe me—and I'll build them very inexpensively. I will build a great, great wall on our southern border, and I will make Mexico pay for that wall. Mark my words [. . .]. When Mexico sends its people, they're not sending the best [. . .]. They're sending people that have lots of problems and they're bringing those problems with us. They're bringing drugs. They're bringing crime. They're rapists [. . .]. And some, I assume, are good people [. . .]. He's not a war hero, U.S. Senator John McCain. He's a war hero because he was captured. I like people that weren't captured, OK, I hate to tell you [. . .]. I want surveillance of these people and of certain mosques. We've had it before; we will have it again [. . .]. I'm putting people on notice that are coming here from Syria as part of this mass migration that if I win, they're going back!*

Franklin D. Roosevelt had these comments about his job:

> *The presidency is not merely an administrative office. That's the least of it. It is more than an engineering job, efficient or inefficient. It is pre-eminently a place of moral leadership.*

Mr. Trump has demonstrated by his venom that he has neither the temperament nor the wisdom to supply such moral leadership. I am confident that clear-thinking citizens will recognize that fact and soon eliminate him from serious consideration. In the meantime, I am waiting for someone in either party to try to approach the poetry and aspirations of the young John Kennedy. In his first press conference, a reporter asked him to define his role as president.

"To exercise power along the lines of excellence," said the poet-in-chief.

FIGHTING FOR CIVILITY

MARCH 8, 2019

Representative Ilhan Omar, a freshman Democrat from Minnesota, recently blurted comments suggesting that some elected officials might have "dual loyalties" to America and Israel. This was a clear anti-Semitic trope that needed to be denounced. What's worse is that Omar has said similar offensive things in the past. While she has apologized for those remarks, her recent ones drew formal action from the U.S. House of Representatives.

Within days of her comments, the House overwhelmingly adopted a resolution condemning them. By a vote of 407-23, Republicans and Democrats clearly said there was no place for anti-Semitism, anti-Muslim discrimination, or any other type of hatred in our public discourse.

They did the right thing.

It is worth taking a moment to be much clearer about bigotry of any form. Omar's past and current comments are unacceptable and unbecoming of anyone—especially someone who holds public office. Period. Speaker Pelosi made that clear in her repudiation of Omar's comments and quickly guided the resolution through the House.

Republicans were quick to point out that the Speaker did grant some leeway to the freshman. Omar was not censured; she did not lose her committee assignments. Speaker Pelosi chose instead to move with some finesse in the china shop that is the U.S. Congress.

Critics will say that Pelosi was too lenient. Perhaps, but consider the freshman class she now leads; they are historically youthful, diverse, and under more scrutiny than previous politicians. There will be gaffes. The challenge for Pelosi, Hoyer, and others is to nurture the idealism and energy of their new colleagues but to be able to rein them in when necessary. This resolution was a good example of leadership walking that fine line.

As for the cries from the Right about "disarray in the Democratic Caucus" or "institutional intolerance" in the Democratic Party, the best response is to quote the vice president and potential presidential candidate Joe Biden: "That's a bunch of malarkey." Attacking all Democrats for some missteps of one member is like benching the entire Phillies lineup if Bryce Harper strikes out. Clearly, a better approach would be to work with your players to improve their skills and make them the best performers they can be.

Democrats remain a party of inclusion and tolerance. Just compare the demographic make-up of the two parties in Congress. Forty-one new Democrats arrived in the House in January. Of these, more than a third identify as people of color. Only 2 percent of new Republicans do.

The 116th Congress features fifty-five black members, forty-four who identify as Hispanic or Latino, and four Native Americans. These, overwhelmingly, are Democrats. *U.S. News and World Report* also delved into religious affiliations in the new Congress. It reports, "More than 99 percent of Republicans identify as Christian compared to 78 percent of Democrats. Less than 1 percent of GOP members are Jewish, while over 11 percent of Democrats say the same. All Buddhists, Muslims, Hindus, and religiously unaffiliated lawmakers are Democrats."

Sadly, over the past two years, it has been the Republican Party—not the Democrats—who have acquiesced to the cruel and hateful rhetoric that streams from the White House regularly. The Republicans have not challenged administration policies that oppress Muslims, minorities, and migrants.

On the issue of immigration, for example, it may be timely to remember what the first Republican president, Abraham Lincoln, had to say after the successful implementation of the Act to Encourage Immigration which was signed on July 4, 1864: "I regard our immigrants as one of the replenishing streams appointed by Providence to repair the ravages of internal war and its waste of national strength and health."

Democrats and Republicans have an opportunity to move forward from the current distraction of a few misguided comments. Lincoln set the example by celebrating the contributions of immigrants and urging tolerance throughout his career. Those are guiding principles that should transcend party politics. As we move forward, it bears repeating that we must cooperate civilly.

Consider the story of President John F. Kennedy, who was at NASA to deliver a speech to inspire the nation to support the Apollo moon project. He took a wrong turn and ended up in a broom closet where a janitor was cleaning his mop.

"What do you do here?" asked the president.

Without hesitation, the janitor said, "I'm putting a man on the moon."

Civility is an achievement as important as any space mission. In that effort, we are all in it together.

THE PRESIDENTIAL MADNESS BEGINS

MARCH 21, 2019

Several years ago, investor and industrialist Warren Buffett made the ultimate sports betting challenge. He offered $1 billion to anybody who could correctly fill out all the NCAA March Madness brackets. Buffett, an expert in risk management, knew his money was safe. According to mathematicians, the odds of selecting the winner in all sixty-three games are 9.2 quintillion to one!

It is literally easier to pick a president than it is to master March Madness, but there are similarities.

Much like college teams invited to the show, most presidential candidates have the prerequisites to play. They have been U.S. senators, governors, or cabinet-level officials. Occasionally a celebrity or a businessman brings a different perspective to the presidential tournament, and most demonstrate quickly that they are ready for the competition.

Another similarity between basketball and politics is that "stuff" happens. Championship teams lose players to the pros or injuries, and suddenly there are no longer top seeds. Candidates have a slip of the tongue or face withering criticism, and they quickly become "also-rans."

Also, like the sixty-four-team field in the NCAA tournament, presidential politics attracts a variety of entrants. The number of participants increases dramatically if the dominant player no longer seems so dominant. It may not be a full sixty-four-team field, but the Democrats will surely bring at least a sweet sixteen to the game. Who will survive the early primaries depends on so many factors that any prediction would be nothing more than a guess.

It would be foolhardy to defy the odds to take on such an errand, but here it goes; on the Republican side, no serious challenge seems to be developing for

President Trump. Yes, Weld of Massachusetts, Kasich of Ohio, and Hogan of Maryland have their followings, but all are likely to fold before the finals.

The Democrats, hailing mostly from the coastal conferences, are another story. Look for spirited contests among the current sweet sixteen and some bracket-busting surprises. While Kamala Harris and Beto O'Rourke seem off to strong starts, Bernie Sanders has a proven, loyal base of supporters and will likely be strong in the early primary states. And don't forget the candidate with the most name recognition and the early lead in the polls, Joe Biden. When Joe announces, the entire tone of the competition shifts and, for most, may end up being a battle for second place on the ticket.

Yes, it looks like a face-off between President Trump and Vice President Joe Biden. I am also confident that the Democrats can avoid the spectacle of personal assaults that plagued the GOP in 2016. Collaboration may be the key to their success in 2020.

The fact that a new team forms right in the middle of the tournament is one of the most exciting nuances of the political process. A Biden-Beto ticket might be a winner in the crucial states of Texas and Pennsylvania. A Booker-Harris ticket covers demographic and geographic ground well.

While March Madness is terrifically entertaining for sports fans, the presidential contest directly impacts us all. It's time for all of us to tune in, make our selections and let the games begin!

WILLIAM BARR AND THE CALL OF DUTY

APRIL 12, 2019

On a Saturday night in October 1973, President Nixon fired Special Prosecutor Archibald Cox, who was closing in on the misdeeds of Watergate. Attorney General Elliott Richardson and Deputy Attorney General William Ruckelshaus resigned in protest. Cox spoke for all three of them when he said, "Whether ours shall continue to be a government of laws and not of men is now up to the Congress and the American people."

While President Trump stopped short of firing Special Prosecutor Bob Mueller, it was not for lack of trying. He made his feelings known to the White House and justice personnel in countless tweets and mutterings. During the investigation, Trump, like Nixon, did everything he could to stymie Mueller's efforts. He stirred up his base with countless charges of a "witch hunt," he fired his FBI director and said on national TV that it was "because of the Russia thing." He publicly humiliated his attorney general until Jeff Sessions left with his tail between his legs. Then, upon release of the report, the president proceeded to take a victory lap based on an utterly false interpretation of what the report said.

The president now comes before the American people with his new, hand-picked attorney general. At first blush, William Barr is an appropriate choice. His credentials are strong. He served many presidents and enjoyed a reputation as a straight shooter.

Recent developments say otherwise.

Barr essentially auditioned for the position of attorney general with a nineteen-paged memo proclaiming that a president could not be indicted for obstruction of justice. In other words, he declared his bias against any alternate recommendation by Mueller before he was confirmed. Then, upon release of the Mueller report, Barr rushed out a summary of the two-year, four-hundred page report designed to give the president his talking point of "no collusion." On the issue of obstruction, Barr substituted his get-out-of-jail-free card even though Mueller clearly stated that he could not exonerate the president on that issue.

The Mueller team has complained about the limited information released and the opportunity for the false narrative it handed to the president. Instead of taking a principled position on getting the full array of information to Congress and the American people, the attorney general told the president what he wanted to hear. Cox, Richardson, and Ruckelshaus sacrificed their careers rather than cut those corners.

But we are not done here. For Barr, there is the all-important matter of what happens next. Barr can redeem himself by releasing an unredacted Mueller report to Congress. Yes, some grand jury and national security excisions must be made, but, for the most part, the American public needs to know just what Mueller found out in his two-year investigation.

This is where Barr is coming up short. In testimony before Congress, he has outlined four different categories of redactions that could result in a Sharpee festival of missing pages.

In addition, he has opined, without proof, that the FBI may have illegally spied in the 2016 elections and that an inspector general's review is underway.

The New York Times reported, "Current and former law enforcement officials have defended their handling of the Russia investigation, saying it was carefully handled based on available evidence, and they have firmly denied engaging in political spying. Those current and former officials have argued they were obligated to investigate allegations that Trump associates might be conspiring with Russians to interfere in the election."

Claiming that our own FBI illegally spied on their candidate may be music to the ears of the MAGA-hatters, but it is exactly the wrong position for the nation's top law enforcement official to take. Mr. Barr must be reminded that he is the people's lawyer, not the president's defender. As one pundit said, "Trump may have found his Roy Cohn." George Santayana wrote, "Those who can't remember the past are condemned to repeat it."

Mr. Barr has one more chance to show that he is up to his office's ethical and historical demands. Release the Mueller report as completely as possible. Let it speak for itself.

RUN, JOE, RUN

MAY 1, 2019

On January 12, 1991, I visited several congressional delegation members in Washington. This was a business trip to round up support for a few important federal initiatives to the state. I was serving as lieutenant governor at the time. While our two Republican U.S. senators were responsive, I couldn't resist scheduling some time with Pennsylvania's other senator, Joe Biden, to talk politics.

The sun lit up the U.S. Capitol outside the window of Biden's office in the Russell Senate Office Building. He looked through slatted blinds directly into those rays for a few moments before he noticed me in the room. We did not talk politics that day; we talked war.

Saddam Hussein had invaded Kuwait, and the Senate was about to vote on a resolution authorizing military force in Operation Desert Storm. While President George H.W. Bush had put together strong international support for the effort, and Hussein's aggression had to be addressed, Senator Joe Biden wrestled with the most difficult decision leaders must make, which is putting soldiers in harm's way. I was stunned when he asked me directly, "What would you do on the resolution?"

"I would support the president on this one," I said.

The gentleman from Delaware shook his head slowly and said, "As Odysseus told Achilles: war is young men dying and old men talking."

Joe Biden walked across the Capitol Plaza and voted for the resolution. It passed 52-47, the closest vote on the authorization of war powers since the War of 1812.

Since that encounter, Joe Biden wrapped up a career in the U.S. Senate, spent eight years as vice president, and put his ambition for president on hold as he grappled with the wrenching loss of his son, Beau. He earned the Medal of Freedom after fifty years of distinguished public service, with President Obama saying forthrightly: "He is the best vice president America has ever had."

The first statement Biden made when he announced his candidacy for president cut right to the essence of the fight and demonstrated the passion and depth of the candidate: "Our country," Biden said, "is locked in a battle for the soul of this nation." He then took his challenge directly to the president: "In the two years since I left the White House, we've seen this administration praise neo-Nazis and white supremacists and rip families apart at the border. This isn't who we are [. . .]. It's time to treat each other with dignity again. Build a middle class that works for everybody. Fight back against the incredible abuses of power we're seeing. It's time to dig deep and remember that our best days still lie ahead."

Even the most partisan Republicans must admit that the announcement was a tour de force. After a bit of fundraising and a rally in the critical electoral battleground of Pennsylvania, Biden was off to Iowa to repeat his message of fairness for working families and a front office committed to solutions, not self-aggrandizement.

In the first three days of his active campaign, his polling numbers shot up to nearly 40 percent in a twenty-candidate field. Elizabeth Warren and Bernie Sanders, the closest competitors, found their numbers stagnating at 12 percent and 11 percent, respectively. To be sure, there is a talented field of other Democratic candidates, and individual political fortunes will ebb and flow in the months ahead. But Joe Biden has climbed onto the bronco and is riding tall in the saddle so far.

One of the reasons for the Democratic warm embrace is electability. While the Mueller report did not exonerate the president and has raised issues that Congress can't ignore, it is safe to say that most Democratic activists were disappointed with its tepid pronouncements. The report did not bring the sky down on President Trump, and it is becoming clear that the voters themselves will have to do that. Democrats, post-Mueller, have gotten serious about one thing: winning.

The surge in Joe Biden's number is directly proportional to his perceived ability to rebuild the "blue wall" of Pennsylvania, Ohio, Michigan, and Wisconsin. Other candidates can present their paths to 271 electoral votes, but Joe Biden has done it before. The barrage of tweets and the puerile name-calling emanating from the White House shows that Joe Biden presents a serious threat.

But Joe Biden is a gifted campaigner and a mature leader who looks ready for the onslaught. He also happens to be able to quote Homer's Iliad.

Run, Joe, run.

TAX CREDITS FOR EDUCATION: A BALANCING ACT

MAY 11, 2019

Pennsylvania's commitment to public education goes back to 1824 when a law called for establishing schools where all children should be admitted and taught without regard to social or financial status. That law was voluntary, and few localities could afford that investment on their own. It was not until Governor George Wolf, a progressive Democrat, called for a state-funded school system that things began to happen. In the 1833-34 legislative session, a joint committee explored the subject and passed the Free School Act with strong bipartisan support.

It was not long before citizens discovered that providing education for all would not be easy or cheap. The threat of new taxes caused a munity in the very next session. The House was flooded with petitions asking for a repeal of the law, and Free Schools seemed doomed.

It was in this atmosphere that Thaddeus Stevens, a young representative from Lancaster, rose to give his famous "Free Schools Speech" on April 11, 1835.

> *So cast our votes that the blessing of education shall be conferred on every son of Pennsylvania; shall be carried home to the poorest child of the poorest inhabitant of your mountains so that even he may be prepared to act well his part in this land of freemen.*

On the strength of his arguments, the legislature abruptly halted the repeal effort and, in fact, increased funding for the public school experiment.

Pennsylvania took its place as the leader in education and went on to enshrine the principle of a "thorough and efficient education" for all children in its Constitution.

Today, education accounts for about 25 percent of the state's expenditures. We spend about $15,000 per student per year. These are staggering numbers that critics say may not meet the efficiency criteria.

There have been movements to alter the current structure of public education. Governors Thornburg and Ridge fought for a voucher alternative allowing parents to move students into private settings. Charter Schools and other options have been added to the mix.

Recently, a creative way of bringing corporate support to education came from the Education Investment Tax Credit (EITC) Program. EITC provides tax credits to eligible businesses contributing to scholarship or educational improvement organizations identified by the State Department of Community and Economic Affairs. The set aside for this program is now $160,000,000, and the House recently passed a bill to increase that amount to $260,000,000 with an annual escalator of 10 percent.

Companies can get tax credits for supporting scholarships to schools of their choice. A win-win deal, right? The problem, of course, is that every dollar set aside for tax credits is one dollar less than the state must spend on education or any program. One House Democrat pointed out that, while EITC is well-intentioned, we are getting to the point that it is becoming a budget buster—especially with the escalator clause. Another points out that, at a time when the Commonwealth has 185 school districts that are still underfunded, the legislature should be looking into investing the money into those established schools and students.

Another concern argument is that EITC monies go primarily to non-public schools that may or may not accommodate low-income students. In fact, recent analyses show that up to 90 percent of the money is spent in settings outside of the public school system. By raising the income threshold for families receiving support to $90,000, the new House bill guarantees that there will be less money—not more—for low to moderate-income families. Education Chairman Jim Roebuck notes that this flies in the face of Pennsylvania's traditional support for all students—a tradition that goes back to the early 1800s and has served us well.

The House vote on expanding EITC was 111-85. This is closer than most expected. Even the governor has weighed in with his reservations about moving too fast and impacting his signature efforts to increase funding to public schools. Still, alleviating companies of a portion of their tax burden makes economic sense. Also, there is something very rational about allowing those companies to spend a portion of their tax dollars as they see fit.

Like most good ideas, the EITC program requires thoughtful oversight and balanced implementation. As the legislature moves into negotiations on the overall budget, I suspect that a compromise on the amount of this tax credit allocation will emerge.

D-DAY

MAY 29, 2019

The Normandy American Cemetery is located at the north end of a half-mile access road on a cliff overlooking Omaha Beach in Colleville-Sur-Mer, France. The nearly two-hundred-acre cemetery contains the graves of over 9,000 Americans who died on D-Day and related battles. When you walk through the rows of crosses and Stars of David, you have a profound sense of quiet, an overpowering feeling that this is sacred ground.

Most families remember ancestors who landed on Omaha Beach or participated in Operation Overlord. My colleague Charlie Gerow has deeply personal stories about heroic General Leonard Gerow and his role in restoring freedom to the planet.

I also stood on Omaha Beach and looked up at the ramparts where the monstrous German cannons rained carnage on the Allies. The invasion was the most complex military undertaking in history and perhaps the most dangerous. On June 6, 1944, one hundred and sixty thousand Allied troops landed on fifty miles of exposed beaches in Normandy, France, to fight Nazi Germany. Thirteen thousand aircraft and 6,000 ships participated in the action. Airmen flew gliders into hedgerows, not landing strips. Paratroopers dropped behind enemy lines and had to fight their way back to secure roads and bridges. Infantrymen slogged through cold, windswept waters with little expectation of reaching the beach.

In one day, the Allies broke through the German lines, but thousands of troops lay dead on the beaches or the cliffs. Stephen Ambrose wrote the definitive book on the D-Day invasion. In it, he relates the stories of hundreds of young soldiers who faced their deaths for something far greater than they could comprehend.

"Our life expectancy was about zero," Private John MacPhee declared. "We were burdened down with too much weight [. . .]. I could endure a lot of physical hardship, but I was so seasick I thought I would die. In fact, I wished I had."

Private Warren Rulien came in with the second wave. Dead soldiers floated around in the water, which had risen past the first obstacles. The lieutenant yelled, "Hey, Rulien, here I go!" and attempted to run to the shore. A machine gun cut him down. Rulien grabbed one of the bodies floating in the water and pushed it in front of him as he made his way to the shore.

Ambrose also pays tribute to a local hero, Lieutenant Richard Winters of Company E, 506th Parachute Division of the 101st Airborne. Winters parachuted in the darkness behind German lines and gathered a squad of others who had survived the jump. They secured their objective—a small town of strategic importance to the invasion and went on to attack entrenched enemy positions.

Winters's squad-sized group had one light mortar, two light machine guns, two tommy guns, and five rifles. But although Winters was outnumbered five to one and was attacking an entrenched enemy, he and his men prevailed. At the cost of four dead, two wounded, Winters and his men killed fifteen Germans, wounded many more, took twelve prisoners, and destroyed four German 105-millimeter cannons.

In his "Order of the Day," General Eisenhower told the troops: "The eyes of the world are upon you. The hopes and prayers of liberty-loving people everywhere march with you [. . .] let us all beseech the blessing of Almighty God upon this great and noble undertaking."

Another soldier who did not forget to invoke the deity was Lieutenant Winters. Just before midnight, after eighteen hours of fierce fighting, Winters, as he wrote later, "did not forget to get down on my knees and thank God for helping me live through this day and ask him for his help on D plus one."

According to Ambrose, Winters promised himself that if he lived through the war, he would find an isolated farm in central Pennsylvania and live in peace and quiet. Dick Winters found that farm in 1951 and lived peacefully in the Hershey area for sixty years.

One of the points that Ambrose makes at the end of his epic on D-Day is that the Allies brought the freedoms of their cultures to the battles with them. They were well-trained and courageous but also capable of independent thought and innovation. The German officers were constrained to take orders from Berlin, and their lockstep adherence to a flawed plan proved fatal.

Freedom matters. People like Dick Winters, Leonard Gerow, John MacPhee, and Warren Rulien demonstrated that and secured liberty for the world. Let us honor them and all who continue to serve this June 6 and every day of the year.

INDEPENDENCE DAY

JUNE 26, 2019

Folklore has it that five of the fifty-six signers of the Declaration of Independence were captured by the British as traitors and tortured before they died. Twelve had their homes burned to the ground. Two lost their sons serving in the Revolutionary Army, and another had two sons captured. Nine of the fifty-six fought and died from wounds or hardships of the Revolutionary War. While some of the details have been clouded by time, the point is that the forefathers bequeathed our nation to us through great sacrifice. They pledged their lives, fortunes, and sacred honor to that cause.

Local Tories kidnapped Richard Stockton of New Jersey just after he managed to evacuate his family from their residence. He spent several years in a British jail like a common criminal.

Thomas McKean, who would later go on to be governor of Pennsylvania, wrote that he had been "hunted like a fox by the enemy, compelled to remove my family five times in three months and at last fixed them in a little log house on the banks of the Susquehanna."

Virginia Governor Thomas Nelson is the subject of several legends. One of these has it that he led General George Washington to his own home in Yorktown, which British General Cornwallis commandeered. Nelson quietly urged Washington to turn the cannon on his own house.

People fought and died as a result of the Declaration of Independence, but the fact is that it was never a sure thing in Pennsylvania before July 4, 1776. According to historian Carl Karsch, "By the spring of 1776, independence fever had spread everywhere—everywhere, that is, except to the State House (now Independence

Hall) where the colonial Assembly was in session. [They] managed to thwart every attempt to respond to events already transforming the future nation."

Wealthy conservatives and timid moderates supported the established order of King George III. The Pennsylvania General Assembly instructed its delegates to the Continental Congress to vote *against* independence. It was the shopkeepers, the craftsmen, and the middle class who rose to oppose their own state government. These "radicals" took their fervor down the street to Carpenters' Hall, where the Continental Congress met. There they committed to taking arms for resistance and independence from the Crown.

Dr. Benjamin Rush led the Pennsylvania delegates to make a clean break with the Tory sympathizers still meeting at Independence Hall. They adopted a preliminary version of the declaration on May 15 and gave Thomas Jefferson an outline for his own famous essay. The "radicals" also went public at a protest rally at the doorstep of the general assembly. Four thousand Philadelphians joined them to demand nothing less than a new state government with the courage to act. Feeling the heat, the Pennsylvania General Assembly disbanded on June 14, clearing the way for the delegates to the Continental Congress to adopt a resolution "for the express purpose of forming a new government in this province, on the authority of the People only."

When they adjourned, the Continental Congress paved the way for disbanding and reorganizing the Pennsylvania government, and it provided a template for a declaration that Thomas Jefferson was writing a few blocks away. Pennsylvania and the nation owe their existence to the liberals willing to take on the existing power structure. It would take six years of war to turn that resistance into true independence.

My favorite Independence Day story involves an extraordinary coincidence that suggests some divine attention to our American experiment. The second and third presidents of the United States, John Adams and Thomas Jefferson, came from different social backgrounds and political camps. They were bitter rivals and kept a wary eye on each other throughout their careers. What bound them together was a love of country and a commitment to independence to take hold in this brave new world. On July 4, 1826, the entire country prayed that both statesmen would live to see the fiftieth anniversary of the signing of that document.

At midnight, Jefferson, aged eighty-three, regained consciousness for the last time and said, "This is the Fourth?" His doctor nodded, and Thomas Jefferson died in peace.

Hours later, John Adams, aged ninety, heard the cannons and a loud voice from the crowd outside his home shout, "Independence forever!" He turned to his granddaughter and asked, "Does Jefferson still survive?"

"Yes," she told him.

Adams managed a faint smile and passed away.

Stockton, McKean, Nelson, Rush, Washington, Adams, Jefferson, patriots all. God bless them, and God bless America.

IMMIGRATION: AMERICA'S STRENGTH

AUGUST 16, 2019

Recently, Ken Cuccinelli, the man who runs the U.S. Citizenship and Immigration Services for the Land of the Free, made it clear that America was no longer interested in welcoming immigrants. He went as far as to suggest that the timeless verse on the Statue of Liberty, "Give me your tired and your poor, your huddled masses yearning to breathe free," applied only to those of European descent.

The *New York Daily News* wrote, "Like his boss Trump, Cuccinelli seems to like only rich immigrants, not the millions of poor strivers fleeing oppression and destitution who sailed past the Mother of Exiles in the harbor. You know, the people who came seeking work, who built this country, who fought our wars, and whose modern-day successors do the jobs the rest of us don't want."

For the record, the Institute on Taxation and Economic Policy released a report recently stating that eleven million illegal immigrants in the United States are paying an estimated amount of $11.64 billion in federal and local taxes annually. Immigrant-owned small businesses account for between 3.7 million and 5.2 million jobs in the formal economy. Of the public U.S. companies backed by venture capital investors, 25 percent were started by immigrants. This percentage includes companies like Google, eBay, Yahoo!, Sun Microsystems, and Intel.

Immigrants are innovators and scientists. The Census Bureau notes that immigrants represent 33 percent of engineers, 27 percent of mathematicians, statisticians, and computer scientists, and 24 percent of physical scientists. Seventy-five percent of the patents won by top universities resulted from foreign-born faculty and students. The Immigration Policy Center estimates that the purchasing power of Latinos and Asians alone is over $2.2 trillion per year.

And yes, contrary to the hysteria fanned by claims that immigrants are "murderers and rapists" or that South American immigrants are an "infestation," study after study has confirmed that immigrants—documented or not—are less likely to commit crimes than native-born Americans.

At a naturalization ceremony at the White House, President Obama put it this way: "Immigration makes America stronger. Immigration makes us more prosperous. No other nation constantly renews itself, refreshes itself with the hopes, and the drive, and the optimism, and the dynamism of each new generation of immigrants."

The level of hypocrisy of the current administration and the president is stunning. The president's grandfather, Frederich Trump, immigrated to the U.S. in 1885. Elizabeth Christ, the president's grandmother, immigrated in 1902. Mary Anne Macleod Trump, the president's mother, immigrated in 1929. Two of the president's wives are first-generation immigrants; Melania's parents, Viktor and Amalija Knavs, relied on family sponsors to obtain their own green cards. This is known as "chain migration," which their son-in-law wants to abolish.

The fact is that we are all immigrants or descendants of immigrants. If all the members of Congress were sent back to their families' countries of origin, four members would be left—the number of actual Native Americans currently there.

I take this attack on immigrants personally. My grandparents came to America with nothing but their religious faith and a dream about a better life for their children. They faced a new world that required back-breaking work to survive. While they were fiercely proud of the customs of their old country, they were even prouder when they became citizens—part of the mosaic of races and religions that is the American masterpiece.

It is time to call out the xenophobia and racism of anti-immigration rhetoric and actions. When the president says that African Americans come from "s—hole countries" but that Norwegians are fine, we understand what he means. We know where he stands when he says that some white supremacists are "fine people." When he separates families and raids factories to arrest immigrant workers for the crime of wanting to provide food for their families, we know exactly what he is up to.

IMMIGRATION: AMERICA'S STRENGTH

There was a time when political leaders, regardless of party, would not stand for this hatred. Real leaders would speak out when the American beacon of freedom and tolerance was dimmed by small minds that did not respect the history or the spirit of tolerance that has always made us great.

The ideals of liberty and respect, and opportunity for people of all nationalities, creeds, and colors are embedded in our Constitution. They are etched in stone on the Statue of Liberty, and any president or anti-immigration *czar* who thumbs his nose at those noble principles fails to perform his patriotic duty as an American.

LABOR DAY

AUGUST 29, 2019

Samuel Gompers was the first president of the American Federation of Labor (AFL). He fought for workers during the darkest days of exploitation of men, women, and children and he was determined to provide dignity to the people who provided the blood, sweat, and tears that powered America's industrial revolution. The AFL grew under his leadership to million members by 1924.

At the height of his organizing career, Gompers (who did not hide his Socialist leanings), was asked what he wanted from the American economy. "More," was his simple answer. More for the steelworker at the blast furnace. More for the coal miner buried hundreds of feet underground, hunched with a pick in hand to pry coal out of two-foot coal seams. More for garment workers who sat for hours at machines stitching clothes at piece rates that required focus and determination to make their quotas.

Labor Day was first celebrated as a parade in New York City in 1882 but was not well received by the monied interests that viewed any organized labor as a threat to their bottom lines. After railroad strikes and violence at manufacturing sites, labor leaders took their cause to Congress and, eventually, won victories for working families. On June 28, 1894, President Cleveland signed the law establishing the first Monday in September as a day of rest and appreciation for labor. The federal holiday was just the beginning of the battle for workers' rights.

The labor movement had not yet matured in Western Pennsylvania when a wave of immigrants sought work in the early 1900s. Most new labor forces came from eastern Europe through Ellis Island and rode the train from New York as far as their meager savings would take them. For many of them, including

Albert Singel, this meant that Johnstown would be the place where he would seek whatever work he could find to start his life in the new world.

My grandfather, who spoke little English, didn't have a union representative when his boss sent him into the mine shafts. He and his crew would arrive before dawn and spend their days with no other light than the bulbs on their helmets. He would walk home after nightfall and, with a shot or two of Imperial Whiskey, spend a full hour stretching his back to his full height again. Albert was a man of faith. He relied on God to help him through the darkness of his labors and received "signs" occasionally. One morning shift, he heard creaking from the timbers at the mine entrance, and he heard the voice of God clearly warning the workers to stay away. The shift boss had none of it and ordered Albert and all the human mules into the mine. Albert stood his ground, and while his boss cursed him out, the mine collapsed. He and 150 other men lived to tell that story.

Another man, a jovial Irishman named John Mertle, was working at the Franklin Freight Car shop for the Bethlehem Steel company. Whether it was a sign or not, a loud metal scraping noise caught his attention. He looked up just in time to see a thirty-ton side of a railcar slip off its crane and head to earth. John Mertle, my other grandfather, jumped back in time to save himself, but all his toes were severed in the accident.

I am convinced that my grandparents survived by God's grace and that I am here because of that divine intervention.

I also firmly believe that corporate America owes its workers better consideration than my forebearers. Workers are entitled to a good day's wage for a good day of work. They deserve the respect and protection that their assignments require. There are now about fifteen million union members in the United States workforce. They all benefit from safety protections, wage increases, and benefits packages won at the bargaining table or through years of labor strife. As John Kennedy said: "Our labor unions are not narrow, self-seeking groups. They have raised wages, shortened hours, and provided supplemental benefits. Through collective bargaining and grievance procedures, they have brought justice and democracy to the shop floor."

One more observation this Labor Day: there is dignity in all work. Dr. Martin Luther King, Jr. said, "If a man is called to be a street sweeper, he should sweep streets even as Michelangelo painted, or Beethoven composed music or Shakespeare wrote poetry. He should sweep streets so well that all the hosts of heaven and earth will pause to say, here lived a great street sweeper who did his job well."

CHRISTMAS GIFTS

DECEMBER 20, 2019

Before we get to the joy of Christmas and to the welcome cleansing that it can bring to all our souls, Americans must face unfinished business.

So much is written about impeachment that it is easy to gloss over the facts and retreat to our partisan corners. My first wish for all Americans is not to let that happen. To my Republican friends especially, I ask: is it proper for any president to solicit foreign interference in our elections? Is it proper to withhold military aid from an ally to pressure them into investigating political rivals? When those actions are exposed, is it acceptable for a president to ignore subpoenas and completely obstruct Congress by muzzling witnesses and refusing to turn over even one requested document?

Abuse of power and obstruction of Congress are exactly the high crimes and misdemeanors the framers had in mind when they provided the impeachment remedy. It is, therefore, appropriate to suggest a gift for the president. As he blusters on about impeachment and the coming trial, I am hopeful that somebody provides him with a mirror this Christmas. Let him look at the real cause of our national anxiety.

But, back to the holiday season, let us focus on minor Christmas miracles. Congress and the president agreed on a spending plan that kept the government open and included goodies for both parties. The plan included increased defense spending, additional dollars for Head Start and other key domestic programs, and funding to stabilize pensions for miners. On trade, Democrats and Republicans came together on the United States-Mexico-Canada Agreement, a replacement for NAFTA. The trade deal would boost U.S. access to Canadian dairy markets, tighten auto-part rules, and ensure higher wages for foreign workers. For these bipartisan efforts, my gift to all members of Congress is the ability to look their constituents in the eyes and say, "We can still get stuff done."

Things have always been less rancorous at the state level, but we had at least one major blow-up on the Senate floor this year. When Lieutenant Governor Fetterman used his gavel in favor of his caucus over established Senate rules, the Senate Republicans unloaded on him. My hope is that both sides can get beyond this flare-up, and my gift to Fetterman and Majority Leader Jake Corman is lipstick, so they can kiss and make up!

Governor Wolf had a good year. He and legislative leaders hammered out another budget with no additional tax increases but still made room for priorities like education, workforce development, and environmental initiatives. He ended the year with a flourish, tightening loopholes that had allowed criminals to get guns, and he made a little progress on increasing the minimum wage. However, all is not rosy in the "Wolf den," as his administration has come under scrutiny for allegedly expediting permits for natural gas pipelines. These allegations must seem hard to fathom to a buttoned-down, by-the-book executive like Tom Wolf. My gift to the governor would be continued candor. We know you are one of the good guys, and the truth will set you free!

To those politicos whose ambitions are driving them toward new heights, I recommend the gift of humility. I am talking to you Mr. Toomey, Mr. Turzai, Mr. Shapiro, Mr. Fetterman, Mr. Torsella, Mr. DePasquale, Mr. Corman. Remember that public office is a sacred trust. Voters who invest that kind of faith in you deserve your thoughtful leadership, not your partisan pandering. They also need to know you have not gotten too isolated to take their phone calls.

To my political sparring partner, Charlie Gerow, I wish you a blessed Christmas and a healthy, happy New Year. During this season and throughout the year, civility matters. I like to think that we both believe in it.

Finally, here is a thought that may be uplifting: Andre Gide said that "Art is a collaboration between God and the artist, and the less the artist does, the better." At this Christmas time, those of us who practice the art of politics would do well to remember that there is a higher power than we, as mere humans, will ever attain. We should all act in that spirit and by the example of the One who started his career in a Bethlehem manger.

PART TWO

2020 OP-EDS

FARM SHOW

JANUARY 1, 2020

An old political story tells about a farmer who suffered a serious cut to his arm while operating his tractor one day. His farmhand rushed him to the hospital, and he waited in the emergency room. Soon, a pregnant woman was escorted ahead of him into the operating room.

"Just one minute," said the farmer, "I have been waiting here with a serious wound. Why did this woman go first?"

"You don't understand," said the nurse, "she's in labor."

"That's the problem with this country today," said the farmer, "everything for labor and nothing for the farmer!"

While labor organizations deserve praise for the steady growth of Pennsylvania's middle class and political leaders recognize its clout, farmers provide more than a backbone for our commonwealth. They keep us fed.

This is the time of year, after the harvest and before the spring planting, when the farming community can relax and take a well-deserved bow. This is the time of year that farmers and consumers flock to the farm show arena to celebrate agriculture—Pennsylvania's number one industry. While the original show featured about 440 exhibits, the 2020 version will have over 13,000. These, along with state-of-the-art equipment vendors, rodeo competitions, and every variety of farm functions, put Pennsylvania's best farm foot forward every year. It is the largest agricultural exhibition in the country.

The first show, entitled the "Pennsylvania Corn, Fruit, Vegetable, Dairy Producers and Wool Show," featured the best corn and dairy products the state had to offer. A hundred years later, it is almost too big to comprehend.

It is spread over the twenty-four-acre complex of the farm show arena and is expected to draw thousands and thousands of visitors over eight days.

The fact is that William Penn himself envisioned the entire farm show week. In the mid-1600s, he organized an agricultural show for farmers to gather and share their knowledge. Like Pennsylvania itself, the show has evolved over the years. The one thing that has remained is its popularity with farmers and families alike.

A new twist to this year's activities should be noted: While the Department of Health is carefully regulating the burgeoning medical cannabis industry, it is not hard to envision its impact on agriculture in the very near future. Already, dispensaries in Pennsylvania have sold more than half a billion dollars of medical marijuana over the past two years. There are 1,200 licensed physicians and 147,000 certified patients that will continue to drive demand for CBD and other products for years to come. This means a new product is grown in huge quantities and will undoubtedly be featured in future farm shows.

CBD oils are already seemingly everywhere, but the real economic driver and job creator, according to economic analysts, is hemp. Industrial hemp is cultivated with only 0.3 percent THC, the psychoactive ingredient that provides the high in cannabis. Hemp, therefore, is not for recreational use. While it can't get users stoned, it has a number of other uses. Beyond medical applications, hemp could replace plastic items like picnic ware, containers, and consumer goods. It is a promising source of building materials. Hemp received a major boost from the federal government in 2019 when it was removed from the federal controlled substances list. To grow in Pennsylvania, farmers need only obtain a license from the state, and Agriculture Secretary Russell Redding says there will be no cap on the number of producers.

In a sense, this means that Pennsylvania will be returning to its roots since it was a leading producer of hemp as far back as the 1600s. The Pennsylvania Hemp Industry Council points out that William Penn encouraged hemp as a cash crop for his fledgling colony.

If your curiosity takes you to one of the hemp product displays, visit one of the world's largest food courts that features only PA products. Maybe I'm biased, but there is nothing like the fried mushrooms and pulled pork sandwiches washed down with a famous farm show milkshake.

This year's farm show is a proud display of Pennsylvania's agricultural history, but it is also brimming with new technologies, products, and promise. You owe it to your family to participate in this uniquely Pennsylvania tradition.

See you at the farm show!

BIDEN BOUNCES BACK BIGLY

FEBRUARY 26, 2020

The magic number is 1,991. That's how many delegates the Democratic candidate must secure to win the nomination. Here is the current count: Biden 595, Sanders 526, Warren 54, Buttigieg 26, Bloomberg 33, Klobuchar 7, Gabbard 2.

Joe Biden's stunning haul of delegates on Super Tuesday made him the front-runner. Since Buttigieg, Bloomberg, and Klobuchar have thrown in with the former vice president, his actual delegate lead has grown to 132. Biden takes momentum into the "mini Super Tuesday" this week with most of the remaining primary map in his favor.

So, what happened here?

From South Carolina through Super Tuesday on March 3 to the cascade of recent endorsements that the Biden camp has garnered, the Democrats are coalescing around Joe Biden. This is noteworthy for several reasons; first, Democrats don't agree on much. The famous Will Rogers observation that "I don't belong to any organized party; I'm a Democrat" applies here. Democrats cover the entire range of perspectives from liberal to conservative, from ardent pro-choice and pro-life advocates to urban minorities to rural traditionalists. What is remarkable is that the emerging movement allows those disparate viewpoints to be included under the tent. The moderate lane that Joe Biden has carefully carved out will also invite clear-thinking Republicans to join in a return to post-Trump normalcy for the country.

Second, the same coalition that resulted in the 2018 blue wave emerged on Super Tuesday. African Americans and suburban voters voted enthusiastically for Joe Biden. They sent a message that they are, indeed, the heart of the Democratic Party and can deliver big wins when they are motivated.

Third, the fusion of Democratic factions happened organically. On Super Tuesday night, one commentator observed, "Joe Biden is mopping the floor in states that he never visited, where he opened zero field offices, and where he spent next to nothing on TV." All true. The surge for Biden is a direct result of today's instant communications. With non-stop cable coverage of the South Carolina results and with immediate social media chatter, Biden translated the critical endorsement of Representative Jim Clyburn and the landslide win in South Carolina into a movement toward the middle and a clear "time to get out" message to all other contenders. Exit polls noted that Joe Biden was the overwhelming favorite for those who waited until after South Carolina to decide. With no advertising budget and little field staff in any of the states, Biden's message permeated the nation as effectively as data disseminated from the mysterious cloud.

Most importantly, Democratic voters from coast to coast made the critical decision that Joe Biden remains the best hope for defeating Donald Trump. They made a judgment about the president's despicable attempts to dig up dirt on Biden and his family and rejected those attacks. They said loudly and clearly that they were repulsed and exhausted by a president with little or no regard for the truth. They showed that they much prefer somebody with empathy and a lifetime of honorable service to his country. While there are still primaries and debates ahead, the Democrats are down to a battle between Biden and Sanders, between moderate pragmatism and progressive idealism. Wherever Democrats fall on that ideological spectrum, they weigh in with this clear message: beat Donald Trump. *USA Today* put it this way: "The only thing Democrats consistently seem able to agree on is that they want to defeat Trump, and they are indeed enthusiastically showing up."

And that's one more bit of good news for Democrats; they're winning the "enthusiasm" battle. Some Republicans tout record turnout numbers for the president in the early primaries. This may be true, but it is equally valid that Democratic turnout in those same primary states was about 40 percent higher. Even in red states like North Carolina, Texas, and Tennessee, Democrats outpaced Republican turnout by large margins. This bodes well for the Ds and the showdown in the fall.

Maybe, just maybe, the Biden Bounce will reach rational Republicans as well. J.W. Verret, a law professor at George Mason and a lifelong Republican, wrote: "Countless Americans today are desperate for reconciliation and a semblance of normalcy. I've never voted for a Democrat, but Biden offers the possibility of just such a political recovery from the nightmare of the past few years. I invite my fellow restless Republicans to join me."

COVID-19: THE REAL ENEMY

MARCH 13, 2020

When President Trump delivered his prime-time televised address to the country last week, he was walking the tightrope of leadership. The stock market had already tanked, and the next day's numbers would reflect whether his words would calm the financial waters. The address was also essential to give hope and reassurance to citizens who have watched the coronavirus invade their country just as menacingly as a hostile army.

In this war-like setting, it falls to a president to take charge.

In the minutes after the teleprompter address, the verdict from news anchors and pundits was the president had failed to calm the waters, and we headed into another market meltdown. One writer put it this way: "The speech was riddled with errors, nationalist and xenophobic in tone, limited in its empathy, and boastful of his own decisions."

The delivery itself was disconcerting. The first rule of crisis management is honesty. People understand and appreciate getting the facts no matter how bad the news is. Trump continued to tout the availability of tests—even though his experts affirmed to Congress that our testing supplies are woefully inadequate. Another rule of crisis management is calmness. Words delivered with calm, sincerity, and empathy reassure citizens and stabilize markets. The demeanor and substance of the president's remarks did neither.

As things worsen with COVID-19, it may be that the president's speech will be remembered much like President George W. Bush's flyover of the Katrina disaster. Julian Zelizer, a Princeton presidential historian, said: "People want to see a leader who has a commanding presence. In some ways, the country is worse off with a message like President Trump's."

When the president finally declared a state of emergency, he made sure to bring the vice president, key scientists, and administration officials with him. It was telling that most of the questions were directed at the professionals. They had less tendency to equivocate and blame others. They were there to get the facts out. While the president deflected some questions, his demeanor and message were focused on the $50 billion that could be mobilized under the emergency declaration to fight the pandemic.

With all of that said, here is a wake-up call for all Americans: we only have one president. In a period of crisis for the country, we need and expect him and all our leaders to make good decisions. We need to lay down the normal political hostilities and deal with the stark reality that faces us without partisanship and rancor.

While it was disappointing that the president chose not to engage directly with Speaker Pelosi on a complete stimulus plan, Vice President Mike Pence and Treasury Secretary Steve Mnuchin did. Leaders from both parties put together a bold plan to accelerate testing and to help pay for coronavirus care. Joe Biden and Bernie Sanders called for paid sick leave, relief for hard-hit workers, expanded unemployment insurance benefits, and enhanced funding for schools and services for low-income families and children. Much of their proposals have now reached the package before Congress.

The immediate priority in the package is to call for free testing and distributing those tests as widely as possible. This is the crucial action required to stop the pandemic. The plan also builds our healthcare response capabilities and directs funding to state and local governments to help affected localities. These kinds of non-partisan actions speak louder than misinformation and political posturing. While it is likely that presidential leadership and character will be a major topic of discussion in the fall, we should all focus on the here and now.

In a particularly silly sidebar during the early discussions of COVID-19, President Trump assigned blame on a familiar target (Barack Obama) despite the former president's capable handling of Ebola, SARS, H1N1, and similar crises. Despite President Trump having eliminated the very health crisis management office in the West Wing, set specifically for our current circumstance.

It is time to move past missteps and misstatements and reaffirm that we are all in this together. COVID-19 is the enemy, and America has the ingenuity and the capacity to tame and destroy it over time. Let us give the president the resources he needs to move beyond the COVID-19, and let us support him fully in that fight.

INSPIRATION FOR DISPIRITING TIMES

MARCH 20, 2020

A silver lining to social distancing is that I am catching up on my reading. Having just finished Doris Kearns's *Leadership in Turbulent Times,* I am reassured that we have had great leaders in the past and that even the toughest times are no match for a kind, united, and courageous country.

The fact is that political courage is rare. Politicians tend to focus on the next election, not the next generation. They live and die by catering to current trends and popular opinion. Courage is about acting in a way they know will damage them politically.

In pushing through the 13th Amendment, Lincoln took on prevailing prejudices to break slavery. Theodore Roosevelt defied his own party to resolve a coal strike crippling the national economy. FDR found himself in the quicksand of a worldwide depression and lifted us with a series of innovative initiatives that benefit all of us to this day. Lyndon Johnson signed the Civil Right Act in 1965, knowing full well that he had written off support from the South for the next two generations.

Whether we are beset by a viral pandemic or a contagion of discontent from some citizens, it is good to remember acts of kindness and courage that have made America who we really are.

In 1983, two hundred and forty-one Marines were killed in an attack on our embassy in Beirut. President Ronald Reagan believed he was in for a lengthy investigation from a hostile Congress—not unlike the eight separate hearings and years of reprisals that Hillary Clinton would face on Benghazi. The president picked up the phone and remarked to Speaker Tip O'Neill something to the effect of, "I guess you are going to have a field day with this."

O'Neill was the opposition leader and the Democratic Speaker of the House, but he was also an American and a patriot. "Mr. President," he said, "You didn't kill those boys."

Congress undertook a brief investigation, produced a bipartisan report containing recommendations for better security, and assigned no blame.

An act of even greater consequence occurred when Gerald R. Ford pardoned Richard Nixon. After what he called the "national nightmare" of Watergate, the president sought to bind the nation's wounds. He knew full well that his action would galvanize the opposition party and lose many of his supporters. He put the needs of the country first; his career came second.

In *Profiles in Courage*, John F. Kennedy chronicles the deeds of a dozen leaders who chose courage over convenience. The story of Edmund Ross (R-KS) is especially dramatic. When the roll was called at the trial of President Andrew Johnson, Ross defied conventional wisdom, political pressure, and the overwhelming opinion of his constituents to acquit the president. In his own words, Edmund Ross "felt like I was looking into my own grave." His actions allowed for a more compassionate reconstruction and may have averted a second Civil War. Sometimes courage manifests itself on smaller stages. Former senator John McCain (R-AZ) is revered as a war hero and a principled public servant, but his star never shined brighter than in a town meeting in 2008 when he was running for president. A supporter had taken the microphone to declare that Barack Obama was unfit for public office. She was concerned because "he's an Arab and a Muslim," but McCain had none of it.

"No, Ma'am," he said, "He's an American and a Christian. He's a good man, a loving husband, and a good father. We just have different opinions about politics. That's all."

And here's one more story that doesn't involve a politician. The most courageous soldiers in the Civil War were often young boys who carried the flag—the regimental colors—into battle. They were unarmed, and while they provided a focal point for their troops to follow, they were also sitting ducks for the enemy, who had them easily in their sights. The story goes that one such color sergeant got too far out in front of his men, and the brigadier general sought to slow him down.

"Bring the colors back to the regiment!" he yelled.

"No sir," shouted the flagbearer, "Bring the regiment up to the colors!"

When Senator Mitt Romney (R-UT) cast his lone impeachment vote, he received the full onslaught of an attack from his own party. His response was simple and profound: "I will tell my children and their children that I did my duty to the best of my ability, believing that my country expected it of me."

These troubling times and all times require that Americans fly their true colors. It is what our children and their children expect of us.

BIPARTISANSHIP PREVAILS

MARCH 27, 2020

As most of us watched the spread of COVID-19 from the safety of our homes, stories of real heroism began to emerge. Across our state and nation, health providers, first responders, and caregivers put themselves directly in the contagion zone to ensure their patients—our neighbors—would be protected. There is a real and present danger for doctors, nurses, or food pantry workers. But given the choice between fighting for others or protecting themselves, they consistently chose to fight.

Americans and citizens worldwide continue to display compassion and creativity in their random acts of kindness. Podcasts of community sing-alongs go viral, young people bring groceries to shut-ins, teachers reach students online, and media outlets provide essential information around the clock.

In terms of governmental leadership, note that the quality of crisis management seems to depend on the individual at the microphone. President Trump established a crisis response team headed by Vice President Mike Pence and some notable healthcare professionals and scientists. It was soon clear that he wanted to dominate the daily briefings, and his demeanor was predictable. After his prepared remarks, the president could not stop himself from attacking the media, blaming others for a slow response to the crisis, and patting himself on the back for whatever small victories he could claim.

At several briefings, it was downright embarrassing to watch Dr. Tony Fauci wince at some of the president's pronouncements; "We have some drugs that will be available soon." *Not exactly.* Clinical trials and safety protocols mean vaccines will not be available for at least a year. "We want to be back to work by Easter." *Impossible.* Fauci and others know that lifting the isolation requirements and sacrificing social distancing too soon would worsen things exponentially.

BIPARTISANSHIP PREVAILS

To their credit, Vice President Pence, Fauci, and other administration officials have been steady, forthright, and helpful throughout the crisis. They understand the first rule for leaders in crisis management: telling the truth.

Governors across the country have also risen to the challenge. Andrew Cuomo in New York stands at the new epicenter of the disease and methodically presses for equipment and safeguards to fight the coming war. States like California, Washington, and Louisiana have worked on a bipartisan basis with the feds to mitigate suffering and economic fallout.

Governor Wolf has received high marks in Pennsylvania for his calm and decisive approach to the darkening clouds. His directives have been timely, and his steady hand has improved a horrible situation. Kudos to Secretary of Health Rachel Levine as well for sharing unvarnished information daily.

Bipartisanship is prevailing in both Washington and at the state level.

The U.S. Congress and Treasury Secretary Steve Mnuchin hammered out an unprecedented response bill to speed relief to families and the American economy. The $2.2 trillion package will get about $3,400 to an average family of four and provide additional unemployment benefits. It will also provide grants and loans for small businesses to get back on their feet. Yes, there is about $500 billion for large corporations, but Republicans and Democrats came together to assure that these companies will have to pay the government back and will be subject to oversight by an independent council and inspector general.

Bill Gates summed up the costly support package by saying that "when bodies are piling up, GDP growth becomes less and less important."

In Pennsylvania, help is on the way in the form of a $60 million COVID-19 Working Capital Access Program for small businesses and another $50 million restricted account to support frontline medical workers and to provide vital equipment.

The governor and Republican leaders ensured these items moved forward—even if it meant voting by teleconference. Senate majority leader, Jake Corman, said: "In Pennsylvania, we worked together to dedicate this money to help those who are waging this extraordinary battle."

One of the most important comments came from Cuomo, who said there was no need to "choose between a smart health strategy and smart economic strategy. We can do both, and we must do both."

The United States now has about 100,000 confirmed cases of COVID-19; Pennsylvania has about 2,000. The flattening of the curve seems a long way off, but leaders and citizens are proving we can weather the storm if we work in harmony and good faith.

EASTER MIRACLES

APRIL 10, 2020

Amid the grim realities of COVID-19, let us take a moment to consider two Easter encounters described in John 20.

And the angels said unto her: "why do you weep?" She said: "Because they have taken away my Lord, and I know not where they have laid him." And when she had said thus, she turned herself back and saw Jesus standing there.

To say that Mary Magdalene would have been startled at the sight of two angels guarding an empty tomb would be an understatement. Turning around and seeing Jesus standing there would have been beyond comprehension.

For Christians, there is no more spectacular affirmation of faith than the resurrection of Jesus Christ. No comparisons can be drawn from other mundane acts of inspiration. Still, when humanity is faced with the dire realities of a COVID-19 pandemic and when politics has been twisted into a blood sport that eschews truth and cooperation, there are some encouraging signs that miracles can still happen.

While deaths rise across the nation, there are glimmers of hope that the infamous curve is flattening. Our social distancing has slowed the spread of the virus enough that we may be able to start handling patients within our existing healthcare system. This is not a final victory but a "new normal" requiring massive changes in our social and economic habits. Still, it is encouraging news.

And while I don't consider them miracles, other developments should be noted. First, the president and his opponent put aside politics for a few moments and discussed the pandemic. Both reported that they had "a good conversation" and went over ideas for what happens next, as leaders should. Biden said the president was "gracious," and Trump said the conversation was "very friendly."

Second, it may be a miracle that Dr. Anthony Fauci and Dr. Deborah Birx are still standing. Americans owe a debt of gratitude to these two consummate professionals for keeping us updated with the unvarnished truth. They are both steeped in science and keep a tight rein on others tempted to mischaracterize the situation and put more lives in danger. The steadiness with which they have imposed guidelines and the knowledge they share under duress—and near exhaustion—has become invaluable.

Likewise, Governor Wolf and Secretary of Health Rachel Levine don't seem to be getting much sleep either. Some have argued that statewide directives are impeding a return to commerce. In a direct and jarring fashion, Levine told the press: "We want to save our livelihoods, but we must save lives first." The governor's recent directive to keep schools closed through June was jarring, historic, and necessary. We can find ways to accelerate learning and allow our students to catch up academically, but we need the strength to take whatever steps are necessary to keep our children safe.

A final occurrence last week that many didn't think possible was the suspension of the Bernie Sanders campaign for president. It should be noted that this took an extraordinary amount of forbearance on Bernie's part. Call him Socialist if you like, but he just helped guide a $2.2 trillion recovery package through Congress that will save countless lives and jobs. He could have insisted that his team continue to "Feel the Bern" through the convention. Like many of the Democratic candidates before him, though, Sanders put aside his own ambition and resisted a strong, vocal network of supporters to do the right thing. The Biden and Sanders camps were quick to issue statements of mutual respect and have begun to set the tone for a campaign that will be united in purpose and focus.

While these examples may not shine as brightly as the sun on that first Easter Sunday, let us hope for a resurrection of sorts. Consider the Apostle Thomas—a realist who, like Mary Magdalene, simply assumed that the Romans had taken the body from the tomb. He was skeptical enough to require that he touch the wounds of the risen Christ before he could believe. But Thomas's doubts were assuaged when he comprehended that extraordinary things happen when faith prevails.

Let us hope that politics and humanity can change for the better. Let us hope that our leaders can inspire us again and that America can rise from pandemics and politics affecting our bodies and souls.

BEYOND COVID-19

APRIL 24, 2020

Singer-songwriter Joni Mitchell wrote about cloud watching in 1968. Her "Both Sides Now" applies some life lessons when we take a moment to appreciate the changing shape of clouds.

Have you noticed that you have more quality time on your hands recently? Many of us have found that we can be productive at our laptops, even if we are working in our pajamas. If your old routine was fighting traffic, reaching your office frazzled, coping with office drama, and dealing with distractions from bosses and employees who always were within shouting distance, you might be surprised at your new-found level of productivity. You may be able to tackle projects, communicate by FaceTime or Zoom, and still have time to walk outdoors without guilt or excuses.

In a recent article, John Malesic boldly asserted that it was time to rethink America's "religious devotion to work." Some people just do not understand this paradigm shift. At the height of the COVID-19 spread in his state, Lieutenant Governor Dan Patrick of Texas said, "Let's get back to work. Let's get back to living. Let's be smart about it, those of us who are seventy-plus. We'll take care of ourselves, but don't sacrifice the economy." Jarring words. Patrick seemed perfectly content to sacrifice thousands of people to get the gears of our economic machinery humming again. He does not comprehend that getting back to work might not be the same as getting back to living.

There may be a more fulfilling existence following the pandemic. People have already discovered that they can read, practice the piano, exercise, and spend time with their kids. Once we recover and heal from the suffering and loss of COVID-19, Malesic argues that "we should not go back to our normal way of working. We need to preserve the best parts of our new work experience and make them accessible to all, especially those who are being hit hardest by this crisis."

One doesn't have to be a futurist to detect some trends.

There will be fewer places to gather. This means that malls, movie theaters, restaurants, taverns, and flea markets will have to find creative ways to accommodate customers in small groups—not through cattle-call jostling. While they may be smaller, these businesses could provide more inviting and pleasant experiences. There will also be many more, meaning new entrepreneurial opportunities will open.

Law firms, real estate offices, banks, and other professional venues will limit human contact. Lawyers could still rack up their billable hours from home, realtors and bankers could service clientele remotely, and face-to-face gatherings would be rare. This means that we should consider new uses for office space that will become available.

In Pennsylvania, we saw this happen before. The surge of school building construction in the baby boom era led to an inevitable oversupply when those structures became outdated or outgrown. State and local officials helped convert those buildings into business incubators, art centers, nursing care facilities, and apartments. This kind of transition is likely to occur again. This time, it will be the renaissance of buildings in our downtown areas that are beautiful but outdated.

Many other aspects of society will change. The way we educate our children can evolve rapidly if we focus on technology instead of bodies in classrooms. The way we watch sports might require some distancing at stadiums. The way we travel might get a little more comfortable as well.

The important point is that we should not fear change. We will face needed policy changes like family leave adjustments and higher wages for frontline workers like first responders, health care providers, and others who do not have the luxury of a new virtual reality. With some creative thinking, we may emerge from this pandemic with a more vibrant economy based on human needs rather than just bottom lines.

Gabriel Garcia Marquez writes vividly about love and loss against the backdrop of a cholera pandemic that lasted fifty years. A couple approaching old age realized they had survived cholera and the ups and downs of marriage itself: "It was the time when they loved each other best, without hurry or excess, when both were most conscious of their incredible victories over adversity. Life would still present them with other mortal trials, of course, but that no longer mattered: they were on the other shore."

It is worth believing we can all reach "the other shore" after COVID-19. When teleworking in the near future, remember what Joni Mitchell suggested long ago: step outside. We could do worse than teach our children the art of cloud watching.

HEROISM IS STAYING HOME

MAY 8, 2020

The news about COVID-19 is not good. While we are all ready to resume our normal lives, the continued infection rates and soaring death rates show that the virus is still very much with us. New York and Pennsylvania are among the states that have been weathering the storm. Both enforced isolation to protect all citizens. The shutdowns in those areas proved absolutely vital in the effort, but leaders in both states urge caution, including facemasks and social distancing for the foreseeable future.

Even with a full array of protections in place, most medical experts agree that there will be a resurgence of the pandemic in the fall. In 1918, the Spanish Flu seemed to recede before it unleashed an even more furious contagion six months later. That is likely to happen with COVID-19, especially if citizens get weary of the battle or insist on their right to get back to their favorite McDonald's.

Clearly, the virus has taken its toll on our economy. The national unemployment rate is at depression levels. Several businesses will likely not return, and there will be challenges for many breadwinners to adjust to some new reality. The anxiety of many Americans is understandable. They have a right to complain and protest.

But recent demonstrations in various states have been irresponsible. Protestors in Pennsylvania brought their slogans and their guns to the state capitol. Ignoring advice to stay home, these people asserted their right to ignore the leaders struggling to walk that fine line between economic recovery and the safety of all citizens. One moment stood out for me: An unmasked protestor with a semiautomatic rifle was confronted by a hospital worker between shifts with this simple truth: "You're putting both of us at risk." Infecting that worker would have taken one real soldier off the battlefield of the pandemic.

In Michigan, the governor grappled with a broken supply chain for critically needed medical equipment. The president was not only unresponsive, but he also supported denying help to "that woman from Michigan." That drama sparked a right wing reaction that continues to get in the way of real solutions.

And a word about these so-called "spontaneous" demonstrations. They are not spontaneous at all. In a disturbing report published by *The Washington Post*, it turns out that mega-donors with connections to the Trump organization supported the COVID-19 protests. Whether the protestors know it or not, they are pawns to make political points with little or no consideration for the health and safety of the public. Disgraceful.

Putting aside the insidious dark money involved in Michigan, the image of a bearded protestor yelling at law enforcement officials in the halls of the state capitol raises the question: is there a right for that man and any citizen to protest in that manner? The answer is absolutely. The Constitution guarantees it. The real question is, are protestors entitled to abuse their First Amendment privileges when their country is under duress?

My friend, Tom Ridge, wrote an article for *USA Today* that pulled no punches. "In recent weeks, we have seen images of Americans carrying weapons as part of their protests to immediately reopen society. What are they planning to do, shoot the virus with their AR-15s?" He goes on to castigate their "false bravado" and says that their actions are neither heroic nor courageous. As a decorated veteran himself, he lays it on the line: "It is difficult and sometimes feels unbearable as economic and emotional stress mount each day [. . .]. But you are not in the trenches of France, not gaining ground inch by inch in the Pacific, not slogging through the paddies and jungles of Vietnam."

Ridge is right: all we have been asked to do is stay home. That helps the real troops provide medical and nursing care to dying people.

For those of us who have spent years upholding the dignity and exceptionalism of our experiment in republican democracy, it is jarring to see how quickly personal or partisan interests prevail when we should all be seeking higher ground. When Madison and Hamilton built some checks into our electoral and governing processes, they intended and hoped that angry crowds would not sway our leaders. They would be alarmed if any demonstrations undermined the fundamental principles of the republic just because citizens were growing weary of their temporary sacrifices.

I give the final words to my colleague, Tom Ridge, who wrote, "We can prevail in this battle if we work together. Forget politics. No time for it now. We can sort it out later. Same team. Same fight. Let's get on with it."

COVID-19 – A LEADERSHIP VOID

JUNE 3, 2020

The COVID-19 virus has now claimed 115,000 lives. One thousand people per day continue to die. The economic toll of the coronavirus is staggering. Thirty-two million people are unemployed; economic growth is at a complete standstill, and the nation seems to have no clear strategy for preventing a second wave of the pandemic.

These are facts, not soundbites. As much as the Trump campaign and his loyalists want to change the subject, these are realities that American citizens and voters understand all too well.

This is not the first time the United States has faced a lethal crisis. We have faced down tyrants overseas, a brutal Civil War, the Great Depression, and at least three pandemics that could have been disastrous. The difference is that our current leadership is incapable or unwilling to take steps to protect us.

No, the loyal opposition is not saying that Trump caused the pandemic, but what is undeniable is that his inaction made the situation much worse. I mentioned in a previous column that academicians have now had the opportunity to analyze the data and the federal actions. Columbia University concluded that social distancing was the correct strategy to contain the virus. Indecision or wishful thinking by the president prevented immediate, large-scale implementation of social distancing. The result is that, of the 115,000 victims, the research shows that earlier actions could have saved almost half of them.

Trump supporters reach for rationalizations: how could he have known? Nobody warned him about pandemics, and their favorite scapegoat, President Obama, is somehow to blame.

Let's set this record straight; warnings about this pandemic go back fifteen years. In 2005, President Bush and the National Institute of Allergy and Infectious Diseases head, Anthony Fauci, released the *National Strategy for Pandemic Influenza*. President Obama, addressing Ebola in 2014, said, "There may and likely will come a time in which we have an airborne disease that is deadly." He created an office on pandemic preparedness as a branch of the National Security Council, which President Trump abolished. On November 18, 2019, one day after the first COVID-19 case was reported, the bipartisan *Commission on Strengthening America's Health Security sent a direct message to the White House:* "Restore health security leadership at the White House National Security Council."

Despite these warnings and an actual tabletop drill conducted during the transition in 2016, the president did not feel the heat from the pandemic wildfire until March 2020, when he declared a national emergency. This was a full four months after the first reported COVID-19 case. It was just days after the president assured us the virus was under control and that it would miraculously disappear. As the virus crept into every part of our country, our president said, "I don't take responsibility at all."

Beyond the sheer lack of understanding of the pandemic, the contradictions from the White House have been astounding. While the Trump campaign has flooded the airwaves with a "too-soft-on-China" campaign against Joe Biden, the president was pandering to China just weeks before. "China has been working very hard to contain the coronavirus. It will all work out well. In particular, on behalf of the American People, I want to thank President Xi!"

As to shutting down travel from China, most European nations did the same thing before we acted. Four hundred thousand Chinese entered the United States when the virus was raging. The president's travel ban leaked like a sieve and failed completely to stop the spread of the infection.

When Trump partisans complain about politicizing the pandemic, they hope you simply ignore these facts. Now, as we face another crisis that has erupted in violence in many parts of the country, the president's approach is to present us with photo opportunities rather than real solutions. His supporters create false narratives about the Far Left or murky stories about Joe Biden and his family. By emulating the full-frontal attack behavior of this president, Republicans are risking their viability in a post-Trump world.

In a recent article, Professor Robert Reich was blunt: "By having no constructive response to any of the monumental crises now convulsing America, Trump has abdicated his office."

Here's the bottom line: we are better than this. We are Americans and know the difference between reality show posturing and real leadership. We have a right and an obligation to object when leadership fails us. That's not politicizing a pandemic; that's trying to bring America home.

INDEPENDENCE DAY 2020

JULY 1, 2020

On this green bank, by this soft stream,
We set to-day a votive stone;
That memory may their deed redeem,
When, like our sires, our sons are gone.

Ralph Waldo Emerson

On Independence Day, Americans pause to recall the heroics of leaders who put their lives on the line. It is a fact that the signers of the Declaration "pledged their lives, their fortunes, and their sacred honor" to the cause of freedom. While citizens today carp about inconveniences like masks and social distancing requirements, the freedoms our forefathers won came at a brutal price. The British hunted the fifty-six signers of the Declaration of Independence. About half of them suffered or died in the Revolutionary War. Many of them lost their homes and fortunes.

While you enjoy your beer and burgers this holiday, give some thought to those who made it possible. Here are a few Pennsylvania heroes to thank: "Mad" Anthony Wayne led his men into battle at Brandywine and Germantown before facing a harsh winter with George Washington at Valley Forge. He led a daring nighttime assault on the British at Stony Point, New York, armed only with bayonets. That's how he got the nickname.

Edward Hand was an Irish immigrant who settled in Lancaster to practice medicine. He took up arms for the American cause in 1775 and served as a lieutenant colonel in the battles of Long Island, Trenton, and Princeton and rose to brigadier general before the war ended. His command at Fort Pitt was marked by securing neutrality from Indian tribes throughout the state.

James Irvine commanded the 2nd Regiment and fought in Pennsylvania, Virginia, and Canada. Captured by the British at Chestnut Hill near Philadelphia, he lost three fingers and suffered a severe back injury in the fight. He was held prisoner for four years but insisted on returning to active duty after his release. He went on to be elected Vice President of the Commonwealth, the equivalent of today's lieutenant governor.

Samuel John Atlee from Lancaster was studying law when he chose to enter the army. By the time he was sixteen, he was placed in command of a small company and rose to colonel. His war record included the Battle of Fort Duquesne and the Battle of Long Island, where he was captured and imprisoned for two years. A member of the Continental Congress, Atlee also served in the general assembly and helped negotiate land treaties with American Indian tribes.

John Peter Gabriel Muhlenberg was a preacher in Virginia when he led his congregation in verse from Ecclesiastes. "For everything, there is a season and a time for every purpose under heaven." He ended his homily by saying, "There is a time to preach and a time to fight. Now is the time to fight." With that, he threw off his clerical robes and revealed an officer's uniform in the Continental Army.

One biographer wrote, "Drums began to roll, men kissed their wives, and they walked down the aisle to enlist." The next day, Muhlenberg brought 300 men from his and neighboring churches to enlist with General George Washington. Muhlenberg moved to Pennsylvania after the war and served with distinction in the U.S. House of Representatives and the U.S. Senate.

Many Americans are sagging from the weight of challenges that seem to have no end in sight. Many have been driven to their ideological corners by a constant flow of information confirming their biases. Some families are overburdened with the reality of making a living and don't have the time for reflection.

The fact is that those who came before us had it much worse. They chose to fight when they had a choice between their comfort or the furnace of battle to forge a nation. They saddled up when threatened with the overwhelming power of the strongest military forces on earth.

I advise everyone celebrating Independence Day this weekend to rise above the news cycle. Think about what your country has asked of you lately. If it is just to stay socially distant to ride out the pandemic, then do it. If it is to share perspectives with members of a different race or religion, try it. If it is to vote, that fundamental act secures this experiment in representative democracy, do it.

We celebrate our forbearers by remembering them. We honor them by being more perfect citizens as we grow into a more perfect nation.

SUBSTANCE AND STYLE AT PRESS CONFERENCES

JULY 24, 2020

It has become clear to the ratings-watcher-in-chief that his numbers are slipping. So much so that he is back at the podium giving personal updates on the COVID-19 pandemic. It's different this time; the president is reading from a binder of notes in a clear attempt to avoid blunders like "I take no responsibility" or "consider ingesting disinfectants" or "we're testing too much."

Still, Trump cannot seem to stop himself. The moment he went off script, he stumbled again. In answer to a question about Ghislaine Maxwell, under investigation for alleged trafficking in children, the president "wished her well." The correct answer would have been, "I hope she helps bring predators and anybody who has abused children to justice." His answer instead signaled that his friendship with Maxwell and Jeffrey Epstein mattered more to him than justice for kids.

Disturbing.

In fairness, Trump is not the only one to buckle under the pressure of the pressers. After losing the California governor's race, Nixon couldn't hide his disdain for the press: "You won't have Richard Nixon to kick around anymore." Harry Truman once threatened to punch a reporter in the nose over his newspaper's criticism of his daughter's opera performance. President Coolidge was approached by a White House guest who had a bet with a colleague that she could get three words from "Silent Cal," to which Coolidge replied, "You lose."

One way to avoid confrontation and gaffes at press conferences is simple: don't have them. In recent years, the office of the press secretary has served as a buffer to the president and has provided information on national and world events to the public. The press secretary has also served another purpose. By taking on the regular chore of mundane updates, they assure that the president commands heightened attention when a matter is grave enough to address. Think of President Kennedy addressing the nation on the Cuban missile crisis, George W. Bush with a bullhorn after 9/11, or Barack Obama assuring the nation that Bin Laden was no more.

Most presidents have a healthy respect for the "bully pulpit" the presidency provides. The finest statements made under the duress of war came from Abraham Lincoln. The Gettysburg Address is sheer poetry in terms of both substance and style. His second inaugural address, which sought to bind the nation's wounds "with malice toward none and charity toward all," was the definition of grace under pressure. From Theodore Roosevelt, through FDR's "fireside chats," to the elegance of John Kennedy's words, we have been blessed with some great oratory. And let's not forget President Reagan, who rightly won the title of the "Great Communicator." This is not faint praise from me since I usually hated the message but had to admire the skill of the messenger.

This gets us back to Trump at the podium. Whether it is in COVID-19 briefings or MAGA rallies or impromptu press gaggles on his way to Marine One, the president expounds with a false bravado that invariably falls short in terms of the truth or civility. It is hard to imagine any other president name-calling opponents or American citizens. Branding someone "Pocahontas," "Sleepy Joe," or "Crooked Hillary" is beneath the dignity of the office. What's worse is that it betrays a tradition of presidential stature that has always commanded respect worldwide.

Even in the friendly embrace of Fox News, this president can't seem to summon the maturity to appeal to anybody but his most frenzied supporters. When Chris Wallace can shred the false data that the president spews when the reporter can clearly show that "defunding police" is nothing but a right-wing talking point, when the POTUS is reduced to bragging about passing a pre-dementia test, it is clear that presidential pronouncements have been seriously degraded. It is hard to accept, but this president's approach to opponents is much like a ten-year-old calling out the poopy heads on the playground.

At one of John Kennedy's first press conferences, he was challenged by a snarky reporter who said, "What is your role as president?"

Without missing a beat, JFK responded, "To exercise power along the lines of excellence."

It was not lost on the press corps that the quote came from Kennedy's knowledge of Greek scholars.

SUBSTANCE AND STYLE AT PRESS CONFERENCES

It may be too much to expect that level of excellence in our leaders, but we are entitled to civil discourse and truth from those who seek to hold the most powerful office on the planet.

SOMETHING IS ROTTEN

JULY 29, 2020

Protests for racial equality and criminal justice reform continue throughout the country. As a direct result of the murder of George Floyd, citizens remain up in arms and are willing to speak out. There has not been a sustained movement like this since the Vietnam War protests. Like today, the population had stark divisions in the 1960s and 1970s. People chose sides based on their political parties or their socioeconomic status. You were either pro "law and order" and against those unruly hippies in the street, or you felt betrayed by a government that lied about the thousands of young men and women dying in a foreign war.

A boiling point was reached on May 4, 1970, when thirteen unarmed students were shot by the Ohio National Guard at Kent State University. Four of those students died, adding gasoline to the fire already burning across the nation.

Today's protests are similar in that a growing cross-section of the population is speaking out. In Portland, community leaders like the mayor are at these street rallies, and people have come together to seek change in race relations. Moms join them in yellow shirts, and dads carry leaf blowers to disperse the tear gas unleashed on them nightly. The overwhelming majority of them are simply exercising their constitutional right to protest.

After getting tear-gassed himself, the mayor of Portland called the federal troops "invaders." He and the mayors of ten other cities have resisted the troops because they add to the mayhem.

On the other side, Attorney General William Barr justifies unleashing armed militia in cities by claiming, "Violent rioters and anarchists have hijacked legitimate protests to wreak senseless havoc and destruction on innocent victims." Yes, there have been injuries and deaths. It is probably true that a small component of the protestors is destructive, and there is no place for that kind of violence under any circumstances. But to deploy thousands of unnamed troops armed with guns, Billy clubs, and mace to protect one federal courthouse is ludicrous. The overreaction from the feds is not only inappropriate but provokes more destruction.

Now the president is committing to "protecting" even more cities. Instead of lending a helping hand to urban areas with admittedly high crime rates and conferring with local leaders to develop real strategies for community police reforms, he prefers a nightly show of force with a splattering of blood for dramatic effect.

Just as Hamlet suspected there was "something rotten in the state of Denmark," we need to open our eyes to some underlying realities during this season of discontent.

The president's poll numbers are crashing. This is largely a result of his bungling response to COVID-19 and aberrant behaviors too numerous to count, and he has just over ninety days to right his ship.

It is not surprising that his messaging has shifted from the painful reality of 160,000 pandemic deaths to a tried-and-true Republican strategy served in shocking doses at the end of many campaigns: get tough on crime. Look no further than the Trump television ads. In one, an elderly woman fears for her life because, somehow, Joe Biden has destroyed the 9-1-1 system. In another, a young mother and her baby crouch under a bed because police departments will no longer be effective under President Joe Biden. These ads are demonstrably false and should not be airing at all. The fact that the president of the United States endorses and "approves these messages" is beyond despicable.

At the recent Barr hearing, Republicans branded Portland protestors as rioters and anarchists. They were all too eager to trot out edited video clips to make their point. You can be sure that you will see this footage in campaign ads in the fall. Here is the president's real message to what remains of his base: "Be afraid, be very afraid, of big city Democrats." After all, they might get enough supporters to enact real change and improve race relations.

Stuck in his biases and obsessed with his own survival, President Trump is not above trampling on citizens' First Amendment rights—protestors or not. Rather than building consensus from Americans of all colors and perspectives, our president is content to invade his cities and blame it on his opponents.

Two generations after Vietnam, America can look back and say we weathered a divisive storm and may have even gotten stronger because of it. Let us hope our children and their children can say the same in 2020.

FROM CHAOS TO STABILITY: BIDEN AND HARRIS STEP UP

AUGUST 14, 2020

In the *Book of Strange New Things*, author Michael Faber wrote, "There was a red button on the wall labeled EMERGENCY, but no button labeled BEWILDERMENT."

In the past four years, Americans have been careened from emergency to emergency, but what has shaken citizens to the core is the bewilderment that comes with a leader who is driven more by personal grievances than by the needs of his people. This lack of focus has resulted in an inadequate response to a pandemic that is killing 1,000 Americans every day. It has plunged the nation into the worst economy in our history, and it has heightened tensions along racial lines. America is divided, and the president encourages that division as a matter of political strategy.

The only time in our history that comes close to this level of confusion was the election of 1920—exactly one hundred years ago. Professor Joe Powers writes that there were 100,000 dead following World War I, and failure to address the "Great Flu" had cost another 650,000 lives. The economy had slid into a deep recession, and "Americans were left weary by all the turmoil."

Not much was expected when Warren Harding took the oath of office, but his leadership quickly restored the nation's physical and economic health. Powers wrote, "The pandemic subsided, the streets calmed, the economy revived, and the twenties roared."

That sound you heard rising from Wilmington, Delaware, and wafting throughout the nation last week was a sigh of relief. As in the 1920 race, voters crying out for leadership shifted their gaze toward a seasoned, earnest team committed to compassionate solutions to the day's challenges.

Joe Biden and Kamala Harris made history with a biracial, bigender ticket that generated immediate enthusiasm among Democrats and Trump-weary Republicans alike. The ticket generated $26 million in donations within twenty-four hours. Most pundits agree that Harris has already energized two key demographics: suburban women and minority voters. Turnout in both groups will be key to victory in the fall.

What was striking about the Biden-Harris introduction was the sheer professionalism of their remarks. Both were direct without being childish, talking about their families and what matters most to them. Both demonstrated a genuine admiration for their running mate and exuded confidence about the future that was believable and suddenly within our grasp.

Biden acknowledged that Harris was a tough prosecutor. The president, predictably, resorted to name-calling. "She's nasty," he said.

"No," said Biden, tough enough to take a punch and throw one if necessary.

"The ticket is too Far Left," was the knee-jerk Republican campaign response. But the reality is that Biden and Harris laser-focused on average working families and the core kitchen table values that are overwhelmingly mainstream.

Harris was at her best in a strong indictment of the current administration: "The president's mismanagement of the pandemic has plunged us into the worst economic crisis since the Great Depression, and we're experiencing a moral reckoning with racism and systemic injustice [. . .]. America is crying out for leadership. Yet we have a president who cares more about himself than the people who elected him [. . .]. The case against Donald Trump and Mike Pence is open and shut."

Another highlight was the humanizing way Harris depicted Biden "riding the rails" between Washington and Delaware daily to care for his two young sons. And this last jab: "Trump inherited the longest economic expansion in history from Obama and Biden. And then, like everything else he inherited, he ran it straight into the ground."

For his part, Biden put to rest any notion that he was tired or ill-prepared. His speech contained equal parts indignation and possibilities. He presented himself as one whose life experiences could be applied immediately to resolving the pandemic and undoing some of the damage it has caused. On issues as diverse as climate change, civil rights, and foreign relations, Biden was not only prepared, but he was also masterful.

As we move into the home stretch of this campaign, we would do well to remember that we are in this together. Rob Reiner posted something worth repeating:

> *The battle lines have been drawn. It's the Union vs. the Confederacy. It's decency vs. cruelty. It's justice for all vs. justice for the privileged. It's the battle for the soul of our nation. And our Union will win again.*

A CONVENTION CHOOSES THE LIGHT OVER TRUMP DARKNESS

AUGUST 21, 2020

There was something different about President Barack Obama when he spoke at the Democratic Convention last week. Yes, the eloquence and delivery of a master orator were still there, but as he looked somberly into the cameras, there was a jarring urgency about his remarks. Barely containing a righteous rage, he went directly at his successor: "One hundred and seventy thousand Americans dead, millions of jobs gone, our worst impulses unleashed, our proud reputation around the world badly diminished, and our democratic institutions threatened like never before." Obama went on to say, "I did hope, for the sake of our country, that Donald Trump might show some interest in taking the job seriously, "that he might come to feel the weight of the office and discover some reverence for the democracy that had been placed in his care. But he never did. Donald Trump hasn't grown into the job because he can't."

As if to make the point, President Trump spent last week legitimizing QAnon, a group that spouts weird conspiracy theories involving cannibalism and pedophilia. It seems the only requirement any fringe group needs to enter Trump's world is that, in his words, "They like me."

Also last week, the Senate Intelligence Committee released a bipartisan report that confirmed close collaboration between the Trump campaign and Russian agents in 2016. This, while Alexei Navalny—the leading opponent of Putin's autocratic regime—may have been poisoned, the Russians have still not been called out on targeting American soldiers in Afghanistan.

Another insult to our democracy and collective intelligence occurred when Congress called The postmaster general on the carpet for tampering with the system he is sworn to protect. Finally, the president's former chief strategist, Steve Bannon, was arrested for fraud—the sixth top Trump aide to face criminal charges.

Thus, in one week, the darkness confirmed what Obama said to the nation: "What's at stake right now is our democracy."

For their part, the Democrats put on an extraordinary virtual show. Some highlights included Michele Obama's stirring keynote address and "real people" testimonials throughout the week. Biden's nomination was put forth by an elevator operator who made the simple point that Joe was "kind." Others, including an eleven-year-old boy with a stutter, described how they benefitted from Biden's special brand of empathy.

The roll call of fifty-seven states and territories was nothing short of delightful. Real people presented their states in post-card perfect stories that showed the diversity of the Democratic Party and its unity of purpose. Gabbie Giffords, still recovering from a gunshot wound to the head, gave a powerful plea for reasonable gun laws. A young Latina told the story about the deportation of her mother. The daughter of a man who died of COVID-19 said powerfully: "His preexisting condition was that he trusted Donald Trump." Working families stepped up to support Biden's plans for jobs and economic recovery, and Jill Biden impressed all of America with her loving tribute to Joe and a plea for a safe return to school. There were surprises like Colin Powell, John Kasich, and a dozen other Republicans who put their country ahead of partisan considerations.

While the nominees were deprived of throngs of supporters interrupting their acceptance speeches with cheers and applause, their performances were strong, emotional, and stirring. Kamala Harris introduced herself to the country and displayed her prosecutorial skills when focused on the current situation. She then flashed a winning smile when she recounted her family background. There is a magnetic appeal to Harris that is undeniable.

Biden accepted the nomination with the strength, sincerity, and energy of a man thirty years younger after several appearances before his moment in the spotlight. He congratulated Kamala Harris in person. He gushed like a teenager with a crush when he crashed Jill Biden's speech. His speech, like Obama's, decried the existential threat of four more years of Trump chaos, then laid out plans for jobs, pandemic recovery, the environment, and our standing in the world. He forcefully put forth his call to arms, "Build back better."

The two-hour nightly shows produced by the Democrats far exceeded expectations. The production values and the mastery of technology were on display. I have attended six national conventions in various roles and this was my favorite. Speakers stayed on the message and conveyed uplifting themes each night. The party put its best foot forward in a way that will mobilize its base and enhance its credibility with any undecideds that remain.

Given the high stakes of this election, that's exactly what was required.

THE CAMPAIGN CRUCIBLE

SEPTEMBER 2, 2020

Historian Samuel Morrison writes that the 1840 campaign was the "jolliest and most idiotic presidential contest in our history." The newly formed Whig Party beat the incumbent Democrat with no platform. They simply avoided real issues like slavery and Western expansion. Instead, they ran a war hero who still had celebrity status from the Battle of Tippecanoe in the War of 1812. People sang ditties dedicated to "Tippecanoe and Tyler, too." The Whigs packaged William Henry Harrison as a common man in a log cabin who liked to drink his hard cider. A Philadelphia distiller named Edmund Booz produced a tin in the shape of a log cabin for his product. After the campaign, Americans bought Log Cabin syrup and enjoyed their "booze."

With rallies and parades throughout the country, 1840 was a carnival, and President Martin Van Buren, still reeling from the effects of the economic Panic of 1837, never had a chance.

As the 2020 presidential campaign moves into the home stretch, neither camp has a sense of frivolity. In the modern era, Labor Day has marked the beginning of political warfare that has been expensive, pervasive, and deadly serious. The year of COVID-19 has added even more drama to the discourse. By election day, 200,000 Americans will have lost their lives to the pandemic, millions will still be out of work, and racial tensions will remain. There will be no sugarcoating that reality with slogans, rallies, or even hard cider. Voters will judge the current administration's effectiveness and whether they want to move in a different direction.

But it is never enough for candidates to be the opposition. It remains for Joe Biden to present his credentials and to convince voters that he can do better than more of the same.

Biden took a giant step in that direction with his first post-convention appearance in Pittsburgh. He went directly at the president: "Trump can't stop the violence because for years he's fomented it," Biden said. "His failure to call on his own supporters to stop acting as an armed militia in this country shows how weak he is."

Biden also laid to rest the Trump assertion that Democrats condone mayhem. While continuing to support peaceful protests, Biden said clearly and for the record that "rioting is not protesting. Looting is not protesting. It's lawlessness, plain and simple, and should be prosecuted to the fullest extent of the law." Biden also made his position on jobs, health care, and energy crystal clear. On the latter item, he spoke to his Western Pennsylvania audience to support fracking for natural gas. It is time for Trump supporters to drop ridiculous notions to the contrary.

The Biden camp has laid out an aggressive schedule of visits to swing states in the post-Labor Day campaign season. This level of energy and the staying power of his lead in the polls is worlds apart from the Trump attempt to brand him as "sleepy."

For his part, Trump boarded Air Force One to visit Kenosha, Wisconsin, over the objections of local leaders and families reeling from the unrest caused by the attack on Jacob Blake. He did not visit the victim but instead continued to fuel the fires of divisiveness with a series of reckless charges and false statements that had even Fox News anchors scratching their heads.

At this contest stage, pundits are famous for pointing out that the race will get tighter before election day. This is probably true, but a glaring difference exists between 2020 and 2016. The polls show that the undecided vote is between 6 percent and 8 percent. That's right, 92 to 94 percent of us have already made up our minds. Moreover, voters from both parties are not likely to change their minds. This means that both sides will be unleashing the rhetoric designed to bolster their base. Look for Trump to play the "law and order" card and downplay the health care crisis and the economic collapse. Look for Biden to remind voters that the mess we are in occurred on Trump's watch, no matter how the president tries to spin it.

Beyond the base, every dime of media spending, every social network message, and every debating point will be aimed directly at a tiny sliver of undecideds—especially those living in swing states. For Pennsylvanians, this means we can expect to see a lot more of the candidates in the weeks to come.

LEADERSHIP ON THE BALLOT

SEPTEMBER 11, 2020

There has been an uptick in my emails recently. People have weighed in on my comments on the presidential campaign, and I am grateful for all perspectives—this includes some colorful ones from "hell or highwater" supporters of President Trump.

Here's the thing: support for your party is understandable and commendable. But confusing blind loyalty with patriotism is not only dangerous to the election process; it's un-American. We are called upon to vote as informed citizens, not in lockstep with someone with the brashest voice, especially when that individual has failed the test of leadership. For most of you, this column doesn't matter. Your minds are made up. But for those of you who are still pondering, consider recent campaign developments.

The past week began with both campaigns testing their messages in key states. Biden has a new focus on jobs as Trump continues his attack on urban violence. A bipartisan group of leaders sought to address any perceived irregularities in mail-in voting, and states are taking necessary precautions.

Kamala Harris bounded out of an airplane in Wisconsin wearing Chuck Taylor Sneakers and skinny jeans—by far the coolest candidate in the race. President Trump launched a Twitter attack, tweeting, "Nobody likes her."

We'll see about that.

The president is still dealing with the fallout from his denigrating comments about fallen soldiers, and one pundit described the ratcheting up of the campaign as "a knife fight in a phone booth."

Then this happened: In news stories about an upcoming book by Bob Woodward, the president, in recorded interviews, declared that he deliberately minimized the risks of COVID-19, although he knew it was deadly serious.

He told Woodward in February, "It's more deadly than even your strenuous flu. This is deadly stuff." At that very moment, the president was deliberately misleading the public. "One day, it's like a miracle. It will disappear. I think it's going to work out fine."

Biden seized upon the revelations calling them a "life-and-death betrayal of the American people."

This moment calls for a pause of conscience for all of us. Putting aside four years of exhausting chaos emanating from the Trump White House, we seem to have arrived at a moment of truth. Former senator Claire McCaskill said this: "Imagine that a Category 5 hurricane was bearing down on the coast of Florida. Do we expect our leaders to downplay the threat and implicitly suggest that folks and businesses just 'ride it out?' Or do we expect candor from our leaders and a brave plan to evacuate or board up properties to minimize the damage?"

If you are one of the few who remain undecided in this election, consider this: all presidents face at least one soul-searching test of leadership. Try as he might, Lyndon Johnson could not rise above the Vietnam quagmire. His failure to lead us out of that war cost him his presidency. Richard Nixon went from a landslide victory to resigning in disgrace because he chose to cover a crime rather than lead the country out of the nightmare. George W. Bush, for all his foreign policy miscues, rose to the occasion after 9/11 and led the country in a resurgence of resolve. Ronald Reagan, likewise, stood firm against communism and helped end the Cold War. John F. Kennedy failed miserably in the Bay of Pigs but passed the test of leadership by accepting the blame and leveling with the American people about the incident.

Over the past four years, President Trump has curried favor with dictators, pressured foreign governments for his own political gain, ignored Putin's threats against our troops, separated children from their mothers at our borders, paid hush money to a porn star to influence a federal campaign, squandered millions of taxpayers' dollars at his golf resorts and committed numerous other transgressions. This has left many of us exhausted and looking for redemption. But, for some of you, the daily dose of disorder from the White House up to this point might not have been enough to shake your faith. What will it take?

At a minimum, we should all expect our president to protect us. We should expect him to level with us when things go wrong. We should expect him to show some backbone, tell us the truth, and lead by example. Wear the mask, for heaven's sake. It is time for voters to decide if the current president's actions justify his reelection. Leadership is on the ballot this November, and we, the people, must decide.

NEXT UP: THE DEBATES

SEPTEMBER 18, 2020

When it comes to debates, few settings are livelier than Philadelphia City Council meetings. In one exchange, a councilman held forth and took direct personal aim against a colleague. That colleague managed to get to the floor and ask as the speaker sat down, "Are you through?" The speaker nodded, and his adversary fired off the best one-liner in Philadelphia politics: "Then wipe yourself!"

There have been flashes of similar, more G-rated wit at the presidential level. In one of the Lincoln-Douglas debates, Stephen Douglas attacked Lincoln's veracity, calling him "two-faced." Lincoln replied: "Sir, if I had two faces, would I be wearing this one?"

Likewise, Ronald Reagan, who was seventy-three during the 1984 debates, came prepared for an attack on his age. He turned it around on Walter Mondale by saying, "I will not make age an issue of this campaign. I am not going to exploit, for political purposes, my opponent's youth and inexperience." Even Mondale got a chuckle out of that one.

Most of us remember Lloyd Bentsen's retort to Dan Quayle's attempt to compare himself to John F. Kennedy: "I served with Jack Kennedy. I knew Jack Kennedy. Jack Kennedy was a friend of mine. Senator, you're no Jack Kennedy." It was a crushing putdown.

Finally, Ross Perot's vice presidential candidate, Admiral James Stockdale, asked publicly in 1992, "Who am I? Why am I here?" It was safe to say that the voters had the same questions.

Debates can be fraught with peril for the unprepared. Gerald Ford made an unforced error about Soviet domination in Eastern Europe and insisted that

NEXT UP: THE DEBATES

Poland and Yugoslavia were free from interference from the Soviet bloc. Nothing was further from the truth, and nothing could have been more damaging to the president's foreign policy credibility at the time.

A gut-wrenching experience for Democrats occurred when candidate Mike Dukakis was asked a blunt question about capital punishment. The moderator asked what he would do if his wife was raped or murdered; would he support a death sentence in that case? Viewers were looking for passion; Dukakis gave them a soulless answer in legalese, leaving them cold.

Given the possibility of such gaffes and the unpredictability of both current presidential candidates, some have suggested that the parties forgo any debates this year. It is true, after all, that most voters have locked in their preference at this point. It is also true that debates serve mostly to affirm individuals' perspectives about issues and their own candidates. People hear what they want to hear in debates.

RUTH BADER GINSBURG AND THE ELECTION

SEPTEMBER 25, 2020

One of Ruth Bader Ginsburg's eulogists called her a "jurist of global importance." They were exactly right. Her leadership and fearlessness were of once-in-a-generation caliber, and her opinions on everything from women's rights to healthcare and immigration reform have provided a thoughtful counterbalance to those who had sought to twist truth and justice toward their own purposes.

RBG's passing happens at a time when politics is sure to encroach on her legacy. Justice Ginsburg expressed her fervent hope that the next president would nominate her replacement in her dying moments.

Her body was still warm when President Trump dashed that possibility.

The fact is that the president and the Republicans in the U.S. Senate are within their rights to nominate and confirm a Supreme Court justice at their timing and pleasure. There are three strong reasons—beyond Justice Ginsburg's dying request—why they should wait.

First, the Republicans are violating their own rules. Ignoring what they did to Merrick Garland in 2016 is the height of hypocrisy. Recall that President Obama's nomination to fill the seat of departed Justice Scalia was ignored for nine months. Why? Because the Republicans said they would not confirm a justice in an election year. They said they would rather have the people speak and let the new president make that lifetime appointment. So here we are, less than forty days before the next election, but that precedent no longer applies somehow.

Second, if we take our political lessons from truly great leaders, think about Abraham Lincoln. Chief Justice Roger B. Taney died twenty-seven days before the 1864 presidential election. The Civil War was raging, and the president desperately needed support from the highest court in the land to uphold some of his jarring actions to hold the nation together. Still, Lincoln delayed his nomination of Salmon Chase until after he won reelection. He did not presume that he would win and did not want to exercise the extraordinary power of installing a justice before the people had their say.

Third, the Merrick Garland maneuver and the full court press by the president and his enablers to push through Justice Kavanaugh have already tilted the Court to the right. This new nomination will push the Court to what may be an insurmountable 6-3 majority. This will invite an onslaught of challenges designed to undo hard-earned social progress in areas like the ones for which RBG fought so long and hard.

If the people vote to reelect Donald Trump on November 3, he will have the power to appoint a new justice and the mandate to do so. But by forcing the issue in the heat of a campaign, the president is pouring gasoline on the fires of division already raging throughout the country and creating a Supreme Court unreflective of mainstream America.

Here's a shocker: he just doesn't care.

Trump has determined that chalking up another win at the Supreme Court will help him at the polls. Republican senators must feel the same since they lined up behind his nominee before he even said who it would be!

The president may be making a huge miscalculation, however. Early polling suggests that Democrats—not Republicans—may be more energized by November. This is partly because the 6-3 majority frightens women, minorities, the LGBTQ community, immigrants, and many other citizens. If suburban women and other critical demographic groups were previously detached, they would surely rock the vote now.

Consider this: at a White House news conference, a reporter asked the president, "Will you commit to making sure that there is a peaceful transfer of power after the election?"

"Well," said the president of the United States, "we're going to have to see what happens."

No, Mr. President. The answer to that question is, and always has been, an unequivocal "Yes." As Senator Mitt Romney (R-UT) said, "This is the United States of America, not Belarus." The peaceful transition of power is what distinguishes us from every other country on Earth.

Donald Trump is telegraphing to all of us that he will accept the results of this election only if he wins. What we see in real time is the exercise of raw political power. A rogue president and a complicit Republican Senate mean our democracy is in for a bumpy ride. True patriotism is about defending the country against this type of destruction.

The ray of hope is that the people may choose a new course in just under forty days.

Do it for Ruth.

THE MAYHEM CONTINUES WITH AN END IN SIGHT

OCTOBER 3, 2020

Over the years, the Paul Simon lyrics from the classic song "Mrs. Robinson" have resurfaced in my mind as America worked through the turbulence of war, disease, politics, and other disruptions. DiMaggio was the essence of style and steadiness. He spent his entire baseball career with the Yankees and lifted the club to the pinnacle of sports. His greatness at the plate and in his service to others became a standard to which several generations of Americans have aspired.

There is no such pinstripe propriety in the political world of today. There is no "normal" in catastrophes that explode daily. When the battle for the presidency was heating up in January, COVID-19 was lurking like a serpent in all our backyards. Today, 209,000 Americans are dead, and the president himself has now been infected. The only appropriate sentiment at this moment is to hope and pray for the speedy recovery of the president and those around him battling the disease.

It is fair to note, however, that reality has caught up with him. The mixed messages about social distancing and wearing masks and the outright disdain for science emanating from the White House allowed the pandemic to flourish. The Republican Convention was staged on the White House lawn with few precautions. The Rose Garden has been the scene of several infection-spreading events, from signing ceremonies with world leaders to announcing a Supreme Court Justice nominee. Signs point to the latter ceremony as a possible cause of the latest round of high-level infections.

It seems like years ago, but just last week, in that barroom brawl of a debate, the president continued to mock his opponent for wearing an oversized mask and for isolating against the virus. He also staged several rallies, including one in Harrisburg, where thousands of onlookers stood within spewing distance of each other. We are now all looking at the results of ignoring science and hoping there is still time to banish the COVID-19 serpent.

But the world doesn't stop. The need for a peaceful demonstration of American democracy has never been more important. The presidential election and every contest on the ballot must proceed with as much normality as we can muster.

Sadly, just before the president was sidelined with COVID-19, he had spread his own infection in our election norms.

In a disturbing end to the first presidential debate, Chris Wallace asked whether both candidates would accept the election results. Specifically, he asked, "Will you ask your supporters not to engage in any civil unrest and accept the results of the election?" The answer that Joe Biden gave was unequivocal, "Yes."

Trump had a chilling response: "We'll see."

He then went on to do the opposite and called on supporters to converge at polling places; he continued to attack the validity of mail-in ballots and affirmed that the rush to fill a seat on the Supreme Court was to have a full bench ready for his election challenges.

Trump's performance did nothing to broaden his base. It was simply an affirmation that, win or lose, he intended to implement a strategy to secure power at any cost. This is nothing less than an end run around democracy. Even the most hard-core MAGA-hatters should be concerned about that.

As we head into the final thirty days of this campaign, we can all agree that we wish President Trump a full and speedy recovery. We should also agree that the election must be about moving away from fear and division. By now, we know the candidates intimately. We know their personalities and their flaws. When we make our choice, it should be about the good of the country and not our affiliation with any party or a cult of personality. It should be about facing the mayhem we have seen over the past several years and finding solutions.

When the Yankees needed to turn things around in the late innings of a ballgame, one thing reassured the team and all its fans: Joe DiMaggio was on deck. For me, Joe Biden represents hope to emerge from the pandemic. He also is the antithesis of the pandemonium that we have seen from the current administration and its policies. He is steady and as reassuring as the Yankee Clipper himself.

The nation turns its lonely eyes to Joe.

SOME NORMALCY AMID THE CHAOS

OCTOBER 10, 2020

The sheer bedlam of 2020 continues.

Last week, law enforcement officials broke up a plot to kidnap the Michigan governor. The FBI confirmed that Far-Right terrorists were responsible and that groups like them were widespread and growing. Still, the president, the man responsible for law and order, tells these groups to "Standby," not "cease and desist." We can expect more violence if the president cannot forcefully denounce armed insurrectionists.

Also, last week the candidates continued to debate how to conduct their next debates as COVID-19 surged at the White House and in hot spots throughout the country. In this environment, watching two candidates vie for the vice presidency in an almost normal debate was reassuring. Vice President Pence and Senator Kamala Harris presented their arguments with the rhythm of skilled debaters. Both carried the banner for their running mates and did their best to advance their party's cause. True, Pence talked over his allotted time and received several well-deserved rebukes from Harris and the moderator. It is also true that Senator Harris flashed some irritation at Pence, which was not a good look for the cameras.

A criticism of both candidates was that neither offered direct answers to any questions. Like small aircrafts, candidates will touch and go on issues. That is, they give a little lip service to the question, "Is climate change an existential threat?" then it wheels up as they tell you how awful their opponent is on fracking or carbon emissions.

The early part of the debate focused on COVID-19. Harris recited the grim statistics: 210,000 dead, 7 million cases, and 30 million jobs lost. No wonder Pence tried to change the subject at every turn. One such effort was to inject a new issue into the discussion. Would the Democrats add more members to the Supreme Court if they get elected? A "yes" answer would bring howls from conservatives who want to protect their soon-to-be 6-3 majority on the bench. A "no" answer would give away any negotiating power the new president might have in the Senate. Biden and Harris ignored the question, but Pence scored some points by raising it.

Predictably, as to who won the debate, each side claimed victory. What is remarkable to me is the passion with which they make the claim. One Republican operative told me that Pence dominated all the instant post-debate polls. This is hard to believe since every media outlet but Fox News reported a win for Kamala Harris. *The Hill* publication reported that six in ten viewers chose Kamala.

President Trump weighed in with his usual invective and personal attack on the first woman of color to be nominated for vice president. "She's a monster," he said. Women and minorities will remember that when they vote in a few weeks.

While Harris ducked the Supreme Court packing question, there were two much worse deflections by Pence. When he crowed about the Trump administration protecting preexisting conditions in health care insurance, Harris was having none of it. "How can you protect preexisting conditions if you are in court right now trying to destroy the Affordable Care Act?" Pence had no good answer, and Harris delivered this zinger directly to the camera: "If you have preexisting conditions, they're coming for you."

And do not gloss over Pence's nonanswer on the peaceful transition of power question. "Will you accept the results of the election?" is a simple question that every candidate and every American must answer affirmatively. The fact that neither Trump nor Pence will do so has already destabilized the process and may cause disruption or worse if the election is close.

Few minds were changed at the vice presidential debate, but it was less gut-wrenching than the presidential mud fest that preceded it. It is not realistic to expect a return to decency in the last days of this campaign, but Pence and Harris showed that there might be hope for more civil disagreements among people who know their craft and their obligations to their country.

In the meantime, the Biden team has been buoyed by polling numbers that are steady and strong. He now holds a double-digit lead nationally, surpassing the "margin of error" in almost all swing states. The Biden message of cooperation seems to be resonating through the chaos.

Three more weeks.

THE SUPREME COURT: WINNING THE BATTLE BUT LOSING THE WAR

OCTOBER 15, 2020

Amy Coney Barrett is a smart, skilled judge. She is about to be confirmed by the United States Senate for a lifetime appointment to the U.S. Supreme Court. Her weeklong job interview with the Senate Judiciary Committee was marked by cautious responses to key policy issues. She remained tight-lipped about every hot-button item and offered no hints about how she would decide on matters like a contested election, women's rights, or Obamacare. While most nominees claim that being specific would jeopardize their impartiality when actual cases arise, some of her responses to "softball" questions were troubling.

Senator Amy Klobuchar (D-Minn.) asked her whether federal law prohibited voter intimidation. Barrett deflected, saying she could "only decide cases as they come to me." Not really. Federal law specifically prohibits intimidation of any kind that interferes with the right of any person to vote. *Period.* Another senator asked whether a president could unilaterally delay an election, which President Trump has suggested. Again, Barrett demurred and said she would "listen to all arguments." Wrong again. Elections are set by the legislative branch. Any election delays must be initiated by Congress.

Senator Kamala Harris grilled Barrett on the Affordable Care Act. "Are you aware of President Trump's statements committing to nominate judges who will strike down the Affordable Care Act?"

Barrett's response strains credibility. "I don't recall hearing about or seeing such statements."

Coming just weeks from a presidential election, a fair question is, what's the rush? It is quite possible that a new president will be elected in November, and surely, that president should have the right to make a lifetime appointment. Note that President Lincoln declined to fill the deceased Roger Taney's seat because he felt that the people had the right to be heard in that election year of 1864. Consider that the Republicans are breaking their own rule on this issue: they refused to even consider the nomination of Merrick Garland in 2016 because it was only nine months before the presidential election.

Another disconcerting aspect of this appointment is that it represents a clear lurching of the Supreme Court to the right.

Women's rights and the Affordable Care Act are considered established precedents, and according to any poll ever taken, both are supported by a large majority of Americans. One pundit said, "Republicans had better hope that Barrett will not be the justice who overturns Roe and the ACA. That will be the death of their party. But go ahead. Because you can "stick it to the Libs" today."

Women are paying attention, and it seems President Trump understands their clout. In one of his whining riffs at a campaign rally last week, Trump literally begged for their support. "Suburban women, would you please like me? Please. Please," he said. "I saved your damn neighborhood, okay?" He mistakenly thinks that keeping minorities out of suburbia by discouraging low-income housing is a good thing. Women reacted immediately to the blatant racism and the patronizing tone of the president's remarks.

Similarly, suburban women and moderate voters are picking up on the signal being sent by the ascendancy of Amy Coney Barrett.

After four years of a White House careening from one blunder to another, it may be that the Supreme Court power play will shine a bright light on key issues for voters. While Senate Republicans put another notch in their political belts, most Americans became more concerned about a 6-3, right-leaning Supreme Court. Amy Coney Barrett on the bench guarantees that there will be challenges to every hard-fought social achievement of recent years.

First up is a challenge to the Affordable Care Act. The president has blatantly called for "his" judicial appointees to fall in line with eviscerating health care protections for millions of Americans. Is *Roe v. Wade* next? Will the Court roll back environmental protections? What about gay marriage?

The citizens of this country will have their say about it on November 3. Poll after poll indicates a strong blue wave of repudiation coming for the president and his incompetence. For that sliver of the electorate still on the fence, the realities of an emerging ideological attack on their way of life may jolt them to seek balance in electing Democrats at the U.S. Senate, House, and down-ballot races.

THE SUPREME COURT: WINNING THE BATTLE BUT LOSING THE WAR

Senator McConnell and the Republicans have the votes to confirm Amy Coney Barrett. They may have won that battle, but on November 3, voters will determine who wins the war.

POST-ELECTION – FIRST IMPRESSIONS

NOVEMBER 6, 2020

Every president has honored the lofty principles of the Founding Fathers and did their best to bring about a "more perfect union." Republicans, Democrats, conservatives, liberals—all understood that our experiment in self-governance was a beacon for the world, and all of them brought dignity to the office, except for Donald J. Trump.

As the nation counted votes, the president sensed his numbers sagging and the presidency slipping away. He could have accepted the harsh reality of government by the people. He could have thanked his citizens for the extraordinary gift of leading the greatest country in the world for four years. Instead, he attacked his opponents, the press, and the republic for which he was supposed to stand. He made false and reckless claims about the integrity of our sacred voting traditions and invited insurrection among his supporters. Donald J. Trump's remarks from the White House on Thursday, November 5, will be recalled by historians as a low point of presidential leadership. They will likely ask voters who supported this man, "What were you thinking?"

The fact is that the post-election tantrum was the culmination of a series of grievances aired by Trump previously. At the pep rallies held in swing states, the president spread more than just the coronavirus. He tossed his usual vitriol to the crowds, and they gobbled it up like fish in a tank. As the pandemic death toll exceeded 250,000 and the economy collapsed, he blithely told his crowds that "we were rounding a corner." His campaign labeled all Democrats as Communists who would "cancel Christmas" and spewed other similar nonsense.

There may still be some twists and turns in the presidential race. Legal teams have fanned out nationwide with conflicting and somewhat irrational attacks. In Arizona, armed protestors wanted all the votes counted and harassed election personnel working around the clock to do just that. In Pennsylvania, they wanted to stop the vote count. This is like saying, "We're leading at the end of the seventh inning. Let's stop the game now." In Michigan, the lawyers wanted to stop the count when they were winning and reversed themselves when they fell behind.

When the smoke clears, Americans will have found their footing again. They will have rejected the petulant, self-serving whiner-in-chief. They will have reaffirmed the peaceful transfer of power, which makes this nation exceptional.

Another reality that emerged relates to the viability of our political parties. Other than eking out a narrow victory for Joe Biden, the Democrats got clobbered in U.S. Senate and House races and state legislatures across the country. There was no blue wave and targeted Republican incumbents protected their turf against an onslaught of campaign advertising. The voters seem to like their current senator, Congress member, or state representative. They were willing to send a message about ending the Trump chaos but did not want to eviscerate the Republican Party. Maybe, just maybe, this is a good thing.

As we all hunger for a return to civility, it may be that Democrats and Republicans can now shake off some of the tribalism that has infected the body politic. I envision a compassionate, experienced President Joe Biden reaching out to Mitch McConnell and both putting country above their respective parties. Both could agree on an actual plan to get us out of the pandemic. Most political leaders agree that an ambitious infrastructure program would stimulate the economy and put millions of people back to work. There might even be room for negotiations on taxes, energy, and other critical issues. The American people have shown by their votes that they are ready for that kind of cooperation.

One more first impression about the campaign: political pollsters blew it. Survey after survey predicted easy wins for Biden and down-ballot Democratic candidates. They were wrong. In fact, their numbers were so bad that the entire polling profession had lost the confidence of candidates, the media, and the public.

The problem, of course, is that without polling data, candidates would be flying blind and unsure of which issues resonate with which voters. It may mean that candidates will spend less time with pollsters and more time with actual voters. Media and technology in campaigns are here to stay, but developing one's message as a candidate might involve something completely different than constant polling. It might be as simple as listening to voters for a change.

TIME TO CONCEDE
NOVEMBER 13, 2020

Karl Rove said, "The president should do his part to unite the country by leading a peaceful transition and letting grievances go." In a *Wall Street Journal* article, Rove noted Biden had an "insurmountable lead" that would require finding tens of thousands of illegal votes to undo. In fact, with Arizona and Georgia in his column, Biden will have won 306 Electoral College votes—the same number that Trump claimed was a landslide in 2016.

It's over. No amount of legal maneuvering or recounts will change the result. Joe Biden is the president-elect. Now the question is when will the current president face that reality and concede? When will he embrace the American tradition of civility and assure a peaceful transition of power?

A *New York Times* op-ed put it this way: "Imagine that a president of another country lost an election and refused to concede defeat. Instead, he lied about the vote count. He then filed lawsuits to have ballots thrown out and used the power of government to prevent a transition of power from starting. We never would have imagined seeing something like this in America." And this from The Washington Post: "Eventually, Republican officials will be forced to make a choice, between breaking with Trump and breaking with democracy."

There have been times in our history when deep personal or political differences have provoked bad behavior. Stinging from a nasty campaign with Thomas Jefferson, John Adams chose to sit out the inauguration of his successor. He left Washington at four o'clock that morning.

Like his father, John Quincy Adams had his presidency limited to one term. Andrew Jackson believed the presidency was stolen from him via a corrupt bargain in 1824. He ran a relentless campaign to unseat John Quincy Adams and succeeded. Interestingly, Adams extended his hand to Jackson and offered the use of the White House for the inaugural festivities. It was the last straw when Jackson refused, and Adams, like his father, left town early.

The only other public example of bad form between outgoing and incoming presidents was when Andrew Johnson ignored the inauguration of General Ulysses S. Grant. Johnson had been denied his party's nomination after being impeached and nearly convicted. On the other hand, Grant was the revered hero of the Civil War who, no doubt, sent Johnson into a rage. The enmity went both ways. Grant made it clear that he would not ride in the presidential carriage with Johnson.

Only three out of forty-five transitions were marred by bad blood. In all other cases, presidents rose above partisan and personal differences to join in furthering the ideals of the American experiment. In all those cases, the incumbent provided guidance and support so the government could survive a transition without losing a step. Every losing presidential candidate in modern history has put the country ahead of their own ego. Losing is hard, but leaving the political stage without dignity would be unthinkable to them.

There have been many cases where vote counts have been much narrower than the decisive result of 2020. Even in those cases, civility prevailed.

Let the record show that both Al Gore in 2000 and Hillary Clinton in 2016 conceded to their opponents and offered the hand of conciliation long before Inauguration Day. It should also be noted that President Obama and Vice President Biden greeted Donald Trump and Mike Pence at the White House within days of the election and initiated a smooth transition of power.

Yes, it is within the rights of any citizen to air their grievances in court. Presidents can bring lawsuits in any state they choose, but the burden is on the plaintiff to show some shred of evidence that those legal actions have merit. One especially absurd charge is that the counting process was secret and prevented poll watchers from observing. Not only were both parties accommodated with front-row seats in every counting venue, but the entire process was also livestreamed for all the world to see.

The bottom line is that Biden won.

President Trump doesn't need to wait for votes to be certified to accept the inevitable. He can do the honorable thing right now. He can begin to erase some of the divisiveness that he, himself, caused by being gracious in defeat. Instead, his sulking and the dismantling of some critical government functions will continue to erode what is left of his legacy.

Man up, Mr. President. Concede and let the country move on.

GEORGIA ON OUR MINDS

DECEMBER 11, 2020

Like most voters, I sat on the edge of my seat as the returns came in on election night. I was confident that clear-thinking Democrats and Republicans would reject the chaos and divisiveness of the Trump presidency, but it was unclear whether the peculiar math of the Electoral College would hold up.

Tensions rose when same-day voters built up substantial early leads for Trump in the critical swing states, but two things buoyed my expectations of a Biden win. First, Democrats took full advantage of the right to vote by mail in Pennsylvania and many other states. It would be overwhelmingly pro-Biden because the president himself had actively discouraged his own voters from using the convenience of voting absentee. He would soon be "hoisted on his own petard." The blue wave would happen just a few days late.

The second glimmer of reassurance I got on election night was by way of the feisty James Carville. Carville was asked which state to watch on one of the network panels as the evening unfolded. Without missing a beat, the self-proclaimed "Ragin' Cajun" said, "Keep your eye on Georgia."

A solid Republican state for forty years, Georgia has supported only two Democratic presidential candidates since 1972—their local candidate Jimmy Carter in 1976 and their Arkansas neighbor, Bill Clinton, in 1992. With its sixteen electoral votes, Georgia has been too important to ignore for either party.

What put Georgia in play in 2020? One very big reason was Stacey Abrams, who lost a close race for governor two years earlier. She and a powerful group of grassroots organizers reached deep into the African American and minority communities. By building coalitions focused on the urban and suburban communities in the state, Democratic turnout reached historic levels—enough to secure a 12,000 win for Joe Biden last month.

GEORGIA ON OUR MINDS

According to most observers, Georgia is considered a swing state, and both parties know it. As a result of Georgia laws requiring runoffs in close elections, the state, on January 5, is hosting two races for the U.S. Senate. Incumbents David Perdue and Kelly Loeffler are facing challenges from Jon Ossoff and Reverend Raphael Warnock. The stakes are high. If Ossoff and Warnock win, the Senate will be split 50-50, with Vice President-elect Kamala Harris having the power to cast a deciding vote. If Perdue and Loeffler win, the Republicans will maintain their current 52-48 majority. Even if one of the two Republicans wins, it could limit President-elect Biden's ability to enact his program or even get much of his cabinet confirmed.

Both campaigns are heavily funded donnybrooks. During the first Loeffler-Warnock debate, nothing was held back. Senator Loeffler opened with a barrage of negatives that attacked Reverend Warnock's faith and patriotism. Warnock returned the fire by noting that Loeffler joined team Trump in the never-ending attack on Georgia officials and voters. Loeffler, he said, doesn't even believe that the president lost.

The airwaves in Georgia and some national programs are full of overheated attacks from all four candidates. During the pandemic, Jon Ossoff branded Perdue a "crook" for questionable pharmaceutical stock deals. Offended by the attack, Perdue chose to forgo his only debate with Ossoff, giving the latter the opportunity to call his opponent a "coward."

When all the invective is spewed, what remains are two contests that will be determined by voter turnout. Republicans are counting on an even bigger vote for their candidates than showed up in November. Democrats are building on the surprising strength of minorities and urbanites who tipped the scale for Biden. A sweep for Democrats in the state would mean that Georgia truly has turned blue and blazed a path for future Democrats who have been stymied in the deep red South in recent years.

Does any of this matter for Pennsylvania? You bet it does. President Biden, with even the slimmest of majorities in the U.S. Senate, would have a chance to put the full array of his programs into place. It means we could have a national strategy to emerge from the pandemic. We could enact a real jobs program targeting working families and reemerge as the leader among our international allies. A Republican majority in the Senate assuredly means Mitch McConnell-driven obstruction that will stymie those efforts.

Take Carville's advice and keep your eye on Georgia. The election results will impact the direction of our state and our country for years to come.

THE BIDEN-MCCONNELL DANCE

DECEMBER 18, 2020

I am not a fan of Senator Mitch McConnell. I watched with horror when he addressed an audience within minutes of Obama's inauguration to announce his top priority: making him a one-term president. From that moment forward, McConnell led his troops in an all-out effort to obstruct any and every initiative that the new president proposed, even those he had previously voted for. With that said, it has been interesting to watch Mitch McConnell negotiate the choppy waters churned up by outgoing Donald Trump and, at long last, step up to his leadership responsibilities.

For his part, Joe Biden has been a model of restraint as he watched the Trump campaign lodge an endless series of baseless attacks on the election. Finally, in his first remarks after the Electoral College vote, he called it like it was—an attempt to wipe out the votes of more than twenty million Americans and to hand the presidency to a candidate who lost the Electoral College, popular vote, and states whose votes they were trying to reverse. Biden said, "It's a position so extreme we've never seen it before. A position that refused to respect the will of the people refused to respect the rule of law, and refused to honor our Constitution."

It is the obligation of elected officials—those who have taken an oath to uphold the Constitution—to do so even if election results are hard to accept. Mitch McConnell remained silent as Trump's advocates spun conspiracy theories and badgered eighty judges who rejected their arguments across the country. It was not until the Electoral College vote that McConnell took to the floor to declare that Joe Biden was, in fact, the president-elect.

Better late than never, I suppose.

In those remarks, however, three important nuances to McConnell's remarks deserve our attention. First, he has freed himself from the demands of a petulant and petty president. To his credit, McConnell has signaled that his concern for an orderly transition of power and democracy itself outweighs his personal loyalty to Donald Trump. While the president was quick to deride McConnell's return to reality, it is McConnell who is now the adult in the room.

Second, McConnell has thrown the gauntlet down for the entire Republican Party. He is presenting his colleagues with a clear choice: continue to grovel at the feet of a president who cannot accept defeat or take up the responsibilities of party and country and face whatever challenges lie ahead. While some grumbling is coming from the fringes, McConnell has told his troops in no uncertain terms that "the Electoral College has spoken." The election is over, and it is time for Republicans everywhere to decide whether they are on Team Trump or Team Mitch.

Third, McConnell has assumed his rightful position as the leader of the "loyal opposition." Especially if Republicans maintain control of the U.S. Senate after the January 5 runoff elections in Georgia, McConnell will be essential to any legislative program President Biden hopes to achieve.

On this third point, McConnell has the parliamentary skills and the tenacity to bargain with the best of them. Just this past week, he demonstrated those skills once again. By dropping his redline demand for liability protections, he got Democrats to back away from a portion of their proposed bailouts for state and local governments. This, in turn, may have helped secure the passage of a $900 billion pandemic stimulus package and turn on the spigot of support for millions of Americans in desperate need. Also, he led his caucus in the discussions to complete work on the entire federal budget.

It should also be noted that a bipartisan group of senators changed the dynamic by insisting on the new stimulus package. It was not necessary for them to oppose McConnell publicly. They had more than fifty-one votes, and McConnell knew it. This has implications for McConnell as leader and Biden as president. The "rank and file" know that they matter and can influence important policy issues anytime they care to work together. Compromise is possible.

But here's the most critical observation: Biden and McConnell know each other well.

By no means are they best buddies; there is enough mutual respect between them to suggest that there will be essential compromises on vital issues like handling vaccine distribution, infrastructure development, energy policies, and foreign affairs.

PA LEGISLATURE TO CONTINUE THE CHARADE IN 2021

DECEMBER 29, 2020

For the record, and for the umpteenth time, Trump lost. I was watching a rerun of a basketball game recently, and the final score was 80-73. Oddly, that is the same percentage of victory Biden had in November. No one suggested that the contest should be awarded to the losing team and that the referees cheated, or some baskets shouldn't count.

Still, the nation was subjected to a whining series of baseless charges from the losing candidate, which failed the test of reality in courts all over the country. Stephanos Bibas, a federal court judge appointed by Trump, stopped efforts to overturn Pennsylvania's votes with this terse assessment: "Free, fair elections are the lifeblood of our democracy. Charges of unfairness are serious. But calling an election unfair does not make it so. Charges require specific allegations and then proof. We have neither here."

Out of six million votes cast in Pennsylvania, there was one arrest for voter fraud—a Trump supporter trying to vote twice in Delaware County. This is evidence that one solitary person committed a crime and, since he was caught doing it, evidence that the voting process is virtually foolproof.

Still, the Pennsylvania legislature has declared it will do a full diagnostic on voting in Pennsylvania. The Republican leadership has already tipped its hand by claiming that the Pennsylvania Supreme Court may have overstepped its bounds by allowing three days to count last-minute mail-in ballots. Put aside the fact that Republicans overwhelmingly supported mail-in ballots in the first place and that the courts applied common sense to handle the unusual volume caused by the new law and the pandemic.

So, in a classic case of overstepping their own bounds, the legislature seems determined to overturn the Pennsylvania Constitution by tampering with how we elect Supreme Court judges. This and other "reforms" are simply opportunistic. They are designed to exploit the skepticism that the president and his enablers have sown about our election process and to twist that doubt into new policies to their own political advantage.

Other states like Georgia and Wisconsin, with Republican majorities, are planning similar charades.

Eli Finkel, a professor at Northwestern, noted that this kind of post-election fever could have long-lasting damage. He noted that it was extraordinary how far Republicans have gone in endorsing beliefs that are disconnected from reality—just to "bind the sect." "When we consider the support for Trump's efforts from officials and the rank and file in the Republican Party, I am profoundly concerned," he said.

True, there may be procedural improvements that can be made that both parties can agree upon. It is also possible that some creative thinking can emerge from this legislative review, but don't hold your breath. Beware of "good government" proponents who cannot count basketball scores or election results.

In other legislative news, each of the four caucuses has outlined its priorities for the coming session.

House Republicans will reintroduce a series of bills designed to make government more efficient. While they continue to support core services, expect reducing regulations and streamlining many government functions to be a part of their initiatives. They will also dust off recommendations from its Transportation Task Force report and offer funding alternatives for meeting highway maintenance and construction costs.

By and large, the House Democrats will support the governor's agenda on budget priorities and pandemic relief efforts. Also, with a clear shift in leadership to the Southeast, House Democrats are drafting bills with an urban flavor. These include a moratorium on evictions and some new housing initiatives. They will also likely revive an environmental package, including the Regional Greenhouse Gas Initiative.

Apart from the election reform effort, Senate leaders have been quieter about their expectations for 2021. One battle already brewing is the decennial effort to redistrict congressional and state legislative districts. The fireworks on that will intensify as we get closer to the 2022 election year.

The governor faces the challenge of balancing a budget pummeled by pandemic impacts. He also must find a way to flatten the curve on infections—with or without vaccine distribution—to enable students to return to school and for businesses to reopen. In fact, the first order of business for the new president, governors, and legislatures throughout the country should be to tone down the political posturing and focus on getting the pandemic under control. Let's see if reason, not political hysteria, can prevail in Harrisburg in 2021.

PART THREE

2021 OP-EDS

SOMETHING BIGGER

JANUARY 15, 2021

Here is a question for students of history and all U.S. citizens: what was the most important event in the history of this country? Some would argue that it was signing the Declaration of Independence, writing the Constitution, quelling the Whiskey Rebellion, or the impact of any decisive battle of the Revolutionary or Civil War. From my perspective, the event that ensured the success of our republic was when John Adams took the oath of office as the second president of the United States.

For the first time in history, a peaceful transition of power occurred, ensuring that America was, indeed, a nation of laws and not personalities. It saw a leader with a huge and devoted following willingly step down and secure a government based on principles that were bigger and more important than any one man.

Some of America's best moments come from leaders who used their inaugurals to instill hope and optimism in the American experiment in democracy. The very best example remains Lincoln's second inaugural address. As the passions of the Civil War still burned, Lincoln made it clear that the path we should take to begin to heal was "with malice toward none and with charity toward all." Other great addresses from Theodore Roosevelt, Franklin Roosevelt, John Kennedy, and Ronald Reagan deserve the attention and admiration of every American.

Most of these orations occurred with the outgoing president participating in the event and thereby giving his endorsement to the seamless continuation of the republic whether he agreed with the policies of his successor or not. It is unfortunate that this week's inauguration ceremonies will be different.

President Trump is shirking his last official duty. He will be a "no-show" at the inaugural and continues to wallow in the fantasy that, somehow, he should be retaking the oath of office.

I learned most of my life lessons from my father. He was patient and compassionate and insisted that all his children treat others respectfully. There was a moment in which we had a sharp disagreement, however. It occurred on an election night with two gubernatorial candidates locked in a race too close to call. When the returns from Pennsylvania's conservative "T" counties began to come in, Mark Singel knew that Tom Ridge would prevail.

"I am going down to the ballroom to concede," I told my father.

"Are you nuts?" was his reaction. We were, in fact, still leading by several thousand votes. I tried to explain the data and clarified that the graceful thing to do would be conceding in time for the opponent to take his bow during the 11:00 p.m. news cycle. It was the kind of graciousness that my father, after all, had instilled in me my entire life. As I struggled with all the speech's emotions, I glanced at my father on the dais and saw his eyes fill with tears. But at that moment, I knew they were not tears of sorrow or regret; they were tears of pride. We had done the right thing for a principle bigger than ourselves.

Election nights and inaugurations are deeply personal for me, not just because I have participated but because I am an American. The light that an American shines as a beacon for the rest of the world depends on our exceptional ability to change leaders and viewpoints without missing a beat. This reality is bigger than any one individual and provides stability vital to world peace.

While it is regrettable that Donald Trump does not understand that truth, Mike Pence does. The vice president has shown great courage in the last few weeks and persevered in certifying the electoral votes for Joe Biden—even when an angry mob threatened his life. It now falls to him to play the role former presidents like Adams, Carter, and George H.W. Bush performed. They summoned grace under pressure to allow the country to heal even after painful election losses. It now falls to Pence to summon the leadership and civility to do what Donald Trump has refused to do.

There is tension in the nation's capital. There is lingering distrust caused largely by an outgoing president who refuses to face reality or his own responsibilities. But we are Americans, and deep down, we understand that patriotism is about working together. It is a core value that is bigger than any one of us.

BIDEN BEGINS THE HEALING PROCESS

JANUARY 22, 2021

A week into the Biden era, you can still hear the sighs of relief from all parts of the country. The best part of the inaugural festivities came from the truth spoken by a twenty-year-old poet named Amanda Gorman. We would do well to continue to listen and reflect on her words.

President Biden then began the healing process at his swearing-in and in the extraordinary celebration that followed. The shining guidepost that he put forth in his inaugural address is that "Democracy has prevailed." He went on to calm citizens' nerves with plain, pitch-perfect language for the day and times.

In another stunning moment of unity, presidents forty-two, forty-three, and forty-four stood shoulder to shoulder and called upon all Americans to work together. They urged that we begin listening to each other and summon the kind of respect for each other that leads to a "more perfect union."

Notably, president forty-five was nowhere to be found in that chorus of patriotism. We need not mention him any further.

However, it is essential to point out that a large swath of Republicans has bought into the lie that the recent election was stolen. Senator Ben Sasse had this to say about the need for the GOP to change its ways. "If the GOP is to have a future, it has to call out falsehoods and conspiracy theories unequivocally. We have to repudiate people who peddle those lies. The past four years have wounded our country in grievous, long-lasting ways. The mob that rushed the Capitol had been fed a steady diet of lies and conspiracy theories." In a standoff "between the Constitution and madness," says Sasse, the GOP "must come home to support the Constitution." Senate Minority Leader Mitch McConnell started to make that same course correction when he called out the lies from the very top of government that led to the deadly siege of the U.S. Capitol.

There also seems to be a new reality check among the insurrectionists themselves. While hundreds of arrests continue across the country, reports are that groups like the Proud Boys are furious that they were misled. They bought into the Big Lie. They thought they were fighting for freedom; they are now fighting to stay out of jail. From our beginnings, Hamilton and others warned of the corrosive effect of lies and corruption at the highest levels. Lincoln called out "mobocracies" that "sustained themselves on authoritarian rejection of law, reason and constitutional constraints."

But the cult of personality is gone, and democracy has, in fact, prevailed. Most Republicans now see the need to move on. He-who-shall-remain-nameless not only lost the presidency, but he also led the party to lose the House and the Senate in one term. Four hundred thousand lives were lost to the pandemic. The tumult caused in the last four years will now be addressed by a second impeachment trial and countless other legal battles that this new private citizen will face.

Accountability is necessary, but looking back is not nearly as important as looking forward. In short order, the Biden administration has set the direction for the country. Jen Psaki, the new press secretary, went a long way to usher in a new era of truth at an extraordinary press conference on Inauguration Day. Covering topics from the pandemic to climate change to immigration reform, she did not engage in a sycophantic spin at the behest of her boss. She did not pretend to have answers on every topic. Instead, she offered the briefing room as a resource for the American public to hear the unvarnished facts of presidential policies.

In addition to a commitment to truth, President Biden made it clear to every member of his administration what he would not tolerate: disrespect, not for himself, but for each other. Unity depends upon communication, and communication depends upon mutual respect. It is a good way to light the way out of our current darkness. This brings us back to Amanda Gorman, who says, "For there is always light if only we're brave enough to see it. If only we're brave enough to be it."

SEEKING COURAGE IN SENATE CANDIDATES

FEBRUARY 12, 2021

The quality I admire most in politicians is courage. We don't expect the stunning bravery of troops facing German guns on the ramparts of Omaha Beach. Their line of work doesn't usually require running into fires or rescuing children from disasters, but voters are entitled to courage from their elected officials.

As of this writing, it appears that the U.S. Senate does not have the votes to render a "guilty" verdict in the second impeachment trial of Donald Trump. Too many Republicans are affected by amnesia when it comes to what happened on January 6. They are turning a blind eye to the worst crime ever committed by a sitting president. They willingly violate their oaths to exercise fair and impartial justice because they fear the lunatic right wing of their party that has fallen for the Big Lie that, somehow, Trump won the election.

Make no mistake about it: voting "not guilty" ignores a mountain of evidence that the former president incited an insurrection. His words and actions before, during, and after January 6 sent a bloodthirsty mob into the Capitol with murder and mayhem on their minds.

Our own senator, Pat Toomey, appears to be an exception to the pandering Republicans. He has spoken out forcefully against the Big Lie and strongly supports a peaceful transition of power. He told the truth to the fringe elements of his party. Some suggest that Toomey's announced retirement gives him this freedom. He's not running, so he doesn't need to grovel at the feet of the muddled MAGA masses. Maybe, but let's credit our senator withstanding his ground, and let's call out the others who turn a blind eye to insurrection and a betrayal of our electoral processes. They are cowards.

So, as we prepare for another crucial election in 2022, who will rise to the level of leadership that we deserve in a U.S. senator? An early entrant in the U.S. Senate race is Lieutenant Governor John Fetterman. At six-foot-eight with a practiced, gruff disposition, he has attracted national media coverage for his outspoken views on the presidential election, gender equality, and legalizing marijuana. He has also irritated colleagues in the Pennsylvania Senate for, in their view, wielding the gavel in a partisan fashion. Within days of floating his candidacy, Fetterman raised nearly $2 million in small amounts from every part of the state. It is too early to declare front-runners, but he is on that track—especially since Attorney General Josh Shapiro is widely considered to be headed for a run at the governor's seat.

Other Democrats being mentioned come mostly from the Pittsburgh and Philadelphia area. Connor Lamb from Pittsburgh has carefully carved out a moderate position that reflects his blue-collar district. The question is, does that sell in the liberal suburban counties around Philadelphia?

Joe Torsella, from Philadelphia, has some statewide name recognition as the former state treasurer, but maybe not enough to burst into the top-tier candidates. Congress member Madeleine Dean from Montgomery County performed well as a manager of the impeachment trial and has impressed many with her poise and leadership skills. She may face a local battle for the nomination if Montgomery County commission chair, Valerie Arkoosh, gets into the race.

It is likely that more than a few other Democrats will emerge.

On the Republican side, several Congress members have shown some interest, including Guy Reschenthaler (Allegheny County), Glenn Thompson (Centre County), and Dan Muesser (Schuylkill County). Note that all these candidates endorsed efforts to challenge the presidential vote count. Just saying.

Two other names of note: Paul Mango lost a primary donnybrook for governor in 2018 but went on to help lead Operation Warp Speed at the federal level. His personal wealth could, once again, propel him to top-tier status in the field. Another dark horse could be Jeff Bartos from Montgomery County. Bartos ran as Scott Wagner's lieutenant governor candidate in 2018 and impressed leaders of both parties with his political skills. A U.S. Senate seat is one of the most desirable prizes in politics. Look for a crowded field in 2022.

Spare us from candidates who, as Senate Minority Leader Mitch McConnell said, "spout loony lies and conspiracy theories." Do not give us candidates who will use January 6 as a rallying cry to stir up extremists. Avoid any candidate who tried to tamper with the results of a safe and secure presidential election.

Above all, look for courage in any candidate who asks for our vote.

LESSONS FROM NEW YORK, PENNSYLVANIA, TEXAS, AND ... MARS?

FEBRUARY 19, 2021

Proverbs 16:18 says, "Pride goeth before destruction, and a haughty spirit before a fall." This was one of my father's go-to passages when he thought that any of his children were getting a little too self-satisfied with school grades or personal accomplishments. He would warn us about getting too big for our britches.

Last week, nine Democratic members of the New York State Assembly called out their governor for underreporting deaths in state nursing homes and for making decisions that may have placed seniors at risk. Governor Andrew Cuomo's staff squabbled with those legislators and made matters worse with a ham-handed approach to keep them in line. It wasn't long before charges of "abuse of power" and "obstruction of justice" began to fly.

Whether the reporting error was intentional or if experts backed the decision to return seniors to nursing care, the governor wanted to ensure that his handling of the pandemic was met with widespread approval. Remember, Andrew Cuomo presented daily updates that were painstakingly thorough—as a direct contrast to the disjointed directives we were getting from the White House at the time. It was also Andrew Cuomo who fired off a book about leadership in the time of COVID-19 that became an immediate bestseller. Like Icarus, Governor Cuomo may have flown too close to the sun. As the wax on his political wings began to melt, a little humility would have been in order.

Pennsylvania had its own brush with vaccine realities last week. It appears second doses of the Moderna vaccine may be delayed for about 100,000 people because they have been used as first doses. Hospitals, clinics, pharmacies, and nursing facilities contend they were following PA Health Department directives to get shots in the arms of Pennsylvania as quickly as possible. To her credit, Acting Secretary of Health Alison Beam faced the press on this glitch and shouldered at least some of the responsibility. They were expecting more vaccines on hand by this time, and they had applied pressure on providers to move quickly.

Governor Wolf and state officials have been under fire from the general assembly for many pronouncements and directives. The Moderna mix-up allowed his detractors to pounce again and second-guess the governor's actions. The usual cries of a lack of transparency and front-office competence surfaced from the sidelines. But it is important to note that Wolf and Cuomo differ in one major aspect; the errors in Pennsylvania reflect good intentions with unforeseen consequences. Moving too quickly on distributing vaccines is an understandable offense. It is much different than Governor Cuomo allowing political calculations to factor into his decision-making.

In Texas, residents suffered a freakish winter storm that left millions without heat or power for many days. Again, hubris and politics interfered with an orderly response to the emergency. Specifically, special interests circulated a story that, somehow, wind turbines were to blame for the power outage. The reality is that the electricity grid in the state was unprepared for temperatures that froze natural gas lines and wreaked havoc on the entire system. The first rule in emergency management is a version of the lesson we all should have learned in childhood: put pride aside and tell the truth.

So, where does one turn for inspiration and uplifting stories in these wintry days of discontent? How about Mars? The U.S. has stepped up its game in the race to Mars and landed the Perseverance rover on its surface. China, the United Arab Emirates, and others are also headed to the red planet, but it is the American project that is already showing the most promise. With the treacherous journey and precise landing behind, the rover is on a mission to probe beneath the surface and answer a question that is profound and exhilarating: is there life on Mars?

We continue to grapple with the debilitating effect of the pandemic. We are sometimes dismayed by the pettiness or arrogance of our leaders as they try to address this and other crises. But, looking beyond pandemics, deep freezes, and politics, we are still capable of great things. Reaching for the stars is only possible if we master the more mundane challenges we face on this planet. Winning those battles depends upon our willingness to put aside our differences and our pride to seek common ground.

ELECTION REFORM OR VOTER SUPPRESSION?

MARCH 5, 2021

In a recent documentary, Theresa Borroughs from Alabama recounted her efforts to register to vote in the late 1940s. Twice a week for two years, she traveled to her local courthouse. Each time, she was met with a new eligibility test. Could she pass a literacy test? Did she own any property? How many red jellybeans are in a jar? It was the Jim Crow South, and politicians did not even try to hide their disdain for African American voters. These citizens were beaten and killed, poll taxes were imposed, literacy tests were concocted, and anyone with any criminal record was denied the vote. The fact is that African Americans often found themselves in jail on the flimsiest of charges, and the criminal justice system conspired with politics to keep them away from the polls.

The Voting Rights Act of 1965 was supposed to end voter intimidation and discrimination. Indeed, every politician talks about the sacred right to vote and pays lip service to this bedrock of our democracy. But, when it comes down to their own elections, they are not as concerned about voter turnout as they are with getting their vote out.

When the Pennsylvania General Assembly enacted mail-in voting on a bipartisan basis, it was hailed to make voting more convenient for everybody. This proved invaluable during the pandemic year when people voted by mail to protect their health. When it became clear, however, that more Democrats would be voting remotely than Republicans, new ploys were developed to discourage the new approach. There was a slowdown in the delivery of mail-in ballots. Huge counties in states like Texas limited drop-box locations, signatures were challenged, and stricter voter ID laws were introduced in the legislature. When the vote count wasn't going their way, partisans alleged widespread fraud.

In the aftermath of the presidential election, every state in the country and courts at every level have proven this allegation wrong.

Just recently, the 2020 loser proclaimed anew the Big Lie that the election was, somehow, rigged. Dutifully, his minions in dozens of states are putting reality aside to weed out this non-existent election fraud.

In Pennsylvania, legislators plan to place new hurdles on registration and make it harder to vote by mail. This, they say, is to assure the integrity of the voting process. One can almost hear the old Alabama registrar saying the same thing about his jellybean test.

It is true that the Pennsylvania secretary of state and the Supreme Court made some interpretations of state law that could be reviewed. But providing three additional days to count mail-in ballots or overlooking signature requirements on outer envelopes does not constitute rampant fraud. It was an accommodation to voters during a stressful time to ensure their voices would be heard.

Just for good measure, the Republican Party has embarked on another quest. Since some Supreme Court rulings did not go their way, they now seek to dislodge as many Democrats as possible from that bench. If they can't reverse a presidential election, they can change how justices are elected and stack the deck for their candidates in the future.

In Georgia, an array of election "reforms" has been proposed. Most are thinly veiled initiatives to interrupt an extraordinary registration and get-out-the-vote effort that has seen record numbers of minorities getting to the polls. In many urban communities, black churches provide transportation to voters in need. This souls to the polls effort is now under fire for one reason: it works.

The New York Times quoted voting rights experts as saying that the legislative onslaught across the country is not about reform but suppression of voters' rights. There is a danger that it could be the biggest rollback of voting rights since the nineteenth century. A counterbalance to the state's actions could be the U.S. Congress, where Democrats now have slim majorities in both Houses.

The House of Representatives has already passed a bill that would expand voting rights. It would increase voter registration venues and make early voting and mail voting more accessible, not less. The reality is that the bill is facing an uphill battle in the Senate. While not all Republican senators are living in denial about the last election, most are ready to put principle aside if it means securing their seat.

It is noteworthy that Americans voted in record numbers in 2020. According to the Pew Research Center, over 158 million ballots were cast, representing about two-thirds of the eligible voters. The goal should be to build on that level of citizen involvement, not to concoct new ways to depress turnout.

VENOM FROM THE RIGHT

APRIL 16, 2021

Like most of us these days, I spend a lot of time hitting the delete key on my laptop. Otherwise, I would be overrun by urgent messages and fundraising pitches from elected officials and candidates that number in the hundreds daily. What is most disconcerting is watching those entreaties turn from a discussion about issues and ideas into overheated attacks on opponents or flat-out lies that are now dropping like hand grenades on social media. I took note of one writer who insisted that the Chinese had already beaten us to Mars. He contended that they were already raising goats on the planet to begin the process of colonization. He was a random citizen entitled to his own bizarre thoughts.

More concerning are actual elected officials who say weird stuff. Representative Marjorie Taylor Greene publicly attacked students who survived the Parkland shooting. She also suggested that the California wildfires were caused by lasers from outer space. And this is from the Missouri senator who openly encouraged the rioters on January 6. Josh Hawley, unrepentant about the attack on the U.S. Capitol or his attack on democracy, said this in a fundraising blast entitled "Comrade Biden." "The media never questions Joe Biden [. . .] they will print any lie told by the White House Communications team. It sounds like Fidel Castro's Cuba, Kim Jung Un's North Korea, or even modern-day China."

Another spinner of right wing dogma is Senator John Cornyn of Texas. Cornyn attacked President Biden for not tweeting enough and presenting measured—perhaps scripted—policy rather than off-the-cuff grunts on the White House lawn. Pundit Paul Begala believes the senator suffers from political dizziness and says, "Remember the Tilt-a-Whirl? You sit in a car that rolls and spins around an undulating track, moving in at least three different ways at once. When you get off it, it's hard to walk. You get the sensation that the ground is spinning and heaving. But it's not. It was the chaotic ride that made the ordinary seem disorienting. Someone who's clearly been on the Trump Tilt-a-Whirl too long is Senator John Cornyn of Texas. The poor man is staggering about, wondering why the Earth is spinning."

Begala asks, "Does Cornyn really miss the last four years of presidential Twitter? Does he not remember the insanity and toxicity that former president Donald Trump unleashed every day on social media? Does Cornyn really think it's a problem that the current president is being "conventional"—that is, steady, stable, normal, and grounded? Biden has been in office for seventy-nine days, and he hasn't attacked the appearance of anyone's spouse nor linked a senator's father to the Kennedy assassination. He has not called American soldiers who died for our country "suckers" or "losers." He has not sucked up to dictators or derided our allies."

Where does all this right wing rancor come from? Consider the tone and substance that erupts from Mar-a-Lago to this day. It seems that the former guy is now focused on former allies for his strongest attacks. Pence was "weak" because he did his constitutional duty. The Governor of Georgia was a "loser" because he counted the votes accurately. Senator Mitch McConnell, the Republican leader, was a "dumb son-of-a-b—h." Remember that the former president raised fearmongering and prevarication into an art form. His political adventure started with the lie that the first African American president was not even a citizen. This birtherism was a complete fraud, but he found many voters who bought into it. He announced his campaign by calling Mexicans rapists and murderers, and the crowd cheered. To him, immigrants come from "s-hole" countries, and even some white supremacists "are good people."

Even after the election, his Twitter machine was in high gear. There was a systematic effort to peddle the Big Lie that he had won. There was an even more blatant campaign to squeeze contributions from followers who bought into that lie, sometimes without their full consent. The short-term effect of that propaganda was a distrust of the election results that caused open insurrection among die-hard believers. In addition, the outgoing president stuffed his coffers with cash to do more damage to anybody he feels is not of his cult.

It is time for both parties to reject the hysteria and hatred of the past. Democrats are not Communists; Republicans are not Fascists. Let there be disagreement among us about issues but let us all resist the flamethrowers who attack each other as a matter of strategy. The optimist in me says that we can get back to an era of American pride that includes all of us. The pessimist in me says that might be as far-fetched as goats on Mars.

COMMON SENSE AND CLIMATE CHANGE

APRIL 16, 2021

NASA reports that global warming has done more damage to the planet in the last seventy-five years than in all the previous years of human civilization. The change in our climate can be measured by an unprecedented increase in the Earth's temperature. Our oceans are heating up, our ice caps are melting, and sea levels are rising at alarming rates.

It is a fact that climate change threatens the very existence of the planet. It is also a fact that man-made emissions have accelerated climate change dramatically. Our burgeoning industrial economies and the energy required to propel them have given us the luxuries of modern civilization. But they have also given us scorching summers, frigid winters, and dwindling water resources. Forests have become tinderboxes, and high-rent coastal properties are watching their shoreline disappear. Most scientists agree that current climate realities are unsustainable. Common sense says that we should do something about it.

To that end, President Biden convened a summit of industrial countries to jump-start discussions on ways to reduce emissions on a global scale. The U.S. target is now a 50 percent reduction in emissions by 2030. The ultimate goal—endorsed by China and other major polluters—is net-zero carbon emissions by 2060.

Pennsylvania has a special stake in this effort for two reasons. First, our heritage requires it. Article 1, Section 27 of the Pennsylvania Constitution grants every Pennsylvanian a right to clean air and water. The only way to protect this right is to ensure our behaviors do not spoil the environment.

Secondly, Pennsylvania proudly participated in the industrial revolution. We were at the forefront of every innovation that provided opportunities to workers and new products to the world. There is a price to pay for mining coal, making steel, and producing the goods and services that the world needs. In the 1950s, headlights and streetlights were necessary to see through the smoke belched from Pittsburgh steel plants, even at high noon. Growing up in Johnstown, I thought the natural color for the hillsides was the rust-orange of sulfur emissions that covered them year-round. Just as Pennsylvania built a robust economy in the last century, we have a chance to reshape it into something better—an economy that taps into our abundant energy resources and into our proven ability to innovate.

Here's where real common sense comes in. Coal provides 20 percent of our energy needs. The 2019 Coal Report of the U.S. Energy Department notes that there are 5,400 coal jobs in Pennsylvania. We produce 7.1 percent of the nation's coal supply. It is just not possible to turn that switch off immediately. Instead, we should embark on a phased-in migration away from coal that includes using existing waste coal and other clean coal technologies. We should accommodate miners with new opportunities in related industries and fund the training required.

Similarly, we can't ignore the huge potential of Pennsylvania's natural gas industry. The Marcellus Shale formation in Pennsylvania is considered the country's largest source of natural gas. Underlying this shale is the Utica Formation, with another sixty years of drilling life. A recent downturn caused by oversupply has caused some belt-tightening in the industry, but 32,000 jobs have already been created, and the upside is still enormous. Wages average about $60,000 per job, and industry sources say the total impact of natural gas on Pennsylvania is about $11 billion annually.

Yes, we must transition to lower emissions, and we have the technology and research support to do that. But common sense says that our approach to climate change must consider the realities of coal and natural gas on the state's economy.

There is one other consideration. Pennsylvania is well on its way to hosting a state-of-the-art "cracking" plant in Beaver County. This facility, funded by Shell Oil and tax breaks from the federal and state governments, will consume huge amounts of the Marcellus Shale gas to make plastic from its ethane molecules. The whole enterprise offers a closed-loop type of manufacturing that utilizes local raw materials to manufacture products without emissions, as we have seen from steel manufacturing or coal-fired boilers.

It is encouraging that the United Mine Workers of America have already discussed appropriate paths for the coal industry. The shift to natural gas is

COMMON SENSE AND CLIMATE CHANGE

underway in our state, and from an environmental perspective, that is a good thing. What remains for elected officials and all of us is to deal with the reality of climate change without fear or rancor. When we reason together, our common sense can prevail.

ALTERNATE REALITIES

MAY 21, 2021

News coverage of the proposed January 6th Committee debate was full of head-scratching moments. Minority Leader Kevin McCarthy opposed the commission even though his negotiators had included every one of his demands to assure bipartisanship. There was Senate Minority Leader Mitch McConnell signaling his opposition to reviewing the events of January 6 even though he loudly condemned the unruly mob four and a half months earlier.

Some House members dug deeply into delusion and claimed the insurrection was no big deal. It was a bunch of tourists who just so happened to be carrying weapons and nooses with the shouted intent of lynching the vice president. Those "tourists" interrupted the transition of power, a sacred tenet of our democracy. Still, McCarthy, McConnell, and most of the once-proud Republican Party tell us, "Nothing to see here. Let's move on." This kind of willful blindness is beyond pathetic. It is irrational. Failure to come to grips with the cause of the insurrection and giving its leaders a pass guarantees that similar violence will happen again.

The same sentiments that launched the Capitol riot are taking hold in states nationwide. In Arizona, believers of the Big Lie are pursuing a sham audit of the 2020 election results. They have concocted inane conspiracy theories and will not stop until they get a result that justifies their delusion that the election was stolen. The election board chairman, Republican Jack Sellers, called the recount (which is being used to raise money for Trump supporters) "a grift disguised as an audit." State legislatures are seizing this same false narrative to pass bills restricting voting rights. The idea is to allow your team full access to the ballot box and keep others away.

This kind of toxicity was completely avoidable. There are winners and losers in politics, and both parties have weathered highs and lows. Until election night, 2020, the tradition of graceful concession was not only a mark of good sportsmanship; it was vital to reassuring both parties that they would live to fight another day with mutual respect intact. By shattering that norm, the former guy lit a fuse that resulted in chaos at the U.S. Capitol and ongoing madness on the part of his base. I spoke with a clear-eyed Republican recently who said, "If I say the sky is blue and you say the sky is red, that does not make it a fifty-fifty chance that the sky has suddenly changed colors. It just means that you are delusional."

After January 6, leaders had a choice. They could dust themselves off and return to the comity of spirited debates or double down on a disgruntled, disgraced purveyor of delusions. In his pilgrimage to Mar-a-Lago, Kevin McCarthy chose the latter. To those like Liz Cheney, who point out that the emperor is wearing no clothes, he and the cult threaten their careers. It takes courage to withstand the onslaught of the emperor's minions.

Here in Pennsylvania, examples of that type of courage are few and far between. In the early stages of the race for governor in 2022, the first two Republicans out of the blocks are boasting about their cultish bona fides. State Senator Doug Mastriano (Franklin County) brags that he spent an hour and a half with Trump recently and came away with a commitment of support. Former Congress member Lou Barletta ran Trump's campaign in Pennsylvania and will carry that credential to every red county in the state. These candidates and others like them are not just content to feed the beast; they are ready to release it into the china shop of our democracy, regardless of the damage it has done and will continue to do.

Back in Washington, U.S. Representative Tim Ryan (D-Ohio) called out his Republican colleagues: "This [opposing the January 6th Committee] is a slap in the face to every rank-and-file cop in the United States. We need two political parties in this country that are both living in reality—and you ain't one of them."

In a ray of hope for bipartisanship and a return to thoughtful discourse, thirty-five Republicans in the U.S. House defied their leadership and voted to review the events of January 6. It is unclear if there will be a similar percentage of senators who put their country ahead of their allegiance to Trump. That would require courage and a clear-headed commitment to extricate ourselves from willful delusion. It could signal a return to the blue skies of our great American experiment in representative democracy.

SWIMMING ASHORE

JUNE 4, 2021

There is an undercurrent in American politics that is continuing to pull us into dangerous waters. It is the continued willingness of citizens to be driven by their biases, not by facts. It is blind partisanship that makes compromise or even handshakes impossible for political leaders. Worse, it is no longer enough to merely align with your tribe; it is now required to demonize adversaries. We cannot swim to shore if we drag each other back into an endless whirlpool of fear and loathing.

It is sad that our leaders at the federal level cannot even agree on a bipartisan investigation of the January 6 riots. It is disturbing that they cannot reach a compromise on infrastructure investment that everybody seems to want. It is ludicrous that the loudest conspiracy voices are the ones that make the news.

Across the country, there is an orchestrated attempt by state legislatures to restrict voting rights. The effort is not about safe and secure elections but trying to tip the scales in their favor in service of a curmudgeon who has them firmly in the grasp of his fantasy. We must hold on to hope if we are to emerge from this sea of confusion.

The noted historian Arthur Schlesinger sounded a tone of optimism in his *Cycles of American History*. His premise is that there is an ebb and flow of politics primarily driven by "we the people." If we can avoid the snare of cults and hyper-partisanship, Schlesinger notes that America's pendulum has always swung back to the center. We have made steady progress when we learn from each other and govern from the informed middle.

Since we are in commencement season, let us take a moment to be hopeful. Listen to some current and past commencement speakers who can help us through turbulent times.

We once had confidence that our country was different from others that had tried democracy and failed. Ours, we believed, had a sturdy foundation in strong, vibrant institutions—Congress, the courts, the press, houses of worship, and the scientific establishment. But we learned in recent years that our institutions were more vulnerable to pressure and manipulation than we ever imagined. Many turned submissive when a powerful leader demanded it. Others went quiet for fear of reprisal. The truth suffered. Verifiable facts were denied. Expertise, experience, education, and evidence were devalued or outright dismissed. Misinformation and disinformation flourished. A huge portion of the public was deceived and radicalized. Our democracy was pushed to the brink. We can either give up on institutions that betray our values, or we can seek to repair them. I urge you to take the latter course. Repair them.

—Martin Barron of *The Washington Post*

You can't do it alone. As you navigate through the rest of your life, be open to collaboration. Other people and other people's ideas are often better than your own.

—Amy Poehler

I have only four instructions for you. Speak your truth. Live in your purpose. Walk in grace. And inspire with your legacy. If you are able to aim for those four guideposts and live your life through them and with them in mind, you will be who you are meant to be.

—Maria Taylor of ESPN

Going further, one of my favorite authors, Kurt Vonnegut, told the graduates of Agnes Scott College in 1999 not to sweat the small stuff. He said you cannot expect others to forgive you for your mistakes if you hold grudges against them. "You cannot live life fostering personal vendettas against others."

Steve Jobs gave an inspirational speech just months before he died. His lesson was powerful and prophetic: "Our time here is limited. Use it wisely because that is what is going to matter most."

Some believe that writer JK Rowling gave the most effective commencement address at Harvard. Despite the international success of her Harry Potter books, she talked about failure.

> *Failure taught me things about myself that I could have learned no other way. I discovered that I had a strong will and more discipline than I had suspected; I also found out that I had friends whose value was truly above the price of rubies [. . .]. We do not need magic to change the world [;] we carry all the power we need inside ourselves already[.] [W]e have the power to imagine better.*
>
> —JK Rowling

I hope that these words are comforting. In our divided political world, I hope they help our new graduates and all of us swim to shore.

PRAYERS FOR TOM RIDGE

JUNE 18, 2021

Tom Ridge is a friend of mine.

We were not so friendly during the heated gubernatorial campaign of 1994. Some old-timers in Pennsylvania politics will remember the spirited tone of that campaign. Just for context, I led the race deep into the homestretch when an incident involving a former prisoner in Pennsylvania upended the race like a bolt of lightning. The Ridge campaign was quick to exploit the incident, and the Singel campaign was drowned with Willie Horton-type ads that were brutal and effective. My son Christopher, seven years old at the time, came home from school to ask me: "Daddy, did you kill somebody?" Tough stuff, but the truth is that the hired guns get paid to exploit those kinds of bombshells.

Here is another largely unknown fact: Tom Ridge and I maintained a bond before, during, and after that campaign. We would often compare notes at joint events and get messages to each other when there was a break in political hostilities. There was a chemistry between us that transcended the warfare.

Early in his tenure as governor, we met to discuss my plans to hang around Harrisburg and to try my hand at lobbying. He could have chosen to derail those plans. He could have made a few phone calls and dried up my prospects. Instead, he was gracious and allowed our friendship to grow. His signature farewell comment to me then and at every subsequent encounter was, "Be well, my friend." You got the sense that he meant it. He also sent the word out to his team that I was one Democrat entitled to access. Key staffers like Mark Holman and Mark Campbell were as gracious as he was during those years—and to this day.

One story about our unusual friendship involves Tiger Woods. In 1996, Governor Ridge and I were invited to the same charitable golf outing at the exclusive

Nemacolin Resort. I was delighted to participate in an event where Woods was the marquee player. Joe Hardy, Nemacolin's owner, had his office call me to make some remarks since it was clear that Ridge could not be there for pre-event festivities. I said to his executive assistant, "You do know that this is Mark Singel, not Mark Schweiker, don't you?" Sure enough, I had gotten the invitation that was intended for the current lieutenant governor. It was Joe Hardy himself who called back to acknowledge the mix-up, but he insisted that I come as his guest anyway.

I arrived at the first tee to hob-nob with the governor, Tiger Woods, Joe Hardy, and other luminaries. "What the hell are you doing here?" asked Ridge. When Hardy and I filled him in, he laughed harder than all of us. We then proceeded to negotiate fairways that were lined with thousands of spectators. As I recall, the governor and I hooked our first drives into the crowd. There were no injuries, save for our egos.

Later, when Governor Ridge became the country's first secretary of homeland security, I caught up with him at a Penn State game. More accurately, I found myself outside a heavily guarded private box and recognized two of the Pennsylvania state police. While chatting, I heard a voice boom from inside, "Is that Mark Singel? Get your butt in here!" For one delightful half of a PSU game, we sat alone and talked politics, world affairs, and the time I weaseled my way into playing golf with Tiger Woods. I also told him how grateful I was that he was serving his country in a crucial way and keeping us all safe.

His private work and mine have aligned from time to time. My company has done some business with the Ridge Policy Group, and we have worked together on projects to promote civility and reform in government. Mutual respect can rise above the mayhem of tribal politics. It requires that we listen to each other and view ourselves as friendly adversaries, not hated enemies. Tom Ridge and I encountered each other in Hershey just two weeks ago. He was as convivial as ever, and we vowed to get in a round of golf soon.

With the news that Governor Ridge has been hospitalized with a serious medical condition, I reflect on a man that continues to matter to the Commonwealth and the country. He served honorably in the Vietnam War as a district attorney, U.S. Congress member, governor of Pennsylvania, and first U.S. Department of Homeland Security Secretary. He kept us safe in the aftermath of the 9/11 attacks. He continues to be a voice of reason in a party being pushed over ideological cliffs. Tom Ridge deserves our respect. In this time of medical challenge, he also deserves our prayers.

Be well, my friend.

THE SUBLIME AND THE RIDICULOUS

JULY 9, 2021

My early summer reading list included the political thriller *The President's Daughter*, authored by former president Bill Clinton and James Patterson. A page-turner, the book has an exciting storyline that involves heroes and terrorists. An interesting aspect of the book was some detail about the origin of Middle Eastern tensions and Islamic principles that go back to Abraham. It reminded me of an experience I had with deeply religious Muslims at the holy mosque in Abu Dhabi.

I was there on a business and academic trip with leaders of Harrisburg University and stood in awe of the splendor and serenity of the mosque. In the prayer section, where faithful Muslims gather six times daily, the wall behind the Imam's lectern features marble panels with Arabic words describing Allah as merciful, all-knowing, omnipotent, and dozens of other attributes. However, there was one panel above the lectern left blank. "Why?" I asked. "It reminds us that we are incapable of understanding the greatness of God," was the answer.

This sublime moment of clarity reminded me not only of the infinitude of the deity but also of the puniness of we who share this speck of a planet. At the very least, I felt that we should strive for something like civility among nations, religions, and, yes, even political parties.

In his 1795 work entitled *The Age of Reason*, political writer Thomas Paine pointed out that going from the "sublime to the ridiculous" is only a step away. Lofty notions of faith, religion, and governance can be subverted by charlatans who whip followers into a frenzy with fantasies that are utterly false. This is the case with much of today's Republican Party. According to recent polls, a disturbing percentage continue to buy into the Big Lie that, somehow, the recent presidential election was stolen. The "pillow man" and his conspiracy-minded ilk are convinced that the former president will somehow glide back into office as early as this summer.

Worse, Republican leaders across the country are too afraid of a base that has devoured this nonsense, and they cater to them. Nearly nine months after the election and six months after results have been counted, recounted, and certified by every single state in the nation, *The Washington Post* reports that more than one-third of the nearly 700 Republicans who have filed initial paperwork to run for the U.S. House or Senate next year support the Big Lie. In fact, they are making it a central part of their campaigns.

This week, state Senator Doug Mastriano, chairman of the State Senate Intergovernmental Operations Committee, notified counties throughout Pennsylvania that he will be conducting his sham audit. Much like in Arizona and several other states, he is determined to find any shred of evidence that points to irregularities in our voting processes.

Privately, Republican leaders will tell you that there is no way that any such audit will uncover enough fraud to overturn the results. Publicly, they grandstand the voters who want to upend democracy itself. So, Mastriano is flexing his authority by making forty-five separate information demands from the counties and threatening them with subpoenas if they do not comply by July 31. His letter to the counties seeks details about election equipment, software, hard drives, personal phone data, voter registration rolls, and enough information to tie up any County Election Bureau for months. Note that county officials have been conducting fraud-free elections since the beginning of the republic. Note also that Senator Mastriano is contemplating a run for governor. He has made pilgrimages to the January 6 insurrection, Mar-a-Lago, and the Arizona audit site—to ensure that the base of falsehood followers know he is their guy.

This is not leadership. It is political pandering.

My friend, Congress member Dwight Evans, used to stir up the crowd at political rallies with this chant: "If it is meant to be [. . .] it is up to us!" The new class of candidates emerging from the shadows of the last administration does not seem concerned with an insurrection and ongoing efforts to overturn an election. Many are willing to inflame the crowds to enhance their chances of winning regardless of truth or our sacred traditions.

As election 2022 heats up, voters must know which candidates bring skill, good faith, and respect for representative democracy to their campaigns. I continue to believe that there are good candidates with ideas and idealism in both political parties. It is more critical than ever that citizens rise to the moment and find them.

"If it is meant to be, it is up to us!"

POLITICIANS NEED TO BE GUIDED BY THE TRUTH

JULY 13, 2021

This just in from Tennessee: according to news reports, Republican lawmakers managed to have the state's top health official, Dr. Michelle Fiscus, fired. Her offense? Encouraging healthcare providers to vaccinate children fourteen years or older. One anti-vaxxer actually sent Fiscus a dog muzzle.

Even as COVID-19 and its new strain surge to dangerous levels across the country, the truth deniers have shut down Tennessee's outreach—not just on COVID-19, but on shots for measles, diphtheria, and polio as well. *The Tennessean* newspaper called it like it is: "It is hard to imagine behavior dumber, more short-sighted and more downright backward than that exhibited by Tennessee and its lawmakers."

A ray of rationality came from Senator Mitch McConnell (R-KY) this week. "Get vaccinated," he said. "Ignore all of these other voices that are giving demonstrably bad advice." However, it may be too little, too late for McConnell's words. The fact is that right wing elected officials, commentators, and social media screamers have been casting doubt on masks and vaccines since the pandemic began. The surge of cases in the South directly results from that ignorance.

In a related sideshow at the federal level, some congressional leaders are clinging to the fiction that the January 6 insurrection was a harmless tourist stunt that should be swept out of our collective memories as soon as possible. Given a chance to review all the facts and to separate the heroes from the felons, House Republicans voted to reject a bipartisan inquiry using the 9-1-1 Commission as its model. When Speaker Pelosi forged ahead but still offered the minority the opportunity to participate in the process, Minority Leader Kevin McCarthy showed his disdain for seeking the truth by suggesting the names of several unhinged conspiracists to assure that the proceedings would be distorted into their absurd reality.

Remember that McCarthy pushed Representative Liz Cheney (R-WY) aside because she asked her party to stop the lies about the election that spurred the Capitol riot in the first place. By appointing people like Representative Jim Jordan (R-OH) and Representative Jim Banks (R-IN), who have given their support to the rioters and who both voted to overthrow the election results, he has shown again that he has bought in, lock stock, and barrel, to the former guy's Big Lie and to pandering to a misguided base.

As Jennifer Rubin points out, McCarthy may be endearing himself to his party's cult leader but "the vast majority of Americans who understand the threat posed by the insurrection will now see the GOP's reaction as mocking, disruptive, dishonest and contemptuous of the lives of law enforcement and of democracy itself."

In another display of fiction over reality, eighteen states have passed new voting restrictions. The response to losing the presidency in 2020 is not "How can we broaden our base and win elections again?" It is "How can we change the rules of the game to tilt elections to our candidates?"

Republicans respond that voter identification and mail-in restrictions are to assure safe elections. This is hogwash. No widespread fraud existed in 2020. Every state in the nation was certified to the count's accuracy, and courts across the nation upheld the vote. The reality is that voter identification is already required for every single voter. If adding more layers of any kind discourages even a sliver of the electorate from voting, it is voter suppression and a defeat for democracy. Similarly, restricting drop boxes for mail-in votes or empowering elected leaders to overrule election results is a way to give politicians one more chance to subvert the will of actual voters.

We should ask ourselves a simple question: do I think that states would be staging phony audits and rushing forward with election reforms if the Republicans had won?

Another question is, does the outburst of self-serving politics at the state level justify a response at the federal level? The For the People Act (H.R. 1) is, in part, a response to the flood of misguided efforts at the state level. It is also a way to ensure voter registration for all citizens, end partisan gerrymandering, curb excessive campaign spending, and enforce ethics requirements. The purpose of H.R. 1 is to encourage voting, not to restrict it.

POLITICIANS NEED TO BE GUIDED BY THE TRUTH

In the climactic scene of *A Few Good Men,* Colonel Jessup spits out the classic line, "You can't handle the truth!" Whether we are dealing with the pandemic, the insurrection, or election reform, leaders must lead. They cannot simply follow the whims of voters who have been goaded into a frenzy of alternate facts. It is time for good men and women across the country to handle the truth.

AFGHANISTAN

AUGUST 20, 2021

In a book of anecdotes about Abraham Lincoln, Anthony Gross relates the story of a group of politicians who met with the president to discuss the habits of General Ulysses S. Grant. They were intent on removing Grant from his command and relayed some juicy gossip about the general.

"He drinks," they said.

"What does he drink?" asked Lincoln.

"Whiskey," they replied, "in excessive amounts."

"Well," said the president, "find out what kind he drinks, and I'll send a barrel to each of the other generals." He then declared the simple, overriding reason for supporting Grant: "He fights."

President Biden has drawn withering criticism on Afghanistan. His mistake was not so much the decision to withdraw from our country's longest war. Most Americans agree that it's time for the troops to come home. His mistake was the flat-footed, disorganized effort to evacuate American citizens and friendly Afghanis.

The fact is that the president thought he had more time. The Afghan government had reassured him that their military would fight to deter the Taliban incursion that began when the American withdrawal was announced. He was under the impression that the 300,000 troops trained and funded by America for twenty years would care enough about freedom to take a stand. He was wrong. Unlike General Grant, the Afghan Army chose not to fight. As a result, Taliban forces walked unchallenged into every provincial capital and seized power in eleven days. This, despite being hugely outnumbered by Afghan soldiers.

To his credit, Biden took responsibility for the chaos at the Bagram air base. His "The Buck Stops Here" speech was what presidential leadership demanded.

He did not shy away from sharing some of the blame, though. He pointed to a deal by the previous administration that had freed thousands of Taliban operatives in exchange for a ceasefire that never occurred. It had Biden boxed in. He chose to end American involvement with the country or commit more troops and extend hostilities indefinitely. It now falls to Biden and the international community to see if the Taliban comes anywhere close to competent governance. Will they ensure rights for women and girls? Will they extract themselves from a history of atrocities as they move away from their characteristic war footing? Can they govern as effectively as they spread mayhem throughout the country?

Sixty years ago, President John F. Kennedy faced the cameras and was forced to admit an utter failure in the Bay of Pigs invasion. Anti-Castro Cubans, with the backing of our CIA, launched an insurrection to depose the dictator. The plan had been hatched in the previous administration, and Kennedy approved the invasion on the advice of all his military advisors. While the mission failed miserably, Kennedy's presentation to the American people did not. Like Biden, Kennedy owned up to his mistakes. As a result, according to the archives of the Gallup organization, 61 percent of Americans approved of his handling of the Cuban invasion even though it was a disaster. Only 15 percent of those polled said they disapproved of the president's actions. The headline in the press after the poll results were released was "Public Rallies Behind Kennedy in Aftermath of Cuban Crisis." Notably, Kennedy's job approval did not go down. It went up to 83 percent favorability.

In today's hypercharged partisan political world, it is inconceivable that Biden will get a bounce from the ongoing confusion in Afghanistan. What he can do, however, is learn from it. Just as Lincoln learned that the personal habits of his generals meant less than their willingness to fight, and just as Kennedy learned not to blindly follow the advice of so-called military experts, Biden should bolster his fact-gathering operations. The CIA, the National Security Agency, and the defense apparatus must have known that the Afghan Army would cut and run. They should have predicted a swarm of humans looking to be airlifted to safety. It is unclear how long the new Taliban leadership will allow the transport of Afghanis to new homes. It is unclear how long it will take for President Biden to fulfill his commitment to evacuate every American. What is clear is that rational foreign policy depends upon solid information and clear-headed rules of engagement. This seems to be a lesson we must relearn in every era of our history.

ORDINARY GREATNESS

AUGUST 27, 2021

PennLive recently did a remarkable story about a World War II veteran named Martin Adler. Adler seemed to have "cleanup" duties as the Nazis evacuated a small Italian village—specifically eliminating any hiding there. At one home, he raised his gun at a large wicker basket and was an instant away from pulling the trigger when a mother jumped in front of the gun, yelling, "Bambini! Bambini!" Sure enough, three small children climbed out of the basket. They were too young to realize their brave mother and a soldier who hesitated momentarily saved their lives. The story goes on to note that Adler, at ninety-seven, reunited with the three children. Those children now have six children, eight grandchildren, and two great-grandchildren of their own.

The story reminded me of another ordinary hero who did something truly extraordinary. Stanislav Yevgrafovich Petrov was born on September 7, 1939, near Vladivostok, Russia. His father had been a fighter pilot during World War II. As a forty-four-year-old lieutenant colonel in the Soviet Air Defense Forces, he had begun his shift as the duty officer at Serpukhov-15, the secret command center outside Moscow where the Soviet military monitored its early-warning satellites over the United States when alarms went off. Ronald Reagan had just made his "Evil Empire" speech, and the Soviet leader, Yuri Andropov, was obsessed with fears of an American attack. Early on the morning of September 26, 1983, Stanislav Petrov watched as his systems detected five missiles incoming from the United States. The estimate was that only twenty-five minutes would elapse between launch and wiping out Moscow. Petrov recalled that, "We knew that every second of procrastination took away valuable time, that the Soviet Union's military and political leadership needed to be informed without delay. My orders were to reach for the phone, to raise the direct line to our top commanders—but I couldn't move. I felt like I was sitting on a hot frying pan."

As the tension in the command center rose, 200 pairs of eyes were trained on Colonel Petrov, and he decided to report the alert as a system malfunction. The false alarm was apparently triggered when the satellite mistook the sun's reflection off the tops of clouds for a missile launch. The computer program that was supposed to filter out such information had malfunctioned. Colonel Petrov later said, "Sometimes we are wiser than the computers." Most people do not even know the young officer's name, who may have averted nuclear war.

Sometimes heroism is about making judgment calls in real time with real consequences. Just as ordinary people step up to do extraordinary things, it is equally possible for folks to fail to do what humanity requires in the heat of the moment. Here is a heartbreaking story from the pandemic front. Samantha Willis, an unvaccinated mother of four, died last week after her battle with COVID-19. Her grieving husband took to Twitter to beg people not to repeat her mistake. "I spent hours in ICU on Thursday [and] Friday with my wife who passed away," he tweeted. "It's real. The numbers are real. Get your vaccine, so you or your family don't have to go through what I have had to."

A Florida radio talk show host was an anti-vaxxer—until he was on his own deathbed. There is no shortage of reckless claims about vaccines. One of the weirder voices claims that the injection "magnetizes" people. That's right; we will soon see forks and spoons attach themselves to our heads.

After painstaking testing and about 200,000,000 doses administered nationwide, the FDA notes that the efficacy of vaccines is well over 90 percent. Simply put, vaccines work. On the other end of the statistics, 98 percent of the deaths attributed to the COVID Delta variant are among unvaccinated patients. It is unconscionable that Americans will not protect themselves and their loved ones from the pandemic. It is ludicrous for them to claim the freedom to infect themselves and others. These are needless, pointless deaths. Consider also that frontline health workers put their own lives on the line as they continue to care for those misguided anti-vaxxers and that there is an economic cost to rejecting vaccines. The economy continues to lag in areas bogged down by growing hospitalization rates.

The government, the CDC, and your neighbors are all asking for one thing: common sense. Accept what medical science established seventy-five years ago when we vanquished polio, diphtheria, and smallpox.

Vaccines work.

No one is asking for an Adler-like moment of clarity that saved generations after World War ll. No one is putting citizens on the precipice of nuclear war. We seek only the ordinary greatness of doing the right thing.

Get vaccinated.

TOOMEY'S TRUTH

SEPTEMBER 10, 2021

In candid conversations, every Republican I know has told me they accept the reality that Biden won in 2020. They may have lingering concerns about the mechanics of mail-in voting, but they understand that no evidence of widespread election fraud exists. To a person, these politicos—some of them key Pennsylvania leaders—say privately that it is time to move on. Does this mean they are willing to repudiate calls for phony audits and election reforms? Hardly.

A recent conversation with one Republican leader went this way:

Me: "Who do you think won the election in 2020?"
GOPer: "We don't need to relitigate that election."
Me: "So, Biden won, and your party is ready to turn the corner?"
GOPer: "Well, there are still some concerns about the election out there. I hear it every time I go to the supermarket."
Me: "Do you tell your voters that Biden won and that it's time to move on?"
GOPer: "Are you kidding? I'd have a primary opponent before I got to the checkout counter."

The continuing saga of election audits and propping up the Big Lie is not about voter fraud or protecting elections; it's about politicians running for cover. It's about elected officials afraid to tell the truth to the people they represent. It's about the sure and rapid repudiation they will get from the fanatical wing of their party.

I have a feeling that retiring U.S. Senator Pat Toomey would hold his ground in supermarket debates and with voters who have willingly jumped on the fantasy voter fraud train. In a recent legislative forum, he was asked a direct question about the future of the GOP and the grip that the former president has on the party. His bold pronouncement was, "I think after what happened post-2020 election, I think the president's behavior was completely unacceptable, so I don't think he should be the nominee to lead the party in 2024."

It took less than twenty-four hours for the wailing from Mar-a-Lago to begin. The former president called Toomey a "terrible representative for both Pennsylvania and the United States." The failed president went on to say, "He ran with me in 2016 and wasn't expected to win, but because of my victory, he did. He still doesn't realize what happened and why—not the sharpest tool in the shed." This is even though Toomey ran well ahead of the former guy when they were on the ballot together.

Over the years, I have disagreed with many of Senator Toomey's positions, but I have always respected his keen understanding of the process and economic policy. He distinguished himself as a hard-working senator and an internationally respected expert in several fields. He is, indeed, "one of the sharpest tools in the shed." Toomey, one of the seven Senate Republicans who voted to convict the former president during the second impeachment trial, tells it like it is. He called Trumpout for inciting a riot at the U.S. Capitol. He stood tall when he defended the certification of votes against the insurrection of a violent mob.

For this, he has earned the enmity of the former guy and his minions. In fact, the inciter-in-chief has gone out of his way to stomp out the Toomey legacy by endorsing a sycophantic, right wing cable news fixture by the name of Sean Parnell in the upcoming U.S. Senate race. Recall that Parnell lost a race for the U.S. House of Representatives to Conor Lamb despite a full-court press from the right in 2020. Putting the Trumpian thumb on the scales in the primary also thumbs the nose at several other candidates on the Republican side who were just gathering steam. Jeff Bartos, a real estate developer from Berks County, ran a strong race for lieutenant governor in 2018. Carla Sands is a former ambassador to Denmark. Congress member Dan Mueser is a credible candidate in his own right. No matter. In today's Republican Party, those closest to the cult leader are the only ones receiving full-throated primary support.

By contrast, the Democrats have half a dozen candidates battling it out for their party's nomination. Each has presented specific policy positions, and each has its own niche in the ideological spectrum. None of them ransacked the Capitol on January 6. None of them perpetuates the Big Lie about the 2020 election results.

As the U.S. Senate campaign heats up, let us recognize once again that truth and honor in politics matter. Let us also note that Senator Toomey has demonstrated both.

PAYING OUR DEBTS

SEPTEMBER 24, 2021

First things first: let's understand what raising the debt ceiling is and isn't. According to Congress, the debt ceiling is the legal limit on the total debt that the federal government can incur. This limitation was first established in 1917 to ensure that we could afford to pay for the commitments made by our leaders at home and abroad. The debt ceiling has required adjustments from time to time to accommodate disasters, wars, critical healthcare, growing human service needs, and other obligations.

Congress and the president have altered the debt ceiling one hundred times since the end of World War II. Republicans led a bipartisan effort to raise the debt ceiling three times in the last administration alone.

The fact is that the need for borrowing and incurring debt has grown exponentially since the early 1900s. Over the years, both parties have agreed that the debt ceiling must be raised to meet our obligations as a world leader. America defaulting on its debts would usher in worldwide economic chaos, and both parties understand this.

The other thing to understand about the debt ceiling is that it has nothing to do with government spending. Raising the debt ceiling becomes necessary when Congress and the executive branch establish new programs or increase budgets for government functions like defense, education, and healthcare. In other words, raising the debt limit is a formality after spending decisions have already been made, and monies have already been allocated. In the simplest terms, the debt ceiling adjustment is necessary to pay for expenses we have already incurred. Imagine taking out a thirty-year mortgage on a home and suddenly deciding that you didn't feel like making the monthly payments. What if everybody in the country did the same thing? The chaos of failing to pay debts—whether in our individual households or at the federal level—is almost incomprehensible.

Mark Zandi of Moody's Analytics wrote that an impasse over the debt ceiling would cost the U.S. economy up to six million jobs and wipe out as much as $15 trillion in household wealth. It would destroy any employment gains made as we came out of the pandemic and plunge the nation into double-digit unemployment again. Then why is Mitch McConnell browbeating his caucus into a "no" vote on the debt ceiling? Why is he risking international economic calamity by running away from America's responsibility to pay its bills?

Because, evidently, partisan politics is more important to him than responsible governance. It is the continuation of a trend of irresponsibility. The GOP continues to peddle a Big Lie about the last election because it fears the backlash of those who refuse to accept reality. The party waffles on vaccination and mask requirements even as more and more unvaccinated, misinformed citizens die pointless deaths. The Republicans slam down any Biden initiative because they benefit from a base that sees any collaboration as selling out the cult. Compromise and collegiality are things of the past.

With the government scheduled to run out of cash by mid-October, will the loyal opposition summon up the statesmanship to do the right thing? Both Democrats and Republicans have acknowledged the disaster that a federal default would be. But Mitch McConnell is willing to play chicken with the debt ceiling to put another dent in the political armor of the president—or just to bolster his talking points with his local Rotary Club.

It may be that Senator McConnell is setting up a political disaster for himself. We have already seen the Republican Minority in the Senate thwart efforts on the pandemic, infrastructure, human services, and even criminal justice reform. It may be that obstruction regarding the debt ceiling will be the tipping point that forces the Senate to amend its rules.

The simple solution to government policy stuck in the mud of politics is to pull out of the puddle. Democrats could, by their razor-thin majority, change the filibuster rule to allow for a simple majority vote on critical issues like the debt ceiling. Then they could proceed with or without their obstreperous colleagues.

This is more than a good idea; it is the appropriate response to the gall of a majority leader willing to tamper with our economic stability to score political points. If the Republicans can threaten to withhold their votes for those purposes, the Democrats can and should vote as a group to keep the wheels of government turning.

LEADERS BEHAVING BADLY

OCTOBER 1, 2021

Last week was a tough test for real government leadership. In congressional hearings, dueling press conferences, and committee meetings, elected officials showed that they were more interested in political grandstanding than in doing their jobs. Let's start with the two-day grilling of General Mark Milley and Defense Secretary Lloyd Austin. The two displayed extraordinary patience and candor as legislators unloaded a barrage of personal attacks on them. Yes, Milley confirmed that he had recommended a different course of action in Afghanistan. But he also staunchly defended the Constitution and his deference to the Commander in Chief.

Representative Matt Gaetz (R-FL), a pretentious conspiracy-monger, launched a scathing attack on the general and secretary, impugning their characters and calling for their resignations. Other Republicans in the Senate and House piled on. It took the remarkable Liz Cheney (R-WY) to set the record straight and describe her colleagues' comments as "despicable."

Senate Minority Leader Mitch McConnell (R-KY) also failed the test of leadership last week. He pressured every Republican senator to drive the United States into default. The issue was suspending or raising the debt ceiling as required by law. Without that action, our country will run out of money sometime in October. According to economists, this would cost the U.S. economy up to 6 million jobs and wipe out as much as $15 trillion in household wealth. McConnell knows that his party raised the debt ceiling three times in the previous administration. He also knows that raising the debt limit has nothing to do with prospective spending—it is about paying the debts that have already been incurred—like the trillion-dollar tax cut for the wealthy that he engineered. McConnell succeeded in turning this basic responsibility into a talking point about "reckless spending" and got his entire party to go along with that charade. *The Salt Lake Tribune* took its Republican senators to task for the blatant partisan grandstanding: "The Republican Party is about to push the global economy into a horrible recession just for the chance to make the Democrats look bad."

What the Republicans were really concerned about was the proposed $3.5 trillion social spending program which remains the cornerstone of the Biden agenda. The talking points on the lips of every Republican were that this is a massive tax increase (although no tax increase is proposed for anyone earning under $400,000 per year), and this will stymie the economy (although economic experts have said that just the opposite is true).

The fact is that the social policy package focuses on landmark issues that have cried out for attention for far too long. Do Republicans really want to tell their constituents that they oppose addressing climate change, providing expanded health and education benefits, and helping low-income families with paid leave and childcare programs?

Here is where I have to parcel out some bipartisan criticism; it seems that the Congressional Progressive Caucus did everything they could to disrupt the largely popular infrastructure program unless they got their $3.5 trillion "human infrastructure" package. Chairman Representative Pramila Jayapal (D-WS) declared that the members of that caucus would not vote for the bipartisan infrastructure bill unless the less popular budget agreement passed as well. Instead of pushing Democrats toward a cliff, she and the progressives could have supported a compromise package of both initiatives that addressed infrastructure, human services, and climate change at a reduced cost. Indeed, this is likely to be what happens as the issues are addressed in the coming days.

At the state level, Senator Chris Dush (R – Jefferson) deserves a reprimand for launching a spectacle in Pennsylvania similar to the bogus Arizona audit that landed with a thud recently. Despite that the Maricopa County review turned up absolutely no evidence of voter fraud—it actually resulted in confirming that Biden won by an even larger margin there—the Pennsylvania Senate is wasting time and taxpayer dollars with a similar fishing expedition.

Two former PA senators, a Republican and a Democrat, wrote a blistering editorial in the Harrisburg *Patriot-News* about the "forensic audit." They pointed out that it is already off to a bad start by demanding private information from every voter in Pennsylvania. Senate Democrats have intervened with a lawsuit to stop this invasion of privacy. What is clear is that the Senate leaders have knuckled under pressure from a certain Mar-a-Lago cult leader. Or, as the aforementioned editorial contends: "The Senate appears to be lost in a fog of partisan ambitions."

PENCE GOES ALL-OUT ORWELL

OCTOBER 8, 2021

I have been a Penn State fan all my life. Through good seasons and bad, through heartaches and scandals, I have had an abiding pride in the quality of the players and their achievements on and off the field. A certain coach once called it success with honor, and I subscribe to that concept enthusiastically. This loyalty to my team does not mean that I spew insults at the opposition. I certainly do not challenge the results when the Nittany Lions lose. My loyalty is strong, but it is not blind.

This week, former Vice President Mike Pence achieved a new level of blind loyalty and political pandering when he downplayed the events of January 6. His blind loyalty to—or his abject fear of—the ex-president caused him to twist the events of January 6 into an attack on the media. This is what he had to say about the worst attack on the Capitol since the War of 1812:

"I know the media wants to distract from the Biden administration's failed agenda by focusing on one day in January [. . .] the president and I sat down a few days later and talked through all of it. I can tell you that we parted amicably."

Let that sink in. Pence spoke "amicably" with a man who had stoked a crowd into a frenzy with specific instructions to stop him from doing his constitutional duty. New details have emerged about how heavily the ex-president leaned on Pence. We also know now that some Capitol invaders intended to do the vice president bodily harm—or worse.

Here is the shocking truth: the mob that invaded the Capitol was headed directly toward the vice president. Because of an alert Capitol policeman, they were directed away from Pence and his colleagues. Had those rioters turned right rather than left, they could have dragged Pence out to the makeshift gallows they had erected.

Until this week, Pence had secured a laudable place in history. He faced personal, political, and physical threats to perform his constitutional duty to certify a free and fair election. It was his most significant service to the nation that he performed as vice president. Now he tells us that the whole insurrection was some kind of media stunt. Now he high-fives his base and the 600 people charged with January 6-related crimes. This level of toadying is worse than a sudden case of January 6 amnesia; this is embracing an Orwellian version of history.

On January 1, 1984, *The New York Times* appropriately printed an article about *1984*, George Orwell's dark, prescient novel that called out the thought control exercised by totalitarians. The book was written when the evil of totalitarianism still burned, and the threat of world domination had just narrowly been avoided. It was written as a warning long before the arrival of the tribal politics that continues to split America apart in the twenty-first century.

The Times summarized the book saying, "Winston, the main character of the novel, lives in a country where individual thought is banned, where only the leader, Big Brother, is allowed to reason and to decide [. . .]. His fellow intellectuals have sold their inalienable right to think freely for security and a semblance of physical well-being."

Inevitably, When Winston succumbs to the groupthink of Big Brother, he becomes just another cog in the machinery of the state. Another drone willing to trade whatever character and morality he had for the comfort of fitting in.

Orwell never expected our country to plunge completely into the abyss of despotism. But it was possible, he said, if we do not "defend our most precious right to have our own thoughts." *The New York Times* article appeared thirty-five years after Orwell gave his dystopian warning. It was written thirty-two years before enough Americans elected a president with Big Brother tendencies and no tolerance for independent thought amongst his minions.

Today, George Orwell would be holding his breath to see if the American experiment in democracy can survive the wanton twisting of the facts and the leaders who buy into the Big Lie.

This week, Mike Pence joined the ranks of Winston and the minions, who meekly put aside what they truly know and believe. It seems that Pence is willing to sacrifice truth for convenience. It seems that his ambitions to run for president in his own right have caused him to relinquish the one characteristic that he displayed on January 6: courage.

POSTMORTEM
NOVEMBER 4, 2021

Democrats took a beating in the 2021 elections. Glenn Youngkin, the GOP candidate for governor in Virginia, won in a state that gave Joe Biden a ten-point majority just one year ago. In New Jersey, the Republicans wiped out a sixteen-point advantage and almost defeated an incumbent governor in a deep blue state. In most states, including Pennsylvania, Democratic turnout was higher than usual for an off-year election cycle. But if the Democrats voted fervently, the Republicans came to the polls in a frenzy. Simply put, the GOP won the crucial get-out-the-vote battle and left Democrats reeling and nervous about 2022 and 2024.

To a degree, the election wounds were self-inflicted. It is a fact that Joe Biden has been aggressive in putting forth bold initiatives to deal with the pandemic. The CARES Act alone qualifies as a major first-year achievement and has provided critical support to families across the country. He has been bold in putting forth other initiatives to reenergize the economy, rebuild the nation's infrastructure, and lead the world in combatting global warming. The highway and bridges infrastructure package would be the largest investment of its type since Eisenhower's interstate highway initiative. The social infrastructure package is equally bold. It features childcare tax credits, universal pre-K and work training programs, and an array of investments in clean energy technologies.

Since the Republicans have resorted to their usual reckless spending arguments and do not intend to provide a single vote for working families, the Democrats needed to close ranks and deliver unanimous support to get the Biden initiatives to his desk.

As the clock ticked to the November elections, the Democrats twisted themselves into knots over the details of the social infrastructure portion of Biden's "Build Back Better" and failed to deliver either of the two bills. This left candidates across the country with a vague framework of a plan but no big win to tout on the campaign trail. Democrats in Virginia and New Jersey hoped to point to victories on roads, bridges, and popular family incentives that draw 70 percent support in public polls. They had hoped to run on a positive record of achievement but, as one Democrat senator put it, "Our timing was horrible."

Terry McAuliffe was reduced to warning voters that Youngkin was the second coming of Trump. Youngkin cleverly distanced himself from Trump to appeal to moderates in both parties but was not above spewing falsehoods and innuendo to energize the MAGA crowd. In true Trumpian fashion, the GOP trotted out a new weapon to frighten parents and stoke racial fears. The notion of attacking critical race theory taught in grade schools was an unsubtle way to suggest that teachers were forcing liberal or "woke" views on their children. (God forbid that student would learn about the role that slavery played in our history.) Also, if critical race theory classes occur, they would be reserved for graduate-level discussions.

That did not stop the GOP from wielding its new weapon in Virginia and many other states. Terry McAuliffe made matters worse by bungling a debate response on the subject and suggesting that parents shouldn't tell schools what to teach their children. This was all the Republicans needed to put their howling misinformation machine into high gear. "Parents matter" became the bumper sticker rallying cry they used to devastating effect.

In an earlier column, I called out similar dark campaigning in Pennsylvania. The winning candidate for the Pennsylvania Supreme Court blanketed the airwaves with a commercial that linked his opponent to hundreds of homicides in Philadelphia. Despite a reprimand from the State Bar Association, the ads had a predictable effect on his opponent. She lost.

Whether candidates are twisting the facts on education in Virginia or going full-on Willie Horton in Pennsylvania, candidates know that there is no bottom to what they can sell to voters. The editors at the *Baltimore Sun* put it this way: "A message that stirs their deepest anxieties, whether unreasonable and factually wrong, is a powerful tool, especially when it's reinforced by the right wing media echo chamber repeatedly. There's a reason why deep-pocketed right wing donors happily finance bogus culture-war campaigns. Sadly, they work."

There really is no way to sugarcoat the losses sustained by Democrats in 2021. Minority Leader Kevin McCarthy is already boasting that the GOP

POSTMORTEM

could win up to sixty new seats in Congress next year. If there is anything positive to take away for Democrats, it is this: you have enough time to help your president do great things for the country. Stop squabbling and start legislating.

Also, expect your opponents to inflame voters with divisive issues. They are good at it. You need better responses. Democrats needed this wake-up call. If they ignore it, they will take a beating in elections for years to come.

OF BIDEN AND BEES

NOVEMBER 26, 2021

With the enactment of the bipartisan infrastructure bill, President Biden has delivered on a promise that has eluded the last three presidents. The second piece of his social and economic package has passed the House and will likely receive Senate approval in the next two weeks. The increase in jobs across all sectors is impressive. As we enjoy this holiday season, we should all be thankful that the Biden administration is focused and successful.

When Americans are asked for their assessment of the Biden agenda, his legislative initiatives are popular. Seventy-eight percent of the population favors the expansion of Medicare; 66 percent believe in affordable housing; 61 percent are for childcare and pre-kindergarten initiatives. But this doesn't stop the flamethrowers on the right from spewing a stream of thinly veiled hate speech at a man doing his job. Many of these personal attacks should be beneath any American citizen. So, from this citizen on this Thanksgiving weekend, I say thanks, Joe.

Another group that deserves our thanks is the Harrisburg University of Science and Technology. It is my pleasure to serve as HU's Board Chairman, and I have a front-row seat to some of the most exciting innovations the university continues to pursue. Already a national leader in medical technologies, robotics, analytics, and advanced manufacturing, HU is turning its attention to the Keystone Agritech Initiative. This global public/private partnership could enhance agriculture production in Pennsylvania and the nation.

The Keystone Agritech Initiative plans to build and operate a thousand-acre organic high-tech facility in Pennsylvania that will put Pennsylvania on the cutting edge of advancements in how we grow food. Sound ambitious? You bet it is. But a delegation of farmers, researchers, investors, and retailers has just returned from a tour of the Netherlands and the latest controlled environment facilities that dramatically increase crop yields while reducing costs and saving the environment.

A model for Pennsylvania is the Agriport A7 outside of Amsterdam. Since 2006, this facility has become the premier climate-controlled indoor agricultural facility in the world. It has created more than 6,000 jobs and has been a wellspring for training. The facility produces vegetables at a rate 10-15 times higher than "traditional" farming. While addressing its development challenges, Agriport A7 has attracted remarkable spin-offs. The facility produces its power and recycles rainwater for irrigation. Using natural crop pollination and protection products minimizes the need for pesticides. By producing its electric power from geothermal and biomass, it has made excess capacity available for other uses. One major success story is the attraction of a massive Microsoft Data Center that has turned the entire area into a thriving, high-tech mecca for food and data production.

The Pennsylvania delegation returned with a wealth of new ideas and close alliances with some of the planet's most innovative growers and horticulturalists. One company specialized in building state-of-the-art greenhouses with autonomous growing to maximize returns. Another firm put artificial intelligence right in the farmers' hands to ensure accurate and perfectly timed application of water, light, and natural fertilization of crops. Another has harnessed the power of bees and beneficial nematodes to assist in pollination and pest prevention.

One of the most promising aspects of the mission was to bring a real-world perspective from a major potential end-user of food products. Based in Carlisle and Amsterdam, Giant Foods sent three executives to observe and brainstorm ways to bring Pennsylvania products to its shelves. The idea is to cultivate products close to its distribution network to assure quality and freshness for its customers.

Again, it is hard to underestimate the role of Harrisburg University in coordinating and nurturing the agritech movement. Notably, Wageningen University in the Netherlands has actively partnered with private industry and visionary government leaders in applying research worldwide. It has impacted over 6,800 employees and 12,900 students in over a hundred countries. This is precisely what the Keystone Agritech Initiative intends for central Pennsylvania and beyond. By finding new ways to make hi-tech farming more accessible and efficient, it can become more profitable and scalable globally. Look for announcements in the months and years to come, but the Keystone Agritech

Initiative is off to a great start with a staggering upside for food production in Pennsylvania and the world.

Progress can be measured in different ways. Federal policies that benefit citizens matter. Harnessing nature and new technologies to feed them is just as important. This holiday season, I am grateful for Biden and bees!

OUR COUNTRY REQUIRES GOOD LEADERS AND GOOD CITIZENS

DECEMBER 3, 2021

This week, Pennsylvania recorded an average of 5,000 new COVID-19 infections daily. In our state, forty-four people die of the pandemic every day. While these numbers are down from this time last year, the Omicron variant threatens to explode in Pennsylvania and elsewhere for one reason: too many people remain unvaccinated.

The vaccine development and rollout were always a race against time. As every medical expert told us, if most citizens had been vaccinated earlier, the Delta and Omicron variants would not have mutated and spread throughout the population. We could have ended the pandemic if citizens had cooperated. Let's just call it like it is: those who still refuse to get vaccinated may be putting us all in danger. This has nothing to do with anti-vaxxers' freedom; it is about doing the right thing to protect our children and our neighbors.

Still, Republicans at all levels of government are digging their heels in against vaccine mandates. In Congress, hard-liners are talking about a government shutdown to oppose vaccines. There is only one way to describe this kind of stance: plain stupid.

Meanwhile, on the other side of the globe, Prime Minister Jacinda Ardern of New Zealand continues to lead her country through the pandemic with effective policies that have minimized infections, hospitalizations, and death rates. In March 2020, she imposed a fourteen-day quarantine on everyone entering the country. At the time, it was the toughest border restriction in the world. She made it clear that New Zealand would remain closed to visitors until her citizens had been fully vaccinated and protected. As a result, the pandemic was contained. Even the Delta spike was short-lived as other countries suffered through new variations. One reporter gave her this praise: "Ardern revealed an empathy, steel, and clarity that in the most appalling circumstances brought New Zealanders together and inspired people the world over."

This was not the first test faced by Ardern. Soon after becoming the world's youngest head of state at thirty-seven, she faced a mass killing at the Christchurch Mosque. Her clear compassion for Muslims and all people shined through her remarks at the time: "Speak the names of those who were lost rather than the name of the man who took them [. . .] he will, when I speak, be nameless." An image of the prime minister embracing a Muslim community member went viral and was even projected on the Burj Khalifa, the world's tallest building, with the word "peace" superimposed.

The most recent ripple of empathy sent out from Jacinda Ardern resulted from a simple gesture that spoke volumes about her personality. Here's how *INC. Magazine* reported the incident:

> *Jacinda Ardern was in the middle of giving a live update on Facebook Monday night on the COVID-19 response in New Zealand when she was interrupted by her 3-year-old daughter. "Mummy?" Ardern's daughter, Neve, could be heard saying off-screen. "You're meant to be in bed, darling," Ardern replied. When Neve called for her again, she responded, "Pop back to bed. I'll see you in a second," before turning back to the camera to laugh about the darling little interruption.*

After a third on-camera interruption, Ardern struck a national chord by asking viewers, "Does anyone else have kids escape like three, four times after bedtime?" You could almost hear the resounding "Yes" from parents all over the world.

This is not just another cute, caught-on-camera moment. This head of state was willing to show her vulnerable side as she handled an uncomfortable situation with honesty and complete transparency. Nick Hobson, a writer for *INC. Magazine,* called the authentic display of compassion under pressure the "best lesson in leadership I have ever seen."

Even the best leaders, however, can crumble under relentless opposition. Biden continues to push forward on initiatives to increase jobs, address the real needs of working families, and secure a better future for our children. What does he get from the very people he is trying to help? Moronic chants about someone named Brandon and a vicious onslaught from leaders interested only in regaining power.

Instead of the current American brand of rabid opposition to its leaders, consider New Zealanders who have come to accept vaccine mandates and harsh COVID restrictions. It is partly because Prime Minister Jacinda Ardern has shown compassion and authenticity at every turn. It is also because her people listen to her rather than shout at each other.

Every nation depends on good leadership. Good leadership requires thoughtful followers. New Zealand seems to have both.

FOOTBALL AND PITCHFORK POLITICS

DECEMBER 10, 2021

Years ago, a football star lit up Friday nights in a small Pennsylvania town. The captain and quarterback of his high school team, the player broke every school record, and the bleachers were filled with fans calling his name. The entire community celebrated when he got the news of a full athletic scholarship to a top-tier California university.

Three games into his college career, the star was sent in to relieve the starting quarterback. Under center for the first time in the big leagues of college football, the star of Smallville decided that he had a better plan for the offense than the play that the coach gave him. He called his own play. The coach called an immediate time-out and gave the player this short explanation: "There is only one coach on this team." For the rest of the season, Smallville tuned in every Saturday only to watch their superstar sit on the bench.

Athletes and politicians are vulnerable to the adulation of crowds. When a freshman quarterback responds to cheers from the sidelines rather than an actual game plan, bad things happen. When senators follow crowd noises rather than science, people die. This week, the Senate voted to roll back mask mandates that President Biden and every credible scientist have said will save lives. Republicans marched in lockstep with two Democrats in tow to pander to their noisy constituents instead. The only weapon we have against a lingering, worldwide pandemic is science. Science has shown that masks and vaccines could relieve the burdens on our health systems and end the pandemic once and for all.

The virus of unbridled populism—mob rule—is the infection that is poisoning our political system. It is causing elected officials to cower away from their responsibilities so they can continue to hear the cheers of the folks in the cheap seats.

Michael Petrou, a Canadian professor of political science, has written bluntly that populism is a threat to democracy. He leaned on examples from world history that included coups and mob uprisings but reached a remarkable conclusion. The biggest threat to democracy doesn't come from foreign enemies or self-proclaimed anarchists. It comes from existing leaders not willing to enforce the guardrails of democracy.

According to Petrou, strong institutions, responsible political parties, and just plain decency are the "soft guardrails of democracy." Decency requires that presidential leadership, like a coach's game plan, be respected. This is especially true when life-and-death issues like war and mortal pestilence are debated. Certainly, there is room for policy debates, and there will always be dissension among the ranks of both parties. But obliterating tolerance, breaking into armed camps, and using every political tool to crush opponents destroys democracy from within. What lies beyond the guardrail, according to Petrou, is an abyss. "Once cultural norms are bypassed, there is little left to stop a populist politician from embracing explicitly undemocratic practices."

Congress will likely enact a scaled-back version of Biden's "Build Back Better" initiative. It is equally likely that it will not garner a single Republican vote. This is not because Republicans oppose childcare tax credits or pre-K education. It is not because Republicans are against investing in new technology and economic development. It is because the marching orders from their leaders are to dig their heels in and fan the fires of division to advance their political objectives.

Even when some bipartisanship flickers into life these days, do not expect any real warmth. House and Senate leaders have, for example, agreed on a path to raise the debt ceiling. Until recently, this routine vote allowed the United States to meet its financial obligation worldwide. It is simply a mechanism to pay debts that we have already incurred. Now, it has become yet another stick of dynamite to light.

Democratic leaders are trying to give the president the ability to operate the government. Republicans provide just enough votes for their minions to lambaste Democrats for excessive spending. What's lost in the debate is the need for responsible, bipartisan government. Instead, we have chaotic responses to crowd noises rather than adherence to coherent game plans.

This is not the system of representative democracy that the founders envisioned. This is pitchfork politics that boils over at a racist rally in Charlottesville or a full-on insurrection at the U.S. Capitol.

Returning to the sports analogy, you may not like the current coach, but since we are all on the same team, we owe him some deference. At the very least, our disagreements should be civil and give us a fighting chance to advance the ball.

PEACE AT CHRISTMAS

DECEMBER 17, 2021

The news remains full of disturbing information about the Capitol riots. It is becoming clearer that the insurgents operated under a game plan discussed and devised at the highest levels of government and that the effort was aided and abetted by elected officials in the U.S. Congress. It is disturbing that the January 6th Committee continues to be rebuffed by witnesses and leaders who should be seeking the truth—not twisting the incident for their own political purposes. The fact is that there were plans in place to nullify a national election, and an alarming portion of the electorate still believes that they have a right to ignore 81 million voters just because their candidate lost.

It is more than bewildering; it is a threat to the very foundations of our government. It is almost too much to think about during this holiday season.

My sister Carol has a solution: Hallmark movies. When she reaches her tolerance level for offensive politics, endless news commentary, and the relentless pandemic, she finds the latest installment of a sugarcoated story on the Hallmark channel. We joke that we can predict the plot and end within minutes of meeting the lead characters. You know: Christmas is coming. John and Jane are alone and getting through some personal issues. Family and friends in some small town help them find each other just in time to change their lives while they decorate the tree.

When her tears well up at the end of each movie, it's not because she has been moved by the production value of some cinematic classic. It is because there is something reassuring about happy endings. There is something important about holding on to peace and kindness when the day's news eats away at our humanity. So, in the spirit of Christmas and a respite from "taking arms against a sea of troubles," here are a few uplifting anecdotes.

PEACE AT CHRISTMAS

An old man came across a young boy tossing something into the ocean. It happens that the boy was trying to return starfish that had washed up on the shore back to the sea.

"What are you doing?" asked the old man.

"If these starfish are still on the beach when the sun comes up, they will die," replied the boy.

"But said the old man, there are thousands of miles of beach and millions of starfish. It doesn't matter how many you throw in; you can't make a difference."

"It matters to this one," the boy said as he threw another starfish into the waves.

Most history students know the story of the Christmas Truce of 1914. A British machine gunner named Bairnsfather wrote about it in his memoirs. On Christmas Eve, 1914, the First Battalion of the Royal Warwickshire Regiment was pinned down in a muddy trench in Belgium where, as the writer put it, his days and nights were "an endless cycle of sleeplessness and fear, stale biscuits and cigarettes too wet to light." The situation was hopeless, and Bairnsfather was sure that his only chance of leaving was in an ambulance.

Then, beyond the barbed wire and from the enemy trenches came an unusual murmur, then a loud sound of human voices. The Germans were singing Christmas carols. The British soldiers began to sing back. After overcoming some language barriers, soldiers declared their own truce and spent Christmas shaking hands and sharing rations.

And this is from an incident that occurred in 2013. Mark Burnett, who has gone on to be a highly successful Hollywood producer, was shooting his miniseries on the Bible in Northern Africa. The series would become a big hit in America, but not before Burnett and his cast experienced some unexplainable events. In a story from the *London Daily Mail,* Burnett talked openly about the hand of God in the undertaking. Venomous snakes appeared mysteriously at the Crucifixion scene. Props and clothing went missing to return to their original locations intact. One scene was filmed during a completely still night in the desert. The character playing Jesus tells Nicodemus, "The Holy Spirit is like the wind." According to Burnett, "At that moment, a wind, like as if a 747 was taking off, blew his hair, almost blew the set over and sustained for [twenty] seconds across the desert."

When our faith in government and leadership is shaken, when rational thinking is being drowned out by partisan shouting, and our very country seems to be at risk, it might be a good time to assure ourselves that there is hope. Whether it is in the form of a boy committed to making a difference, soldiers putting down their weapons, or a whisper of grace that is carried on the wind, there is hope.

May Christmas bring you peace and happy endings.

JANUARY 6: AN ALARMING ANNIVERSARY

DECEMBER 31, 2021

As we approach the one-year anniversary of the January 6 riots, the revelations coming from the House Committee investigating those events are jarring. The criminal justice system has been focused on those who perpetrated crimes and were caught on camera. Several hundred have been charged, and many are now going to jail.

The legislative inquiry is moving more methodically because it is focused on the people who planned, encouraged, and funded the insurrection. What is most disturbing is the emerging picture of highly placed elected officials scheming to overturn the election. These people who swore to uphold the Constitution were actively shredding it right before our eyes. Some realized their efforts were misguided and, in the mayhem of January 6, tried to tame the beast that they helped to unleash. Messages to the president's chief of staff included, "We are under siege here at the Capitol."

"They have breached the Capitol."

"Hey, Mark [Meadows], protestors are literally storming the Capitol. Is Trump going to say something?"

Even some Fox News hosts (the very people who now downplay the coup attempt) chimed in. Laura Ingraham wrote, "The president needs to tell people in the Capitol to go home. This is hurting all of us. He is destroying his legacy."

Sean Hannity wrote to Meadows, "Can he [Trump] make a statement? Ask the people to leave the Capitol?"

We are now hearing lurid details about insurrectionist "war rooms" at the Willard Hotel. And, worst of all, we now know that more than a few Congress members were in on the whole thing. Here's a local connection that cannot go unnoticed: Congress member Scott Perry is being questioned about his role in attempting to install a Trump appointee as attorney general in the days leading up to the riot. Perry, who helped lead the effort to oppose certification of the election results, also reportedly supported replacing the attorney general with a deputy who could be counted on to defy the election results. The move would have upended the Constitution with an astounding overreach by a chief executive on his way out the door.

Some want to move on from this ugly chapter in American history simply. Some believe that unleashing a murderous mob to trample all over the Constitution was, somehow, patriotic. They should listen to what DC policeman Michael Fanone said, "I was grabbed, beaten, tased, all while being called a traitor to my country [. . .] I heard chants of 'Kill him with his own gun.'"

U.S. Capitol Police Sergeant Aquilino Gonnell told NPR recently about his own experience at the hands of the mob: "I could feel myself losing oxygen and recall thinking to myself, 'This is how I'm going to die, trampled defending this entrance."

Both Fanone and Gonnell have said that it is unnerving that the very members of Congress that they risked their lives to protect are now promoting the Big Lie about the presidential election and downplaying the violence of January 6. Gonnell told NPR, "We risked our lives to give them enough time to get to safety. And allegedly, some of them were in communication with some of the rioters and with some of the coordinators or in the know of what would happen [. . .]. We did everything possible to prevent him [Pence] from being hanged and killed in front of his daughter and wife. And now he's telling us that that one day in January doesn't mean anything. It's pathetic. It's a disgrace." The House panel has announced they will release an interim report by the summer of 2022.

As we head toward the 2022 election cycle, it is important that voters of both parties ask their candidates some pertinent questions: Do you accept the results of the 2020 elections? Do you believe the planners and participants in the January 6 riots should be brought to justice? Are you willing to tell the truth about the Big Lie, or will you continue to inflame the anger of your base for fear of losing their votes?

The ramblings of the former president will likely continue. Statesmen must arise in both parties to stop accepting that blather and to get back to some semblance of public policy based on mutual respect and respect for our Constitution. That is how we will get past the stain of January 6.

PART FOUR

2022 ARTICLES

BIDEN'S MESSAGE GETS DROWNED OUT
JANUARY 21, 2022

The White House had prepared a detailed summary of President Joe Biden's successes in his first year in office. "In spite of unprecedented crises and opposition from congressional Republicans, the president and congressional Democrats got an enormous amount done for the American people in 2021" was how the note began. The brief went on to point out that he had gotten 490 million vaccine shots into the arms of citizens. While the stubborn anti-vax crowd has prevented the eradication of the virus, Biden and his team can rightfully claim that his leadership helped save 1.1 million lives and prevented more than 10 million hospitalizations.

Biden's notes also included the reopening of 99 percent of schools, direct assistance to families through the American Rescue Plan, and a Bipartisan Infrastructure Law that will create millions of good-paying jobs rebuilding roads and bridges across America. The White House also pointed to a booming economy. Nearly six million jobs were added last year—more than any first-year president in history. The unemployment rate fell to 4.2 percent, and unemployment claims reached their lowest since 1969. The American Rescue Plan and other Biden initiatives have pushed the GDP to grow by 5-6 percent—the best number since 1964. Americans have an average of $100 more monthly in their pockets, and child poverty has been cut in half.

On the thorny issues of inflation, supply chain interruptions, and gas prices, the reality is that much has been accomplished. Through executive orders and jawboning of shipping interests, the number of containers stuck at the docks has been reduced by more than half. Because of a historic release of products from our Strategic Petroleum Reserve, gas prices are coming down again.

When Joe Biden faced the press to review his first year in office, he did his best to focus on these and other achievements. The problem is that two of his most hyped projects (voting rights and the Build Back Better program) were mired in a partisan standoff. Both initiatives required a robust and full contingent of Democratic senators to succeed. Both fell two votes short. Worse, at the very time that Biden should have been taking a bow for a very good year, Senator Joe Manchin (D-WV) and Senator Kyrsten Sinema (D-AZ) derailed the bills and drowned out his message by stepping on his airtime. Dana Milbank of *The Washington Post* said, "It was the split screen that has bedeviled the Biden presidency. There they were Wednesday afternoon, in the exact same time slot: The two Joes. The president, and the man who is destroying his presidency."

As soon as Biden got through the positive points of his first-year achievements, the press went into attack mode. "Why can't you deliver Manchin and Sinema?" "Did you overpromise on voting rights and Build Back Better?" The president got drawn into a vortex of explanations about the filibuster rules and, according to some observers, stumbled in his attempt to offer a clear and reassuring message.

Biden's frustration with the logjam in the Senate and his passion for protecting his initiatives spilled into some contentious moments. During the two-hour ordeal, the press questions became increasingly confrontational, and the president became increasingly annoyed.

There was also a foreign policy misstep. When asked about Russia's next steps in Ukraine, Biden admitted that he expected some kind of incursion. While he quickly added that any such action would be met with a swift and proportionate response, Ukraine and NATO Allies were taken aback. The following day was spent reassuring allies that we would forcefully oppose any Russian adventurism. What should have been a victory lap for a solid year of achievements devolved into a spat about the president's capabilities.

President Biden has faced unprecedented challenges, including a stubborn worldwide pandemic, a former president that stokes the fires of sedition daily, and an opposition party that has chosen to coddle extremists rather than seek common ground. But this is all part of the job. In an era when media outlets gleefully broadcast falsehoods and lesser leaders fail to rise to their responsibilities, the president must raise a standard around which we can rally. If his opponents are conniving, he must be smart and transparent. If the media perpetrates lies, he must present truths that resonate with the public. No position on the planet requires clear-eyed, visionary leadership like the Presidency of the United States.

No other president—except Abraham Lincoln—has faced an era that could make or break our democracy. Joe Biden must do more than win battles in Congress and the press room. He must win the hearts and minds of citizens daily.

LEGISLATORS SHIRK THEIR DUTY

JANUARY 28, 2022

When Pennsylvania voters go to the polls this spring, they will likely face several proposed constitutional amendments. Last year, Republicans in the general assembly vented their displeasure with the Wolf administration by pushing two amendments that limited the governor's power to declare and manage state emergencies. Buoyed by their success, they ask voters to dramatically alter state government by shifting responsibilities from the executive branch to themselves. They argue that they are simply "letting the people decide" through a statewide referendum on these issues. What is really happening is a concerted effort to undermine the governor's prerogatives and to use the constitutional amendment process to achieve what they could not accomplish legislatively. As complicated as the amendment process is, it precludes any gubernatorial veto and, instead, relies on the voters to put up a "yes" vote— regardless of their familiarity with the issues.

As a refresher, constitutional amendments require that both chambers in the general assembly pass them in two consecutive sessions, followed by a statewide referendum. If a majority of voters approve the amendment, it becomes law and a new section of the Pennsylvania Constitution.

While this sounds daunting, the record shows that the majority of amendments placed before the voters get approved. Since 1968, forty-three of the forty-nine proposed amendments have been adopted. In the current legislative session, lawmakers have already proposed more than seventy amendments to the PA Constitution.

A sampling of those amendments includes:

- Creating a two-year window for victims of childhood sexual abuse to allow for the filing of civil suits.
- Expanding the general assembly's power to override executive orders.
- Changing how we elect lieutenant governors.
- Requiring audits of elections.
- Eliminating or altering property taxes.
- Repealing mail-in voting.
- Reducing terms of judges and putting salary decisions in the hands of legislators.
- Establishing merit selection rather than popular election of judges.
- Cutting the size of the PA Legislature.
- Moving to a two-year state budget process.
- Eliminating any right to an abortion under the PA Constitution.

Some legislators have decided that they have a better chance of convincing a surly electorate to pass these and other controversial items through a statewide vote than by working through the complexities of the legislative process. Some feel they can simply bypass the governor and his veto pen just by taking it to the people.

The problem, of course, is that this undermines the delicate balance between the executive and the legislative branches of government. Both the U.S. and PA Constitutions clearly delineate the powers and limits of both branches. The Founding Fathers would be rolling over in their graves to see current elected officials overstepping their roles. They would also be appalled that elected representatives were abdicating their roles as the elected representatives—charged with exercising their judgments and making tough decisions based on compromise with their peers.

It bears repeating that we do not live in a democracy; it is a republic. We elect representatives who, presumably, are educated in the day's issues and capable of making informed decisions on our behalf. If every controversial matter were simply put before the people, there would be little hope of thorough discussion and understanding. Instead, media campaigns, special interests, internet influencers, and talking heads would bombard voters with their version of the facts. Why elect legislators if voters can weigh in with a simple "yes" or "no" on matters of public policy? Why not give every voter a button to push so that even the most detached, uninformed voter can thrust his thumb up or down like Romans in the Coliseum?

Alexander Hamilton was straightforward on this point. "The body of people often do not possess the discernment and stability necessary for systematic government [. . .]. They are frequently led into the grossest errors by misinformation and passion."

Plato outlined a system of enlightened leaders who would be free from temptations and capable of governing excellently on behalf of all citizens. He warned that "Democracy ruins itself by excess—of democracy."

Does this mean that elect officials should ignore popular opinion? Certainly not. They wouldn't be around long if they were continually out of synch with their own voters. But it does mean that elected officials must live up to the requirements of representative democracy. Instead of casting about for the cover of constitutional amendments they should take on even the tough issues and consider them in the spirit of what is best for their community and state. They need to educate their own constituencies when it is required. They need to face down the passions of the people when they are wrong. They need to assume their proper role in this republic—if we are to keep it.

SENATE CAMPAIGN CIRCUS

FEBRUARY 3, 2022

In today's political environment, the unofficial start of any U.S. Senate campaign is filing the end-of-year report with the Federal Elections Commission. This is where the candidates must come clean about their fundraising prowess and cash on hand. Due on January 31 of the election year, the report helps to separate the contenders from the pretenders.

On the Democratic side, the numbers show that Lieutenant Governor Fetterman has a decisive financial lead over his closest rival, Congress member Conor Lamb of Pittsburgh. With $5.5 million to his opponent's $3.0 million, Fetterman is sure to have staying power at least through the primary. The other candidates have not cracked the magic million-dollar mark. Without competitive funding, they will be vying for whatever attention they can get without a big advertising campaign. It looks increasingly like the Democrats will have a two-person horse race.

On the Republican side, former hedge fund manager David McCormick did not file an annual report, but he is said to have $5 million cash on hand with much more to come from his friends on Wall Street and corporate America.

Dr. Mehmet Oz, the race's television celebrity, jumpstarted his campaign with a $5 million personal loan. Much of that has already been spent on television ads. Likewise, Carla Sands, a former Trump official, dug deep into her own pockets for a $3.5 million loan which she appears to have invested in the media and on administration in the early going. Her remaining $1.5 seems inadequate to fend off more well-heeled opponents. Jeff Bartos, a real estate developer from eastern PA and former candidate for lieutenant governor, reports having $2 million cash on hand. While he continues to enjoy good relations with party activists, he will likely be outspent by the newcomers in the race.

At about this time eight years ago, a relatively unknown candidate for governor in Pennsylvania named Tom Wolf did an extraordinary thing. He bet on bad weather. Wolf's campaign bought big chunks of time on stations airing the 2014 Winter Olympics. With much of the voting population snowbound by record storms, they saw an endless series of introductory television ads that gave Wolf a decisive lead when the final medals were handed out.

Look for all the candidates to follow that model this year. Indeed, Dr. Oz has already covered the airwaves like a blanket of snow. His chief opponent David McCormick has begun to respond in kind. Here's where campaigning begins to grate on voters like fingernails on a chalkboard. Dr. Oz began his media foray with some chest-thumping about Dr. Fauci and some direct shots at McCormick. The former was a direct effort to attract MAGA supporters who have weaponized their anti-vaccine, anti-mask positions for the past two years. The latter attack included a broadside against McCormick, whose hedge fund made some investments in Chinese corporations. McCormick tried to outdo Oz on the issue of China by pointing to his work in international trade as an official in the George W. Bush administration. He proclaims his support for "American capitalism, not socialism." A banal but effective bumper slogan for GOP partisans.

Counter ads are starting to pop up and are likely to get snarkier as the campaign goes on. While there have been no big ad buys from the Democrats yet, stay tuned. It is only February, and there is plenty of time for attacks and counterattacks.

Therein lies my objection to big money and small-mindedness in politics. U.S. Senate candidates should be respectful of the office they seek. They should have some historical knowledge of real leaders who came before them. Instead of emulating Clay, Calhoun, Webster, LaFollette, Taft, Dirksen, and other giants, they succumb to hired guns whose obsession is not statecraft but stagecraft. Instead of presenting themselves as lions of the Senate, they are content to roar and preen like lions in a circus.

While the Democrats are biding their time, the Republicans are actively pandering to the faction of their party that clings to the Big Lie and other delusions. This is the exact moment when leaders of both parties must rise to their calling and tell their voters the truth. Instead of spouting their undying loyalty to the former guy, they could be blazing a trail toward excellence in the greatest deliberative body on earth. Instead of inspirational rhetoric, we get bumper sticker slogans, fearmongering, and outright fantasies about previous election results.

There will always be legitimate differences between the parties. There is also still time for the campaign to take on a more uplifting tone. Until that happens, voters have every right to tune out the circus.

APPLYING THE CONSTITUTION

FEBRUARY 11, 2022

Education has become a hot political topic. Parents of every political stripe complain that their children are not getting the preparation they need to succeed, and most agree that there is precious little understanding of our Constitution and our system of government to enable them to become good citizens.

The reality is that there is a deficit of any real knowledge about history and our democratic norms that spreads far beyond the classroom. Politicians and the people they represent fall well short of what should be considered a minimum level of civic knowledge in political campaigns, in the halls of Congress, and at neighborhood gatherings. In a country that depends on the informed consent of the governed, Americans show an appalling lack of understanding of our experiment in representative democracy.

For example, voters should be aware of certain constitutional restrictions on candidates seeking office or reelection. On June 13, 1866, Congress passed the 14th Amendment to the Constitution. The states ratified it on July 9, 1868, and it has proven to be one of the most consequential pillars of our governmental structure since that time. Known primarily as the amendment that granted citizenship to recently freed slaves, it also enshrined the notions of due process and equal protection for every citizen. It has been the touchstone for Supreme Court decisions and subsequent legislation affecting a wide range of rights for all citizens.

It is less known that the amendment also clarifies that certain candidates who defy their own country and its laws should be disqualified from seeking office. Section three of the 14th Amendment reads: "No person shall be a Senator or Representative in Congress, or elector of President and Vice-President, or hold any office, civil or military, under the United States, or under any State, who, having previously taken an oath, as a member of Congress, or as an officer of the United States, or as a member of any State legislature, or as an executive or judicial officer of any State, to support the Constitution of the United States, shall have engaged in insurrection or rebellion against the same, or given aid or comfort to the enemies thereof. But Congress may, by a vote of two-thirds of each House, remove such disability." With the ongoing investigation of the January 6 riot, we now know that many members of Congress may have engaged in the very insurrection or rebellion that the 14th Amendment describes.

The truth is that the original amendment was passed during a time when the country was licking its wounds from the Civil War. The dominant factions in the Congress wanted to ensure that Southern Congress members who had taken arms against the Union or who had participated in the insurrection of any kind could not return to their old seats—or any seats at the federal or state levels. Today, there are active lawsuits filed against elected officials who may have broken their oaths of office in the events surrounding the January 6 uprising.

Even after a violent mob ransacked the Capitol and stormed its halls with chants to "Hang Mike Pence!" Even after it was made clear that the intention was to overturn a presidential election, even after five people died in the mayhem. One hundred and forty-seven members of Congress voted with the rioters to delay or disrupt the certification of electoral votes for the president-elect. Following that low moment in history, more than 125 House Republicans signed an amicus brief backing a lawsuit brought before the Supreme Court that sought to overturn election results in four states—including Pennsylvania.

The latest outrage relates to an attempt to send counterfeit electors to the Electoral Colleges in seven states. The Justice Department has begun investigating this scheme to subvert the election, and the Congressional Select Committee has subpoenaed some fake electors. They want to know how the fake electors were recruited and who orchestrated the scheme. State attorneys general are considering charging them with election fraud.

In Pennsylvania, the list of participants in this scheme reads like a who's who of Republican politicians. Two of them are candidates for governor. Another candidate attended the rally on January 6 and now touts his actions as some twisted form of patriotism. One can make the case that these candidates are ineligible to hold future office according to the 14th Amendment. Is it likely that political candidates will be thrown off the ballot for their anti-government behavior? Probably not.

But it is essential that citizens factor in their bad behaviors when they go to vote. As citizens, we are entitled to know that our leaders are aware of the language of the Constitution. We are entitled to leaders who respect our country and its laws.

WE ARE UKRAINIANS

FEBRUARY 25, 2022

Malcov is a village in the Presov region of northeast Slovakia. It borders Poland and Ukraine and is the ancestral home of Byzantine Catholics and Russian Orthodox Americans who emigrated to the United States in the early 1900s. Many of the founders of Malcov were Russians who sought religious freedom from the *czar* and crossed through Ukraine to practice their faith free of the control of the state. The next step for the following generation was to seek an even better life in America.

The Pennsylvanians who arrived from Malcov—like my grandfather—worked in Pennsylvania coal mines and steel mills and spent their lifetimes providing for their families and holding on to the richness of their Eastern European traditions. St. Mary's Byzantine Catholic Church and Christ the Savior Greek Orthodox Church in Johnstown, Pennsylvania, are filled with people who know their roots. Theirs is a history intertwined with Carpatho-Russians from Slovakia, Hungary, the Czech Republic, and yes, Ukraine.

My own lineage includes a grandfather whose surname was changed at Ellis Island from "Czingel" to "Singel." He took the train until his money ran out and started his new life in Johnstown, Pennsylvania. He married a young woman named Keblish, who was also born on the Ukraine border, and together, they would raise nine children who taught their children about the ways of their old country.

My first memories of music, art, faith, and family came from church. *"Vosklinite Hospodevi vsja zeml'a"* or "Shout joyfully to the Lord all the earth" was the first musical phrase I ever heard—sung by sopranos who sounded like angels to me. The basses and tenors followed with booming voices that filled the hearts and minds of everyone in the pews, all under the watchful eyes of the saints on icons throughout the church. By the time we reached elementary school, my brothers and sisters could all sing the Divine Liturgy in Old Slavonic—a version of Russian—in four-part harmony. My grandfather insisted on hearing the prayers in Old Slavonic: "God doesn't listen to English," he said.

When I look at the news reports and the faces of Ukrainians under siege, I see my extended family. Our traditions are their traditions. We prefer halupkis and perogies at St. Mary's to any fancy steak dinner. Beer and homemade wines flow freely at Easter and Christmas when folk songs and polkas fill the air. When sworn in as lieutenant governor, I posed for pictures with two leading Byzantine Catholic prelates in my Harrisburg office. We were holding up the inaugural ceremonies for Governor Casey a bit, but he understood the magic of the moment.

Bob Casey was very fond of our respective immigrant cultures, and we talked

about our heritage often. Years later, as lieutenant governor, I recited the "Our Father" in Old Slavonic to a group of visiting Russian businessmen who had just shaken off Communist control. They told me how they just recently felt comfortable saying *"Otce Nas"* in public. Several of them wept. My family also wept openly when we said goodbye to our father with one last acapella, *"Bohorodice Divo,"* the Hail Mary, his favorite hymn.

The entire Carpatho-Russian culture—including Ukrainians—allows itself the presumption of proximity to God. *"S'Nami Boh"* (God is With Us) is the chant that still rings from choir lofts during holidays. It is also a bit of a password with my family that has gotten us through difficult times. This closeness to God also engenders great humility.

The phrase *"Hospodi pomiluj"* (Lord, have mercy) is uttered over a hundred times during Sunday liturgies. It was also the catchphrase that our grandmother used to express occasional exasperation.

Perhaps the most meaningful chant of all the Byzantine and Orthodox rituals comes when the priest lifts the chalice with the body and blood of the Savior close to heaven and pleads: *"Spasi l'udi tvoja Hospodi, i blahoslovi dostojanije tvoje"* "Save your people, O Lord, and bless your inheritance." All members of the Carpatho-Russian family reply with firm and faithful voices, *"Amin."*

Vladimir Putin betrays his own culture by murdering innocent people. But the atrocities of Putin in no way reflect the character of the Russian people. I know that our forbearers and distant families in Ukraine and Russia today are as heartbroken as we are with his current madness. In Dostoyevsky's *Crime and*

Punishment, the author provides hope under the direst of circumstances. *"Chem temneye noch', tem yarche zyezdy. Chem glubzhe gore, tem blizhe Bog."* "The darker the night, the brighter the stars. The deeper the grief, the closer is God."

God bless you, my Ukrainian brothers, and bless your inheritance.

REALITY CHECK

MARCH 18, 2022

One candidate for governor looks earnestly into the camera and tells us that he would do the opposite of everything that Wolf does. Immediately after that, the news reports that Pennsylvania's unemployment rate has fallen to its lowest rate in years and that the state has bounced back and gained back virtually all the jobs lost during the pandemic. We also learned that Governor Wolf is actively dispersing infrastructure and education funding to assure that job growth continues. I guess the opposite of that approach is to squelch job growth and stop the infrastructure program.

Another candidate bemoans inflation and gas prices and says that "Biden and Wolf caused this mess." Really? Or could it be that the economic upheaval and choking off Russian oil are the direct results of actions made by a murderous thug named Vladimir Putin?

Yet another candidate—this one an aspirant to the United States Senate—embraces the cult of the former president. When he says he is with Trump, I guess that means he has no problem with an egomaniac who trampled all over the Constitution trying to hold on to power. Worse, it validates the continued deception of the former guy and, by association, trivializes the insurrection at the U.S. Capitol that his role model instigated. Can we also assume that he agrees with Trump's assessment of Vladimir Putin? Does Dr. Oz think that Putin—who is murdering hundreds of Ukrainian citizens every day—is a genius?

As the campaigns ramp up, the airwaves are sure to be full of cheap shots and pandering to voters that are just plain dumb. Much of it is also just untrue. I was on a dais with a Republican strategist recently who shared with me his secret for campaign success. "The guy who wins is the one who tells the best story," he said. Not, "I'm supporting the best person for the job," or "My guy believes in working with everybody to get things done."

No. Usually, the best story means touting a person's biography in a way that seems to place him on the verge of sainthood. Next is engaging focus groups to ferret out what is bothering voters. This is followed by a candidate recording slick commercials where they profess to understand those concerns and, by God, they are going to fix them.

Finally, add in a cringe-worthy helping of negative attacks on whomever the opponent happens to be at the moment, and you have your best story that you can splash on the brows of the electorate relentlessly. When it comes right down to it, very little truth emerges from this exercise.

Such banality plays out in the national media as well. Tucker Carlson twists himself into an incomprehensible pretzel when he criticizes NATO and the U.S. response to the Russian invasion of Ukraine. Even as the bodies pile up, he is incapable of summoning up support for those who are in this existential battle against authoritarianism. Carlson's Fox News colleague Jesse Watters would be equally disturbing if he weren't so ridiculous. On a recent broadcast, Watters implied that Joe Biden—not Vladimir Putin—was responsible for the attack on Ukraine. Who was his source? A computer repair shop owner claims that, somehow, Hunter Biden's laptop is at the core of all evil. Let's get real; we are at war.

Someone who understands this is NATO Secretary General Jens Stoltenberg. He called out Russia and announced that the thirty-country organization was doubling down on its support for Ukraine. NATO is expanding its defenses and sending a clear signal that Russia's efforts to destabilize Western Europe have already failed.

Today's real hero, Volodymyr Zelenskyy, also faces the realities of war and death daily. He has precious little time for political posturing as hospitals and children's shelters are being bombed. Zelenskyy faces grim facts in the body counts that add up every day. His crushing reality makes our current state and federal political campaigns look like a game of Trivial Pursuits.

The realities that Zelenskyy, Biden, and NATO face every day make the sloganeering of political wannabes seem insignificant. Voters deserve more from people interviewing for real jobs with real consequences. Candidates are the people who may find themselves at the helm when the ship of state gets into choppy waters. Show us that you are more than just a caricature or a good story. Show us that you can lead.

ENEMIES: FOREIGN AND DOMESTIC

APRIL 15, 2022

Vladimir Putin is a murderer. The bodies of innocent men, women, and children pile up in mass graves as he and his troops slam their missiles into Ukraine. This is wanton destruction in a sovereign nation that is as immoral and repugnant as any invasion in recent history.

America's response has been clear and strong. As the world's leader, we cannot abide this assault on a key ally and a thriving democracy. In fact, our Constitution requires that we defend ourselves against all enemies—foreign and domestic. Failing the Ukrainian people would invite further erosion of Democratic states and of the American experiment in self-governance that has been the beacon for the world for 250 years.

Why, then, are Pennsylvania politicians retreating to their corners and clucking about mere distractions when they should be giving full-throated support to the Commander in Chief and the war effort? Why is the cost of gasoline and inflation the thrust of their television ads? Of course, we all feel the sting when costs go up. But these are short-term prices to pay to move beyond Russian oil and to adjust to supply chain disruptions caused by disease and war.

Experts point to several factors that have caused our current levels of inflation. Ports have been clogged, trucks are in short supply, Russian oil supplies have dried up, and formerly pent-up demand is now outstripping supplies of all goods and services. Still, economists like Emily Stewart are hopeful. "Production capacity will get moving again. Demand will cool off, adjustments will be made. It would be nice if there were one neat trick to solve inflation. There is not. The good news is things will improve."

The reality is that bread may cost another thirty cents a loaf for a while, but mothers in Ukraine have nothing at all to feed their children.

In this context, the current political season has become absurd. Candidates toss grenades at each other and would have you believe they alone can fix it, whether that refers to inflation, healthcare, or keeping critical thinking out of our classrooms. This was the brash claim of the former president, who now imposes his will on weak-kneed candidates. Like the Putin threat to democracy, Trump is the domestic threat the Constitution warned us about.

One by one, the candidates trek to Mar-a-Lago to grovel at the feet of the provocateur-in-chief. This is despite it becoming more apparent that Trump and his henchmen planned, funded, and incited a riot designed to disrupt his government.

A federal judge has concluded that "it is more likely than not that Trump engaged in criminal activity." The January 6th Committee has now seen thousands of documents, including tweets from Trump with the message "Be there. Be wild." This launched the effort to disrupt power transfer, even with violence. It is the definition of an insurrection. You would think that candidates would distance themselves from that behavior, not embrace it. But embrace it they do. Bill McSwain was singled out for some harsh words by the former guy. It seems that McSwain refused to violate the Constitution and steal the election for Trump in Pennsylvania. That earned him the steamroller treatment from Mar-a-Lago.

It also impacted another candidate. Jake Corman was reportedly getting little traction in his campaign and was planning to withdraw. Instead, he trotted out his credentials as a proponent for "election reform" in Pennsylvania and got on the phone with Trump. It looks like he received enough of a seal of approval to restart his campaign engine, much to the dismay of other candidates like Lou Barletta and Doug Mastriano, who were counting on a MAGA boost.

One bright spot in the primary season came when Jeff Bartos, a Republican candidate for U.S. Senate, finally broke through the fog of the Big Lie and told the truth. On a Sunday morning talk show, he was asked if Joe Biden was the duly-elected president of the United States. "Yes," he said, "it's time to move on."

Thanks for making sense, Jeff, and for showing your colleagues how to answer an easy question directly. Voters are tired of hearing baseless claims about fraud. They are smart enough to know that the rantings of a sore loser have infected our political anatomy. Yes, it is time to move on, and it is also time to gird ourselves against foreign and domestic threats. Voters should be careful to support those candidates who understand the need to support the Constitution. They should strongly oppose those who are too timid to do so.

CODE RED

APRIL 15, 2022

In the military courtroom drama *A Few Good Men,* Lieutenant Daniel Kaffee, a navy lawyer, tries to ferret out the truth from a crusty Marine colonel about the suspicious death of a young Marine under his command. The climactic scene occurs when Kaffee grills Colonel Jessup demanding the truth. After some suspense, Jessup spits his disdain for the young lawyer by sneering, "You can't handle the truth." Then, in a flourish of hubris, he incriminates himself by acknowledging that he ordered the Code Red that killed what he considered an "inadequate Marine."

More than a year after the Capitol riots, the January 6th Committee continues asking: "Who sparked the insurrection?" In other words, who ordered the Code Red? Like Nathan Jessup, the former president is dug into his position that there was no crime committed at all. In fact, he continues to promote the delusion that he is the rightful president. What's appalling is that the rank and file who have fallen in behind him continue to wallow in that delusion.

The Marine Corps in *A Few Good Men* comes to the ethical conclusion that there are boundaries in the chain of command. The military tribunal correctly punishes Colonel Jessup for murder. In today's political climate, there are few candidates strong enough to defy the hold that the former guy exerts as he promotes his fantasy.

I mentioned in a recent column that a noteworthy exception to that groveling came from Jeff Bartos, a Republican candidate for U.S. Senate. The question was whether or not Joe Biden is the duly-elected president of the United States, to which the candidate answered directly, "Yes, let's move on." Trying to find other good men or women in the Republican ranks who are ready to separate from MAGA egomania has been difficult.

The Greek philosopher Diogenes is known for holding a lantern up to the faces of the people of Athens in search of an honest man. He was cynical enough to believe that citizens were incapable of truthfulness. Instead, they followed the faction's whims that controlled the day's politics. In the birthplace of democracy, the ancient Greeks sowed the seeds of their demise by failing to live up to the requirement of truth—in their politics and daily lives.

Of course, there are nuances to the truth that are necessary for human interactions. We hold back our opinions of a person's appearance if we know it will offend them. We do not react to friends' comments if we know it will prolong an argument. It was Emily Dickinson who wrote: "Tell all the truth but tell it slant [. . .]. The Truth must dazzle gradually. Or every man be blind."

But the observation does not mean we should embrace any fabrication just because it is presented as truth. It is essential to call out lies to ensure they do not take on the veneer of truth.

The current political season in Pennsylvania and throughout the country is an appalling display of fiction over facts. We are in trouble when candidates cannot accept that a peaceful transition of power has occurred and that rational partisan discussion can ensue outside of the Big Lie. When that happens, it is impossible for any government or social institution to thrive. There is no current fact base on which we can even begin rational discussions about policy.

The situation is exacerbated when America is trying to rally the world to stave off the murderous adventurism of authoritarianism. At the very least, can we put our hyper-partisanship aside until we rid Ukraine of the menace that Putin represents? Can we agree that problems like inflation and energy production are issues that deserve bipartisan attention—not irrational extremism? Can we agree that those who spout deliberate lies should be called out?

Most Democrats know that their Republican neighbors are not fascists. Most Republicans know that their Democrat neighbors are not Communists. We need to meander back to the middle, where the power of a fair-minded America resides. Assuming we can handle the truth, it is not too late to avoid the Code Red that threatens our representative democracy.

BOOK BURNINGS AND OTHER OUTRAGES

APRIL 29, 2022

The Republican-led Tennessee state house passed a bill just this week that would require public school librarians to submit to the state a list of book titles for approval. When asked what he would do with the banned books, the Republican sponsor of the bill said, "I would burn them."

There are no words to adequately describe the stupidity of this exchange. But there is history. On May 10, 1933, forty thousand people attended a rally sponsored by Joseph Goebbels and the Nazis and burned a mountain of books deemed un-German. It was a shocking display of authoritarian arrogance that showed the world how depraved the Nazis had become. Where is the outrage in Tennessee today? What has happened to the Republican Party? Is no one in that state or Pennsylvania who will stand for freedom of speech and the U.S. Constitution?

It gets worse. One of the leading candidates for the GOP nomination of Pennsylvania governor has aligned himself with QAnon. Recall that this group provided much of the hysteria for the January 6 riots. Among other things, QAnon claims that Democratic "elites" are engaged in sex trafficking and demon worship. They question the Kennedy assassination, and the Twin Towers' collapse on 9/11. That didn't stop PA Senator Doug Mastriano from attending a Far Right conference in Gettysburg that featured QAnon activists and presentations. In fact, he accepted financial support from the event organizers.

And what about that field of Republican candidates for the U.S. Senate? A fundamental requirement for holding office is to respect and uphold the U.S. Constitution. This includes accepting wins and losses in elections and acknowledging the critical importance of the peaceful transition of power. But, of the seven candidates running for Senate, only two have said they would have voted to certify the 2016 presidential election. All the others are shamelessly exploiting the lie that there was widespread fraud in the election—enough for them to admit that they would have tossed out the votes of 150 million Americans to suit their political agenda. Candidates who cannot uphold their constitutional duty should be disqualified from running for office. Period.

On the gubernatorial front, the most recent debate featured the candidates competing for the attention of Donald Trump. They were grown men chirping like needy birds for whatever worms they could get. WHYY reported that they were all "battling to prove who can be most conservative and, perhaps more importantly, most like former President Donald Trump." Even Bill McSwain, the former U.S. prosecutor Trump dissed for not joining the conspiracy to overturn the election, tried to burnish his credentials with the MAGA crowd. He pointed to the fact that he was the only candidate who served in the Trump administration.

This level of groveling by these Republican candidates is more than disturbing. It raises the question of how they could possibly govern if elected. Would their loyalties lie with the myriad of responsibilities they would face on behalf of all Pennsylvanians, or would they be locked into the permanent puppet hood of Trumpism?

Here's one clear signal that things do not look good. Every single GOP candidate has called for reform or elimination of mail-in ballots. Some have called for draconian measures to suppress voting or to reject voting results through handpicked partisan officials. This even though Pennsylvania has been handling absentee ballots for fifty years. This even though the convenience of mail-in voting has dramatically increased citizen participation for both parties.

It turns out that all the candidates are hiding behind rhetoric about fair elections. Not one of them is willing to admit that they are really buying into the national Trump voter suppression campaign. GOP candidates are not standing for full and fair elections. They are using the issue to send more love notes to Mar-a-Lago.

From the outrage of book burnings to the craven sycophancy of candidates who dare not step out of line, we should be alert and angry as citizens. One can only hope that the general election brings a more balanced presentation from the emerging candidates. The hope is that even those making outrageous claims today will understand the fundamental nature of Pennsylvania's voters by November. We care about the truth. We care about leaders who care about us. We are inclined to support pragmatic leaders who can stand on their own principles and not whip up passions by embracing extremism.

THE ATTACK ON WOMEN AND DEMOCRACY

APRIL 29, 2022

There is no way to sugarcoat it. The recently leaked Supreme Court draft decision is an affront and an all-out attack on women. The Court quickly pointed out it was only a draft and that the official decision would not be rendered for months. Still, the author, Justice Sam Alito, made it clear what the majority's intentions were that *Roe v. Wade* was, in his opinion, "egregiously wrong from the start and must be overruled."

For the record, *Roe v. Wade*, combined with the subsequent *Planned Parenthood v. Casey* decision, enshrined the right to privacy for women under the 9th and 14th Amendments to the Constitution. Together, these rulings protected the right to choose while allowing states to impose reasonable restrictions on abortions. This accommodation to one of the most difficult and politically explosive issues of the modern era has stood the test of time. It has been considered a settled precedent for fifty years.

That is until the current Supreme Court justices—including three handpicked by the Far Right Federalist Society—got their hands on the issue. It should be noted that at least two of those justices took a completely different tone when they met privately and publicly with senators during their confirmation process. Senator Susan Collins says she is deeply disappointed in Brett Kavanaugh and Neil Gorsuch since they told her they accepted *Roe v. Wade* as settled law. That meant to her that they would take a hands-off approach to the issue. I don't know which is worse: Kavanaugh's and Gorsuch's deception, which borders on perjury, or Collins's naivete, which borders on stupidity.

So here we are with a Supreme Court about to allow the imposition of government mandates rather than trust women to make decisions about their own lives. Democratic leaders, from President Biden to Governors and candidates across the country, are sounding the alarm that it will not likely stop there. What is to prevent a radically conservative court from chipping away at other freedoms? Contraceptives? Gay rights? Civil rights? Voting rights?

Ironically, the party that objected to putting a piece of cloth over their mouths during a pandemic because it was an assault on their freedom now says that it is acceptable to tell 150 million women that the government will now control their bodies. At a time when we are in an existential battle with authoritarianism halfway around the world, it is stunning that the United States of America is about to roll back the rights of its citizens.

To those who wear the mantle of being pro-life, let's call it like it is. Republicans have had the opportunity to support prenatal care, family leave, comprehensive health care, and family tax credits, and, in most cases, they have walked in GOP lockstep opposition to this help for working families. Yet, it defends life from conception to birth. Today's Republican Party is not pro-life; it is pro-birth. After that, families are on their own.

And don't think for a minute that this is just about shifting responsibilities to the state governments. One leader of the anti-choice movement has already stated that the next step is to push for completely abolishing abortion as a matter of federal law. To their credit, one group has stepped up to call out the hypocrisy and cruelty of moral judgments replacing individual rights. Catholics for Choice says, "We're fighting a religious movement. We have religious ideology being codified into law, and we have to have people of faith rising up and saying, 'Not in our name.'"

Democrats across the country are sounding another alarm. "Wake up, America. Make sure you take into account where politicians stand on the fundamental question of denying women's rights when you vote." Most American voters do not want to abandon *Roe v. Wade*. A Public Religion Research Institute poll last week found that 61 percent oppose overturning Roe, and 36 percent support overturning it. When asked the more generic question, "Should abortion be permitted in some circumstances," 81 percent of Americans said "yes." Only 19 percent of the population said "no."

This will be a political issue in the critical midterm elections and for years to come. Clive Crook, a conservative writer for *Bloomberg News*, put it this way: "Better to limit the damage already done to American politics than to push the country toward something even worse." There is nothing ambiguous about this moment.

Democracy cannot be strong if the rights of women are under attack.

LEADERS NEED TO SERVE

MAY 13, 2022

I was asked recently to reflect on the life and times of Robert P. Casey, the former Governor of Pennsylvania. Since I had served with him as lieutenant governor from 1987 through 1995, I had a front-row seat on the character and the vision of this truly decent public servant.

We had a strong, productive relationship that resulted in a number of policy innovations for Pennsylvania. These included groundbreaking programs to stimulate economic development, a national model for recycling and environmental protections, education reforms, and a robust effort to extend health care to all—especially children. The record will show that we agreed on most of the day's critical issues and worked tirelessly for the people of the Commonwealth.

Truth be told, we disagreed on one or two things—like my future. I like to tell people that we enjoyed a father-son relationship, and I just wanted to take the car for a spin once in a while! But the lessons learned from that period stay with me today. The recent interview included the question, "Why did Bob Casey run for office?" I know the answer because I had that exact conversation with him in 1986. He told me the story of encountering a homeless man on a steam grate in Philadelphia when he and two of his law partners were headed to lunch. "Here I was, successful and comfortable, heading to the Palm Restaurant," he said, "and this man hadn't eaten in two days. That's just not right." He decided to make his third run for governor right then and there. Years later, in a private conversation about responsibilities and our purpose on the planet, he said this to me, "Mark, I'm not sure about a lot of things, but I am dead certain that we are here to help each other."

The 2022 primary season is wrapping up in Pennsylvania with no such clarity. We have been bombarded by inane advertisements from candidates whose purpose is to demean others and insult our intelligence. Instead of presenting a plan to help each other through the serious business of life, candidates are busy scurrying like gerbils for their morsel of acceptance from a leader who can't seem to admit that his day has come and gone. We get bombarded by ads and social media attacking anyone who seems to be gaining momentum. Currently, Senator Doug Mastriano and Kathy Barnette are in the crosshairs.

Other ads are geared toward stoking fears of immigrant invasions, drug epidemics, and the content of books in our classrooms. Meanwhile, several of the candidates who have emerged as front-runners on the Republican side participated actively in the riots that occurred on January 6. At least one of them maintains connections with the conspiracy-addled group QAnon. One local Congress member faces a subpoena to explain his actions during the insurrection.

On the Republican side, the campaign has been a clown show. In the closing moments of the primary, the establishment seems to have figured out that those emerging from a multicandidate mud bath may win by as little as 19 or 20 percent of the primary vote. And, with all the candidates marching resolutely to the Far Right, it will be impossible to chart a moderate course for the general election, where most of the voters remain.

Some see these dark clouds forming. Jake Corman pulled out at the last minute to try to add his votes to a candidate who may be acceptable as a candidate for governor. But Majority Leader Kim Ward is pulling for another candidate, and there still is no consensus. The reality is that it is too little, too late. In the U.S. Senate and governor races, the Republican Party is about to nominate candidates that may have made themselves unelectable in the fall. Their wounds are self-inflicted.

While the Democrats have a competitive race for U.S. Senate, the candidates have been careful to toe a line close to our purple state's moderate leanings. And Josh Shapiro, who has the luxury of being unopposed, has already begun his general election campaign for governor on a positive note. An ad across the state introduces us to Josh, his family, and his record. It relays a clear ideal reminiscent of leaders who have given us a similar message in years past. "Help others and do the right thing." Voters should act accordingly.

DEMOCRATS FIND THEIR FOOTING

MAY 20, 2022

In an earlier column, I discussed something I call the "red sky phenomenon." It is very simple: if I say the sky is blue and you say the sky is red, that does not make it a fifty-fifty chance that the sky has suddenly changed colors. It just means that you are delusional.

In an unprecedented move, *The Philadelphia Inquirer* declined to endorse anyone in the recent Republican primary. Why? Because six of the seven candidates they interviewed clung to the delusion that the 2020 presidential election was invalid due to widespread fraud. Only one of the candidates could bring himself to affirm that Joe Biden was the duly-elected president of the United States. The others were too afraid to alienate an extreme base that had bought into the red sky delusion.

And it got much worse as primary election day neared. Candidates for governor and senator scampered to curry favor with an ex-president who is the ultimate purveyor of delusion. They spent more than $50 million proclaiming their allegiance to Trump, and they are now stuck wearing his label when they face a much more moderate electorate in the fall. As Jimmy Buffett says, this kind of tattoo is a "permanent reminder of a temporary feeling."

It did not need to be this way. After the January 6 riots, Republican leaders could have regrouped and returned to the civil discourse on which the country depends. Instead, they doubled and tripled down on allegiance to the Big Lie and hung independent thinkers and moderate voters out to dry.

In the Pennsylvania primary, Republicans nominated a candidate for governor who may be the most extreme candidate in the country. State Senator Doug Mastriano is unabashed about peddling false election theories. He participated in the January 6 uprising and presented his Trumpian credentials to anyone who would listen. The fact is that this kind of political toadyism is just what the base wanted to hear. The most extreme wing tends to be the loudest, and, in the case of Mastriano, they made sure that less dogmatic candidates were pushed off the stage.

Again, GOP leaders acquiesced. They should have learned from recent history that too many candidates in the field could result in someone eking out a win with his small but vocal minority. The establishment acted too late to coalesce around a less provocative standard bearer. The result is that they have nominated a candidate who may be unelectable in the fall.

While the race for the Republican nomination for U.S. Senate remains undecided, both David McCormick and Mehmet Oz have given the Democrats plenty of ammunition for the fall. Their advertising campaigns were less about introducing their credentials to Pennsylvania than about inflicting pain on each other. The overall theme was "Who was Trumpiest." They were not just content to feed the beast; they helped release it into the china shop of our democracy--regardless of the damage it has done and will continue to do. Whether McCormick or Oz emerges as the candidate, they will find their willingness to coddle the MAGA cult toxic in the fall.

As to the Democrats, Josh Shapiro had the unheard-of luxury of running without opposition. His ads were warm and fuzzy. They presented him as a family man with real accomplishments and the potential to lead with actual bipartisanship. He also spent some of his war chest painting Mastriano as an extremist, previewing what will come.

While John Fetterman faced some legitimate challengers in the Senate primary, he dominated his opponents. In fact, Fetterman won every single county in the state and racked up a lion's share win of 60 percent, while McCormick and Oz managed to get about a third of the Republican primary voters.

It appears that Democrats have found their footing in Pennsylvania. Republicans, on the other hand, must dig themselves out of the hole of extremism to return to the electable middle. Given the fracas of the primary season and the positions taken by the candidates, some Republican leaders are expressing doubts. At least one major money player told me they "will be focusing on the down ballot." Look for a shift in priorities among the insiders that pour money into U.S. Congressional races and the battle to control the PA General Assembly.

Maybe, just maybe, that portends a return to genuine discussions about state and local issues. The 2022 election cycle in Pennsylvania may help us move beyond hysterical red-sky posturing and back to governing.

ENOUGH

MAY 27, 2022

On the afternoon of the Uvalde, Texas shooting, U.S. Senator Chris Murphy (D-CT) took to the floor. He challenged every senator by asking what could be more important than the safety of our children. "Why are we here? If not, try to make sure that fewer schools and fewer communities go through what Sandy Hook has gone through. What Uvalde is going through. What are we doing? Why are we here?"

One commentator said that shootings happen so frequently that we can't even mourn the losses of one before the next one occurs. Movie theaters, churches, synagogues, concerts, nightclubs, grocery stores, and schools are no longer safe.

According to the FBI, 288 attacks on classrooms in the United States have occurred over the past thirty years. The second highest number of such incidents is in Mexico: eight. That's right. The U.S., more than any country in the world, has allowed gun violence to become a way of life. Here's one more chilling fact: guns kill more American children than any other cause, more than illnesses or accidents.

Before the first responders left the site at Uvalde, politicians rushed to the cameras to offer thoughts and prayers but not solutions. They once again trotted out the 2nd Amendment to argue that the shooter's rights outweighed the families' grief. Even more outrageous is that the NRA is conducting its annual conference just down the highway from the Uvalde massacre. Who are the speakers? Senator Ted Cruz and Texas Governor Greg Abbott will burnish their credentials with the gun manufacturers while their constituents bury their loved ones. It has been reported that conference attendees cannot bring their guns to the speeches. The NRA seems more willing to protect its politicians than our children.

So, what can be done?

Some are willing to take on the NRA and consider reasonable gun safety measures. Two background-check bills have passed the House and are sitting in the Senate right now. Senator Murphy and Senator John Cornyn (R-TX) came close to an agreement last year on a compromise that would stop sales of guns from unlicensed dealers. There is some support for laws that would allow family members or law enforcement to petition the courts to take away a person's guns if he presents an extreme risk to himself or others. And, if we can't ban them altogether, we should at least raise the age to purchase assault weapons from eighteen to twenty-one. But there is no sign that the NRA will release politicians from its stranglehold even for these common-sense restrictions.

Senator Pat Toomey (R-PA) and Senator Joe Manchin (D-WV) got themselves in hot water for suggesting even a modest expansion of background checks after Sandy Hook. It is not clear whether they will fight that fight again.

Other nations have tackled their gun problems head-on. In 1966 at an elementary school in Dunblane, Scotland, sixteen children and their teacher were killed by a gunman. Leaders in the United Kingdom put their political differences aside and passed gun registration laws and other restrictions, including a ban on assault weapons. There has not been a mass shooting at a school in the UK since.

One of the most poignant passages I read in the last few days was from a writer reporting on the scene: "In Uvalde in Texas, 19 elementary school kids crawled out of bed, ate their favorite breakfast cereal, bunny-looped their sneakers, packed their school backpacks, and headed off to school—excited to get through the final two days of class before summer vacation. They did not return home that day."

Enough is enough.

I am a citizen, and I vote. For this and every election to follow, I will ask every candidate one simple question: "Do you support reasonable gun safety laws?" If candidates— Democrats or Republicans—cannot vote to protect our children, I will not vote for them.

After children watch their friends suffer and die, they face a lifetime of trauma. Counselors are assigned to help them through the early stages of that grief. They assign a code word that any student can invoke at any time to get help. After Sandy Hook, that word was "monkey." Today, a new code word should ring out from all of us when politicians are too timid to act: courage.

Our children are dying at their desks at school. Our elected officials must have the courage to do something about that, or we should elect leaders who will.

RISE UP AGAINST EVIL

JUNE 10, 2022

Who will stand up for me against evildoers? Who will take his stand for me against those who do injustice?
—Psalm 94:16

The House Committee on the January 6 riots began its public hearings with new revelations about an extensive conspiracy to overturn a presidential election. We saw with our own eyes an insurrection that featured an armed mob intent on disrupting the government and threatening to lynch the vice president. We now know that elected officials at all levels directed and abetted the mob.

Chairman Bennie Thompson (D-MS) said it best. January 6 was a "sprawling, multi-step conspiracy" and the "culmination of an attempted coup." Numerous political actors appear complicit in the riots and a related scheme to steal the election with a phony slate of electors. Representative Scott Perry (R-PA) was singled out for his alleged role in meddling with the Department of Justice to tilt the election results in Trump's favor.

Republican leaders and the right wing media are turning a blind eye to what may be the most serious threat ever made to our democracy. They want you to believe that there is nothing to see here. The fact is that there was real evil at work, and America needs to confront it.

Liz Cheney (R-WY) did just that by warning her Republican colleagues that, "There will come a day when Donald Trump is gone, but your dishonor will remain."

Meanwhile, Congress wrestles with gun safety legislation in the wake of yet another unfathomable act of violence against children. Dr. Roy Guerrero is a pediatrician in Texas. He said this after the Uvalde school shooting "Keeping children safe from bacteria and brittle bones, I can do. But making sure our children are safe from guns, that's the job of our politicians and leaders."

The House of Representatives heard from an eleven-year-old who smeared blood over herself and played dead. Others testified that the bullets from AR-15 ripped through the faces and bodies of the children with such ferocity that they were unidentifiable. Some Congress members wept openly at the testimony. Others sat impassively and made it clear that their passion for guns was more important than the lives of children.

The House passed some aggressive gun restrictions, including banning high-capacity magazines for guns and increasing the age to purchase semiautomatic weapons to twenty-one (the Uvalde shooter bought his AR-15 the day he turned eighteen). The House package will likely be watered down by the Senate, where most Republican members remain unmoved by the blood that splatters the classroom walls of our nation.

And one more outrage this week came from a Far Left fringe maniac. Some lunatic armed himself and traveled across the country with the apparent intent of killing Supreme Court Justice Brett Kavanaugh. It doesn't matter what issue he was espousing. It doesn't matter that he may have viewed Justice Kavanaugh as an impediment to his cause. What matters is that the U.S. Supreme Court represents the epitome of our justice system. To threaten one of its members is to threaten our entire nation of laws and our very structure of government.

These are three clear examples that cry out for political leadership. Whether we are ferreting out the facts of an attack on the peaceful transfer of power, preventing the carnage caused by beasts with access to guns, or protecting the institutions of government that make us unique, the time has come for elected officials to strip off the labels and act as compassionate Americans.

Real Christians know that the entire New Testament can be summed up in this command: love one another. It may be that we are too cynical and too selfish to achieve real love for anything but our own biases. It may be that we are entrenched in political camps that make it impossible to see real evil and do something about it.

If we are incapable of love, I'll settle for outrage.

It is time to rise up against evildoers. If leaders will not lead, it is time for citizens of this great country to take on the task themselves and replace them.

MIKE PENCE: AMERICAN HERO

JUNE 17, 2022

On May 22, 1856, Representative Preston Brooks of South Carolina walked onto the floor of the U.S. Senate and beat Senator Charles Sumner of Massachusetts with a brass-topped cane into unconsciousness. Trapped at his desk, Sumner took thirty blows to the face and head until, in the words of Brooks, Sumner "bellowed like a calf" and collapsed in a pool of his blood.

The attack was provoked by a speech given by Sumner on whether Kansas should be admitted to the Union as a free or slave state. Sumner did not hold back as he attacked pro-slavery senators. He called Stephen Douglas a "noisesome squat and nameless animal" and cast similar aspersions about Andrew Butler, the junior senator from South Carolina. When Preston Brooks charged onto the Senate floor, he avenged the slander of his kinsman, Andrew Butler. When Sumner was carried away, Brooks walked calmly off the floor. In fact, he became a hero in his southern state, where he was reelected to his House seat. Constituents sent canes and walking sticks as replacement weapons. The U.S. Senate's official history records, "The nation, suffering from the breakdown of reasoned discourse that this event symbolized, tumbled onward toward the catastrophe of civil war."

The violence and magnitude of the Brooks/Sumner incident were unmatched in American history until January 6, 2021. The current congressional hearings on the riots have now demonstrated that the insurrection was based on a sitting president's refusal to accept the will of the voters in a free and fair election. Witness after witness has testified that Trump knew that his plan to simply ignore electoral votes from key states was illegal, unconstitutional, and ludicrous. Still, he lit the fuse of the mayhem by targeting his vice president for violence or worse.

The mob dutifully stormed the Capitol chanting, "Hang Mike Pence!" They also had marching orders to "drag Nancy Pelosi out by the hair!" And they searched the halls for AOC and other targets that Trump and his zealots put in the crosshairs.

Before the congressional hearings, Judge David O. Carter found that "it is more likely than not that President Trump corruptly attempted to obstruct the Joint Session of Congress on January 6, 2021." Saying efforts to overturn the 2020 presidential election was "a coup in search of a legal theory," the judge ruled that if Trump lawyer John Eastman and President Trump's plan had worked, it would have "permanently ended the peaceful transition of power, undermining American democracy and the Constitution."

At the end of the rioting, five Capitol policemen were dead. Hundreds were injured, and like in 1856, the nation was pushed into bitter divisions caused by one man's shocking irresponsibility and dereliction of duty.

On the third day of the January 6 hearings, Chairman Bennie Thompson pointed to one man who stood up to the pressure of a delusional president. He said, "We are fortunate for Mr. Pence's courage on January 6. Our democracy came dangerously close to catastrophe."

Trump ran an unrelenting pressure campaign on his vice president before, during, and after the attack. The president made personal phone calls to urge Pence to proclaim Trump the winner simply. In typical coarse language, Trump called his vice president a "wimp" and a "p—y." When he heard that his rabid supporters were intent on hanging the vice president, he remarked that "they might have the right idea."

Meanwhile, the vice president was on the phone with legislative leaders, ensuring they were safe. Pence—not the president—called Homeland Security and the Defense Department to bring in reinforcements. Above all, Mike Pence stayed at his post and made sure that the certification of the electoral votes would continue. At great risk to himself, Mike Pence assured that willfully blind followers of an unhinged president would not subvert 230 years of American commitment to the rule of law.

Judge J. Michael Luttig (a conservative Republican appointee) said, "America's democracy was almost stolen from us on January 6. Had the vice president of the United States obeyed the president of the United States, America would immediately have been plunged into what would have been tantamount to a revolution within a paralyzing constitutional crisis." Luttig also warned that Trump's collaborators who are emerging as candidates for office at all levels of government represent a "clear and present danger to American democracy."

Look for the January 6th Committee to focus next on the labyrinth of lies that permeated state Capitols in the days leading up to the insurrection. Some of Pennsylvania's politicians have explaining to do.

In the meantime, let us hold on to at least one shining light of courage and patriotism. Mike Pence is an American hero.

HUBRIS AND THE DOWNFALL OF DONALD J. TRUMP

JULY 1, 2022

No leader in the history of our country comes close to the arrogance of Donald J. Trump. His emergence as a presidential candidate was complete with the brag that, on the healthcare system, "only I can fix it."

He didn't fix it. Trump made constant references to his genius and disrupted relations with allies as he elbowed his way onto the world stage. His performance as president earned two impeachment proceedings and awakened the American electorate in time to deny him a second term.

Shakespeare's *Macbeth* put himself above all others and touted his destiny to rule. He committed murder to become king, but, in the end, his pride and inflated ego left him defeated and alone. After the latest hearing of the Congressional Committee to Investigate the January 6 riots, it should be clear to every American that Donald J. Trump deserves that same fate.

According to *The New York Times*, "The fundamental story of Jan. 6 is clear: A United States president who lost reelection was aware of—and encouraged—a violent attack on the Capitol intended to prevent the transfer of power to his opponent."

But, for those who question the objectivity of *The New York Times*, consider another source. The *Washington Examiner* has been a brash source of right wing opinion before and throughout the Trump administration. It highlighted the ravings of Rand Paul over the science of Dr. Fauci. It has placed the loudest Trumpists like Ted Cruz and Ron Johnson on its editorial pedestal. The newspaper produces an unending flood of criticism of Joe Biden and anything with Democratic credentials. It is the go-to source of information for many conservative pundits. Here is what the *Washington Examiner* had to say about the testimony of Cassidy Hutchison and what it means for Trump and his followers:

> Former White House aide Cassidy Hutchinson's Tuesday testimony ought to ring the death knell for former President Donald Trump's political career. Trump is unfit to be anywhere near power ever again [. . .]. She gave believable accounts of White House awareness that the planned January 6 rally could turn violent. She repeated testimony that Trump not only knew that then-Vice President Mike Pence's life had been credibly threatened that day but also that he was somewhere between uncaring and approving of Pence's danger [. . .]. Trump is a disgrace. Republicans have far better options to lead the party in 2024. No one should think otherwise, much less support him, ever again.

Representative Liz Cheney (R-WY) was even more direct. "You can support the Constitution, or you can support Donald Trump. You can't do both."

The fact is that Trump knew the January 6 mob was armed. He knew they could harm someone, but he didn't care—if he wasn't their target. He lit the fuse to attack the Capitol and our Constitution and did nothing to stop the riot for hours.

The Atlantic had this to say about Trump's behavior and the Republican Party's subservience to his cult: "If, after the latest January 6 hearing, House Republicans persist in their policy of pro-Trump cover-up, American democracy is in dire peril. House Republican leader Kevin McCarthy is on record condemning Trump's coup at the time that it happened. Since then, he has shriveled into the enabling role he has played over the past [eighteen] months [. . .]. Is there any flicker of decency and independence alive in the Republican who may soon lead the House majority?"

The other disturbing revelations about Trump's behavior should give us all pause. Most of us would not allow our six-year-olds to throw food in a temper tantrum. Most of us know enough about the Constitution to consider the transfer of power sacred and would not take extreme measures to stay in office. Most of us would not turn our backs on colleagues and incite physical harm to them.

I pose this question to my Republican friends: when is enough enough? With hundreds of Trump conspirators finding their way onto the ballot for positions ranging from U.S. Senate and governor to Bureau of Elections officials, the danger has not yet passed.

Surely, as the *Washington Examiner* has suggested, the Grand Old Party can sever ties with an arrogant, delusional loser and find its way back to the legitimate policy discussions that have enriched our political discourse over the years. It is time to move past the Trump era and the vile taste he has left in the mouth of our republic.

As we celebrate our pride in America and its Constitution this Independence Day, let us hope that conservatives and liberals, Republicans and Democrats, can move beyond the embarrassment.

HUMAN SUFFERING

JULY 8, 2022

About suffering they were never wrong,
The old Masters: how well they understood
Its human position: how it takes place
While someone else is eating or opening a window or just
walking dully along.

—W.H. Auden, Musee des Beaux Arts

In today's world, newsworthy events occur constantly and are transmitted instantaneously through the media and social networks. It is exhausting for those of us who are simply observers. For those who are in the business of presenting breaking news in a truthful and coherent way, it can be overwhelming.

For the past several years, I have had the pleasure of watching broadcast professionals do their jobs with unflinching skills. The folks at CBS-21 were kind enough to let me add some commentary to political events, and I was happy to be a part of their *Face the State* show and some news broadcasts. It never failed to amaze me that a team of writers, producers, technicians, and reporters could react in a matter of seconds when the public needed to know how the tides of fate had shifted; what new monster had been let loose among us?

People like Robb Hanrahan and others like him were unflappable. I watched him scrap his notes and look beyond the teleprompter many times to deliver even the most jarring news when it intruded on our lives. There is no such thing as an easy broadcast. Remember that those faces you see at six and eleven o'clock are in just as much pain as when the images splatter on the screen.

HUMAN SUFFERING

When mass graves in Ukraine cry out for explanation; when classrooms and children are riddled with bullets; when disasters wipe out human lives by the thousands, the on-air messengers have no choice but to soldier on. Add to that the pressure of getting it right and getting it first, and you have the components of a job that would test the nerves of the strongest among us.

Here's what I liked best about Robb Hanrahan. He was not stoic; he cared. The daily dose of confusion that he confronted had an impact on him. He had strong opinions about the direction of our country. He questioned politicians—sometimes directly—when they went off the rails. He loved his young son so much that he had real trouble dealing with stories about child abuse or human trafficking.

He operated under some constraints that must have been excruciating. There was never enough time to explore critical issues. There was a show to put on. There was a format to follow to keep the banter flowing and the sponsors happy. Robb bit his tongue on numerous occasions and did his job, even if he felt like letting out a scream once in a while.

It seems clear that his first heart attack was the result of the pressures and demands of the profession that, for all its challenges, he loved. It made sense for him to seek less intensive pursuits as he recovered, and I am sure that he found a new level of happiness with his wife, Stacey, his son Van, and his daughter Hannah at the top of his priority list.

The inspiration for W.H. Auden's poem was the story of Icarus daring to fly toward the sun with his wings of feathers and wax. As the wax melted and Icarus plunged into the sea, merchants in ships and farmers in the fields took little notice of the extraordinary sight of a boy falling from the sky. They simply went on with their lives.

Robb Hanrahan and broadcast journalists cannot look away. They are the ones who tell us what new tragedies have befallen us. They are the ones who see the raw footage and present it to us through their tears. The next time someone sneers at the "lamestream" media or talks about "fake news," remember that these are the people who absorb the gut punches of reality when the rest of us are eating, opening a window, or just walking dully along.

Robb Hanrahan died too soon. But his legacy of hard work, fairness, and compassion will live on. For me, Robb changed my perspective on the news. He reminded me that we are all in this life together. Our stories intertwine. We are not allowed to just look away. If Robb had one last late-breaking admonition for us all, I'm sure it would be, "Be kind to each other."

VISION

JULY 15, 2022

"Alexa, play soft rock."

Two or three songs in, I am treated to the old Paul Simon classic "So Long, Frank Lloyd Wright."

Considered by the American Institute of Architects as the "greatest American architect of all time," Wright said that "the mission of an architect is to help people understand how to make life more beautiful, the world a better one for living in, and to give reason, rhyme, and meaning to life." From Fallingwater in Pennsylvania to Taliesin West in Arizona, he changed how we live.

This past week, NASA released extraordinary photos that may also change our lives. We have been given a glimpse of what the universe looked like billions of years ago. Our whole perspective on time and space has been altered because of the deployment and successful operation of the James Webb Telescope. One article described the spectacle as "young stars tugging at one another." Some stars were forming, and others were "dying, swirling out gas and dust in a final dance."

It takes a full eight minutes for light to travel the ninety-three million miles from the sun to the Earth. The light that we see in the Webb photos is billions of lightyears away. What look like specks to us are entire galaxies that began to send their light to us just after the universe was born.

With these new images, puny citizens of this speck that we call Earth can get at least some sense of the vastness of creation. They can help us make discoveries and even search for signs of life in the cosmos. One writer from *The New York Times* said, "These stunning images are a major achievement for us Earthlings. And given everything absurd we've witnessed on Earth of late, they are more than that. If nothing else, the humongousness of the universe ought to put our problems into perspective. A little insignificance isn't such a bad thing."

The creativity of Frank Lloyd Wright and the immenseness of the universe starkly contrast with the pettiness of our current politics. It seems contradictory that we can harness great art and stunning science while we don't even try to calm the choppy waters of self-governance.

If we can look to architecture and the stars, why can't we do better in our political discourse? Why can't we, for example, agree on global warming and at least try to save our planet? If we can build telescopes and park them in orbit to reach back fourteen billion years, why can't we weave our human experiences together and achieve the consensus required of self-governance?

It may be that the brilliant truth that emanates from distant stars is too bright for us to bear. It is easier to bungle through daily life with limited interests and even less compassion for each other. While we are treated to stunning images from space, we are stuck in the mud of tribalism that allows terrible political actors to distract us from the better angels of our natures.

Oddly, Alexa plays another Paul Simon song. I recognize "El Condor Pasa," which laments man's limitations and the sadness of being earthbound.

I prefer to cling to hope. Just as art and science can inspire creativity and progress, as young scientists look to breakthroughs at the edges of the universe, we have a right to believe that our elected officials can spend less time bickering and more time governing. The Webb telescope shows that the American government can get it right once in a while. We should make that the norm rather than the exception.

POLITICAL TOURISM

JULY 22, 2022

The term "carpetbagger" found its way into our language during the Reconstruction Era. For the most part, it referred to people from northern states who went into the South to take advantage of political and economic opportunities. Some claimed they were lifting former slaves out of poverty by providing jobs and education, but many became wealthy landowners who simply substituted sharecropping for slavery on their plantations.

In 1875, Hiram Revels, the first African American U.S. senator, wrote to President Ulysses S. Grant, "Since reconstruction, the masses of my people have been, as it were, enslaved in mind by unprincipled adventurers, who, caring nothing for country, were willing to stoop to anything no matter how infamous, to secure power [. . .] in order that they may aggrandize themselves by office, and its emoluments." See James Wiilford Garner's *Reconstruction in Mississippi* for more of this history.

Over the years, carpetbagger has been adapted primarily to politics. It crops up in campaigns to identify political candidates who seek elections in areas without local ties. In a recent *City and State Magazine* article, Zach Williams points out several examples from New York. Rufus King moved from Massachusetts to New York City to become one of the state's first U.S. senators. Hillary Clinton moved to Chappaqua to make her own run in 2000. After serving as attorney general, Robert Kennedy also found a new home in New York. His famous name and powerful organization were enough to overcome the carpetbagger label.

Closer to home, Congress member John P. Murtha, the longest-serving member of the Pennsylvania delegation and the patron of Western Pennsylvania, was born and raised in West Virginia. He had solid credentials when he came to Pennsylvania, however. He ran for his first office as a highly decorated Marine and was the first veteran of the Vietnam War to get elected to Congress.

While numerous examples of political adventurism exist in the states, they can usually be expected to draw fire from opponents. In the race for U.S. Senate in Pennsylvania, the carpetbagger attack on Dr. Oz seems to be resonating much more than the "Socialist" attack on John Fetterman. In fact, the battle of labels fits right into Fetterman's campaign style. The Fetterman camp has had some fun with the issue of Oz's true residence and loyalties. They began by pointing out Oz's various mansions in several states and followed up with an airplane banner flown over the busy New Jersey shore that welcomed Oz to his "real" home at the beach. Even Snooki of the *Jersey Shore* television show got into the act to ensure voters knew Oz was a political tourist in the Keystone State.

As to the Socialist label that Republicans want to hang on Fetterman and Democrats in general, a spokesperson for the Fetterman campaign handled it adroitly. "John is not like Bernie, or Biden, or any other politician in Washington for that matter," campaign spokesperson Joe Calvello said, "He's John Fetterman, and there is no one else like him. The people of Pennsylvania understand that, and if Dr. Oz was actually from Pennsylvania, he would, too." The Fetterman campaign can also point to the primary campaign where his closest rival tried to paint him as Far Left and failed. In fact, Fetterman won all sixty-seven counties.

Meanwhile, Mehmet Oz has to face some early campaign questions. His ads in the primary touted his 2nd Amendment support and his ownership of a hunting ranch in Florida. It appears that he never had a license to hunt in that state. Doctors around the country signed a searing letter to Columbia University questioning Oz's medical credentials.

Notwithstanding residency issues or early political attacks, the lingering shadow over the Oz candidacy is the willful acceptance of Trumpism. He has joined the chorus of voices promoting baseless election conspiracies and shown that he is more about appeasing the MAGA base than finding rational solutions to problems that face the U.S. Government daily.

Voters in Pennsylvania have proven themselves to be independent thinkers. When a candidate's political tourism includes bringing into our state delusions about the transfer of power and blind allegiance to a sulking wannabe, they recognize the danger. The first order of business of any senator is to profess allegiance to the Constitution—not to take orders from Mar-a-Lago. Whether that candidate is homegrown or a newcomer to the state, the oath of office requires at least that level of integrity.

THE COST OF LIES

AUGUST 5, 2022

Far-Right conspiracist Alex Jones has used the power of his podcast to stir up fear and hatred among his millions of listeners. Among his most offensive and incendiary rants was that the 2012 Sandy Hook Elementary School shooting wasn't a tragedy at all. In fact, said Jones, it was a "hoax" drummed up by children performing as "crisis actors" and parents trying to make a point about gun control. He desecrated the memory of the twenty elementary school children and six teachers who lost their lives. He motivated his listeners to launch social meetings and other personal attacks against parents still grieving from the deadliest school shooting in American history.

Lies have consequences, and Alex Jones is facing a judge and jury that has begun to slap him with millions of damages for his false claims. On the final day of testimony in a defamation lawsuit against him and his media company, Jones claimed to have changed his mind and admitted that what happened at Sandy Hook was "one hundred percent real."

This realization came too little, too late for the plaintiffs. Neil Heslin and Scarlett Lewis had a son who died in the classroom that day. According to Heslin, Jones's hurtful words poured salt into deep wounds and "made their lives a living hell."

When radio celebrities and media empires deliberately spread assertions that they know are false, they must be held accountable. As Neil Heslin put it, "Alex started this fight, and I'll finish it."

That's one citizen taking on an empire of delusion.

This reminded me of a moment in our history when another man was forced to face down evil and deliberate lies. The effect of such lies is even more dangerous when it is done on an international scale. In 1962, the Soviet Union reassured us that their armaments in Cuba were defensive only. It wasn't until American spy planes photographed dozens of missiles pointed directly at the United States that we understood the depth of the Kremlin's lies and the real scope of their intentions. This was after the Soviet Union told lie after lie and hid the warheads under tarps and mud ninety miles off American soil. After intense negotiations that Robert Kennedy outlined in his book *Thirteen Days*, President Kennedy implemented a naval quarantine until the missiles were dismantled and removed.

This tidbit of history begs the question: is there anything more dangerous or corrosive than a nuclear threat camouflaged by lies from a foreign power? It seems to me we are living through an example of that today. The only thing more dangerous than a threat from foreign powers is a threat from within. The forty-fifth president of the United States tried to hold onto power at all costs. The failure to concede the election and his efforts to use every legal and illegal weapon to challenge that election have delivered a gut punch to American democracy from which we may not recover.

The lingering contagion of election lies has spread to millions of voters. They seem incapable of accepting the reality of the former president's loss. They are, therefore, openly expressing a willingness to subvert any future election that does not result in a win for their side. This mantra has launched hundreds of campaigns by candidates who say they would willingly abandon the Constitution to benefit their delusional leader. Abject loyalty for a MAGA endorsement. It is the stuff of third-world autocracies.

The venom of lies spewed on podcasts can destroy people's lives. Those who engage in such reckless behavior should be brought to justice. It appears that Alex Jones may soon reap what he has sown. Foreign powers that lie about nuclear stockpiles and put the world on edge need to be disarmed. Armed with the truth, President Kennedy fought a war of nerves with Nikita Khrushchev and may have saved the world. But the reality is that the most pernicious source of lies we face today comes from a domestic source. When those lies emanate from a man once entrusted with the leadership of the free world, there is only one course of action open to Americans. We must stand up to the deceptions and reject those who follow them.

There is reason to believe that many Republicans are willing to put principle above party if that is what it takes. Democrats should welcome those acts of courage to face down the threat.

RINOS TO THE RESCUE

AUGUST 12, 2022

Let's be clear about something. The Presidential Records Act, enacted in 1978, establishes that presidential records belong to the country, and any outgoing president must transfer control of them to the National Archives when he leaves office. More specifically, 18 U.S.C. § 2071 makes it a felony to attempt to remove, mutilate or destroy any presidential records. This is a crime that could be punishable by fines and imprisonment. The law also says that a violation requires the individual to "forfeit his office and be disqualified from holding any office under the United States."

Earlier this year, the National Archives disclosed that it had been forced to retrieve fifteen boxes of records from Trump's Mar-a-Lago residence, and *The New York Times* reported that some of those boxes contained classified records.

In addition to breaking the law, removing classified materials from secure archives puts us all at risk. Imagine that those documents identify U.S. personnel in sensitive positions overseas or list black ops information that could fall into the wrong hands. Reckless handling of documents could endanger our very national security. That is the reason for the Presidential Records Act and the harsh penalties it prescribes.

Recently, after receiving information that more materials existed at Mar-a-Lago, the FBI obtained a federal court warrant to search the property and recover whatever materials rightfully belonged to the United States. They found eleven more boxes of documents. The FBI and the Department of Justice did their job. No more, no less. This did not stop the ex-president from claiming their actions were "foul." It was the former president himself who broke the news of the FBI search. While none of us expect contrition from an utterly shameless man, it was remarkable that he turned what is very likely a flagrant violation of federal law into a rallying cry to his base. Worse, he pointed to Merrick Garland and the FBI as the offending parties. He launched another conspiracy theory that the Department of Justice raided his residence and could no longer be trusted just because they wanted their documents back.

The level of hypocrisy is astounding. We all remember that Hillary Clinton was charged and persecuted by Trump at countless rallies chanting, "Lock her up!" Why? Because she supposedly handled classified documents recklessly. During that campaign, Republican leader Kevin McCarthy was all too eager to condemn Clinton for her "total disregard for protecting and handling our nation's highly classified secrets." This time, it seems that McCarthy has no problem with document abuse. Like Trump, he would have you believe that the Department of Justice and the FBI are the criminals for doing their job. It was a sorry sight to see a dozen of his Republican colleagues rally around the cult leader at his Bedminster Golf Club. Instead of supporting the rule of law, they were posing for selfies with a man who held himself above the law, who faces investigations on several fronts and may be guilty of federal crimes.

In earlier times, Republican leaders showed more spine. In August 1974, the leaders of the Republican Party, including U.S. Senator Hugh Scott of Pennsylvania, went to the White House to tell Richard Nixon that he had lost their support and the support of the American people. Within days of that meeting, Nixon resigned. Republicans who dare to place country above party today are viciously attacked. They are called RINOs—Republicans in name only.

Some notable RINOs like Representative Liz Cheney (R-WY) and Senator Mitt Romney (R-UT) and others who have called out the former president for his lawlessness and his unhinged rantings will be remembered in history for their courage.

Perhaps the most prominent RINO of all was Abraham Lincoln himself. While he suffered through the bloodiest conflict in our history, he was attacked relentlessly by the radical Republicans who controlled Congress. In his second inaugural address, he dared to suggest that the way to proceed with reconstruction was "with malice toward none and charity toward all." This earned him scorn from his party, who had plans to punish the South unmercifully.

Aside from a few profiles in courage, where are the Lincolns and Scotts today? Surely, Republicans can see the difference between principled leadership and egomania. Surely, they understand that their duty is to protect the fundamentals of our democracy and its Constitution— and not shred it every time a disgruntled ex-president has a grievance to spew.

I have been hearing some encouraging comments from some Republicans recently. They are ready to step away from the mendacity of MAGA-ism and return to the original principles of the GOP. One such friend put it this way: "If that makes me a RINO, so be it." Independents, reasonable Democrats, and moderate Republicans hold the key to a return to thoughtful, less divisive government. It may be that RINOs will play a vital role in that rescue operation.

SHE DIDN'T TAKE THE SOUP

AUGUST 12, 2022

The most recent example of a political climate that wallows in revenge rather than respect is the defeat of Congress member Liz Cheney (R-WY). A Republican House leader with solid conservative credentials, Cheney made a mistake that put her in the crosshairs of Donald Trump and his cultlike followers; she told the truth.

Cheney won reelection in 2020 with 70 percent of the vote. The fact that she lost in 2022 overwhelmingly says only one thing: she could have easily saved herself by going along with the Big Lie. Like a handful of Republican leaders, she chose to take a principled stand that said "No!"

No, there was no election fraud that could have swung the election to Trump. It is not acceptable for a president to destroy the concept of a peaceful transition of power in the United States of America. No, it is not appropriate to incite a mob to storm the Capitol on the very day that the votes for president were being affirmed. It is wrong for a rogue leader to care more about his interests than the country and Constitution he swore to protect.

She was ostracized because she refused to go along with the cult of Trump. She was drummed out of office and continues to be the target of hatemongering from those who cannot begin to understand her courage level.

We are in a campaign season where the only thing that matters to the leader of the "Republican Inquisition" is abject loyalty and a suspension of belief. Candidates have been primaried and defeated because they won't tell the Big Lie. Other less honorable candidates willfully embrace the alternate reality that Trump has built.

In 1845, when Ireland was still a colony of Great Britain, mold swept through the farmlands and wiped out crops in what became known as the Potato Famine. That famine would last for seven years, leaving over a million Irish citizens dead and another million forced to wander to other countries as refugees. Amid starvation, there are stories of Protestant Bible Societies that reached out to the largely Catholic farming community and offered warm soup if Catholics accepted Protestantism.

When millions of starving Irish Catholics could almost taste the lifesaving broth their Protestant neighbors offered in the 1800s, many chose to risk starvation rather than betray their faith. People who converted for the food became known as "soupers." But even though it was excruciating, most families resisted the food because it would have been worse to renounce everything they believed in.

The soup ladled out by the tyrant-in-waiting at Mar-a-Lago is the fiction that he somehow won reelection in 2020. Millions of followers have bought into the Big Lie because they are as delusional as the chef who cooks it up or afraid of losing their place in the political soup line.

Liz Cheney could have taken the soup. She did not. As *The Atlantic* stated, "Liz Cheney told the people of Wyoming and America to snap out of their Trump-induced trance." In her concession speech, Cheney said, "I believe deeply in the principles and the ideals on which my party was founded. I love its history, and I love what our party has stood for, but I love my country more." She also pointed out the continuing clear and present danger that Trumpism means for America. "There are Republican candidates for governor who deny the outcome of the 2020 election and who may refuse to certify future elections if they oppose the results. We have candidates for secretary of state who may refuse to report the actual results of the popular vote in future elections [. . .]. No American should support election deniers for any position of genuine responsibility, where their refusal to follow the rule of law will corrupt our future."

Liz Cheney has lost the battle for her congressional seat, but she remains a central figure in the war to restore sanity to the republic. The coming midterm elections will demonstrate what we stand for as Americans. Republicans and Democrats cannot afford to "take the soup" of fear and lies. It is time to move on with leaders like Liz Cheney and others who are willing to put country before party.

THE FEVER IS BREAKING

AUGUST 26, 2022

As we head into the home stretch of the midterm elections, there are signs that the nation's long-running disease of deception and denial may be coming to an end. Special elections, recent breakthroughs in Congress, and a handful of defections by Republicans who are no longer in the thrall of the Big Lie seem to indicate that the Trump fever may be breaking. While it is too early to claim that we are on the road to recovery, there are definite signs that the body politic may be finding its way back to health.

A candidate named Pat Ryan won a special election in a swing New York Congressional District by laying out an agenda that may be a template for Democrats in the fall. While his challenger was busy hammering away at inflation and socialists and blaming everything on Biden and Democrats, Ryan raised the level of discussion to larger, more powerful themes. He focused on overturning *Roe v. Wade* and the hysteria of election deniers. His message was clear: women's rights and our right to vote are at stake. By the end of the campaign, polls showed that voters cared deeply about fighting for personal freedoms and democracy. Ryan won decisively.

In Florida and other recent primary states, Democrats ran ahead of expectations and fine-tuned their messages. Congress member Charlie Crist now appears to be a legitimate threat to the current governor and would-be presidential candidate Ron DeSantis. Congress member Val Demings' recent polling has her edging ahead of U.S. Senator Marco Rubio. Closer to home, Democrats John Fetterman and Josh Shapiro enjoy strong leads in their respective races for senator and governor.

Recently, I attended an event and had conversations with several Republican elected officials. Even though they all personally rejected the Big Lie, they were not quite ready to face the wrath of Trump enablers. Still, it is a good sign that leaders of both parties now talk—at least privately—about moving beyond the spectacle of the Trump era.

Without question, it will still be an uphill battle for Democrats in November. Republicans need to flip just five seats to take back the House. The U.S. Senate is still considered to be up for grabs. It is also true that several Trump loyalists have prevailed in the primary season. There are a dozen or so safe Republican seats that will be occupied by Trump devotees next year.

But, according to Sarah Chamberlain, president and CEO of the Republican Main Street Partnership, most new Republican candidates are distancing themselves from the cult leader. She points to "governing Republicans" seeking bipartisan progress and an exit ramp from the antics of a certain former president.

In the 1950s, Wisconsin Republican Senator Joseph R. McCarthy dominated public opinion with his Cold War allegations against Communists in the government. After years of cruelty that ruined countless lives, McCarthy was finally called out by an attorney named Joseph Welch. At a televised congressional hearing, McCarthy directly attacked one of Welch's legal assistants. It was too much for Welch, who looked the senator in the eyes and said, "Until this moment, senator, I think I never really gauged your cruelty or your recklessness. Let us not assassinate this lad further, senator. You have done enough. Have you no sense of decency?" It broke a national fever and ended McCarthy's career.

Breaking our current fever may not result from one such tipping point. Instead, the best strategy to overcome the overheated rhetoric of the Far Right is to govern from the center. Even with razor-thin majorities in Congress, President Biden has racked up some significant accomplishments. These include historic pandemic recovery and infrastructure programs, ten million new jobs, and spearheading the fight for Ukraine. In the last two months, the Inflation Reduction Act, the Microchips and Science Act, the Burn Pits Assistance Act for Veterans, and debt relief for student loans have demonstrated that leaders can still get things done. Moreover, the new programs have been implemented without increasing the deficit. A midterm review from the Department of Treasury shows that the deficit has been cut by $2 trillion from the previous administration.

These solid achievements put Biden and the Democrats in a new positive light. As President Biden's favorable numbers go up, the prospects for Democrats in the fall improve. For voters of both parties, the elections in November provide an opportunity to regain our political health.

SHELTER FROM THE STORM

SEPTEMBER 9, 2022

Queen Elizabeth II is dead. She passed away at Balmoral Castle, her summer estate in Scotland, surrounded by her children, including the next King of England.

The Queen's actual title was "Elizabeth the Second, by the Grace of God, of the United Kingdom of Great Britain and Northern Ireland and of Her other Realms and Territories Queen, Head of the Commonwealth, Defender of the Faith." It signifies an awesome range of responsibilities she handled with grace for seventy years. She witnessed the installation of fifteen different prime ministers. She interacted as the head of state with every American president since Eisenhower.

Over the years, Queen Elizabeth has weathered every imaginable crisis, from warfare to economic upheavals to deeply personal family issues. She put her high office and country ahead of her interests and never once wavered from her duties. The respect that she commanded made her a stabilizing force for the entire world. She provided shelter from the storm.

As Great Britain gathers to mourn its matriarch, America had its moment of peace and comfort last week. Barack and Michelle Obama returned to Washington for the unveiling of their official portraits. At the White House, the Bidens hosted what amounted to a family reunion. In stark contrast to the darkness that self-serving leaders and hyper-partisanship have caused, the ceremony reminded us of brighter days. It has only been six years since the Obama administration, but we have suffered through what seems like an eternity of enmity.

President Obama, like all presidents, exercised immense power in the most significant job on the planet. But here is what he had to say about his time in office: "When you're sitting behind that desk, you are aware that presidents and first ladies are human beings like everyone else. We have our gifts. We have our flaws. We have good days and bad days. We feel the same joy and sadness, frustration, and hope." This is a level of humility that was sorely lacking in the administration that followed his. The Obama unveiling event would have traditionally been held during the Trump presidency, but Donald Trump refused to host it.

It was Michelle Obama who turned the event into a lesson for all of us. She didn't have to mention his name, but Michelle Obama was very clear about who is behind the current threat to American democracy. She spoke about those who insist that Trump won the 2020 election. "You see the people, they make their voices heard with their vote," the former first lady said. "We hold an inauguration to ensure a peaceful transition of power. Those of us lucky enough to serve work as hard as we can for as long as we can, as long as the people choose to keep us here. And once our time is up, we move on."

Her message comes when America braces for midterm elections featuring an array of candidates who are election deniers. Some of these candidates are handpicked by Donald Trump and have stated openly that they would defy the people's will if future elections do not go their way. Michelle wants you to know that such extremism is unacceptable. Most voters in America want less contentious politics. They want leaders who respect election results and orderly transfers of power.

By presenting a statesman's calm, assuring demeanor, Barack Obama reminded us why he would be considered by history to be a consequential president. By stepping up to protect the constitutional norms that have sustained us for over two centuries, Michelle Obama reminded us that we can all rise to the threats we face. Together, they gave us some respite. They provided a moment of shelter from the current storm of malignant politics.

Queen Elizabeth's lifetime of service and the Obamas' message should motivate all citizens to do better. Their examples should motivate us to guard against demagogues and autocrats who would undermine what truly makes both nations great.

THIS IS NOT NORMAL

SEPTEMBER 23, 2022

At last count, former President Donald J. Trump faces over thirty separate investigations and legal proceedings. Lingering charges of sexual assault have been revived. His business entities face fraud charges in New York that could amount to $250 million in damages. The Department of Justice is assessing the damage to our national security because the former president walked off with 11,000 documents, some of which were top secret or highly classified.

For the record, the Presidential Records Act makes it clear that all such papers are the property of the U.S. Government. Removing even one document constitutes a felony punishable by fines, imprisonment, and forfeiting the right to hold office again. The next question has to do with espionage and the reason that the documents were pilfered in the first place.

This is not normal.

After the chaos that has swirled around Trump for years, it is time to make a clear-headed break with Trumpism. We have had more than our fill of a reckless autocrat who spewed venom from his very first political pronouncements. We watched him attempt to extort a foreign leader to dig up dirt on an opponent and saw him try to explain away a payoff to a porn star.

But putting all of that aside, here is the transgression that cries out for prosecution: in our proud tradition of self-governance, Trump is the only president we have ever had who has refused to accept defeat. The utter lack of class to whine about the election results ignited an insurrection of supporters at the Capitol. It launched a legion of candidates who now threaten to spread the infection of self-interest through our system.

This is not normal.

And it comes to this: the former president reasserted that the documents previously mentioned were, somehow, declassified before they were strewn about Mar-a-Lago. In fact, he took his autocratic tendencies to a new level when he observed that a president could achieve that objective "even by thinking about it." Consider the ramifications for the country if any president asserts that he has the authority to take actions without checks and balances and without regard for established procedures. It is enough for him to simply rattle a thought around in his own head. Public be damned. They'll just have to get better at mind-reading.

This would all be considered lunacy if it came from anyone but Donald J. Trump. But the smitten cultists who hang on every word he utters treat it like the gospel truth. This is why *The New York Times* reported recently that 40 percent of Republican candidates running for office are either election deniers or will not commit to accepting the results of their own campaigns unless they win. In addition, candidates are running for governor and positions like secretary of state who openly affirm their loyalty to Trump over their obligation to the constitutional process of free and fair elections. We could very well find ourselves saddled with autocrats who, like Donald Trump, believe that democracy is beneath them. What matters is their own political egos.

With sixty days left in this year's election cycle, it is time to face this cancer head-on. It is time for all of us to rise to the level of participation that the founders envisioned when they espoused active participation of the citizenry. Here is a suggestion: make sure you understand whether the candidates on the ballot stand for something other than themselves. Make sure that they can put Trumpism behind them and articulate a reasonable set of ideas that would be expected of a leader.

Would you like a litmus test that you could apply to any candidate of any party? Here it is: ask anyone and everyone running for office in 2022 the question, do you believe that Joe Biden is the duly-elected president of the United States?" Any candidate who hesitates with their answer is not worthy of your vote. Any hem and hawing like, "Well, there were irregularities" or "the process is flawed" is unacceptable. We all deserve to know that our candidates, at the very least, respect the Constitution enough to support the peaceful transition of power. Not only should election deniers and wishy-washy candidates be defeated at the polls, but they should also be disqualified from holding office. The oath to uphold and defend the Constitution still means something to most of us. We need to know that candidates can break free of the tarpit Trump created when he failed to concede his election defeat. This is how we get back to normal.

CRISIS BRINGS LEADERS TOGETHER

SEPTEMBER 30, 2022

Long before social media technology turned every voter into an opinion machine, our country depended on elected leaders' good faith to lead. Elected officials were not bombarded with factions and fiction that demanded subservience to any notion that went viral. More importantly, the two parties found common ground when it came to addressing the country's critical needs and ignored the occasional charlatan attempting to bend one party or the other to their own will.

As we enter the final days of the midterm elections, we are still in the throes of a phenomenon that continues to be a clear and present danger to the republic. The Republican Party has been overrun by zealots without interest in thoughtful, bipartisan governance. We have reached a point where the dominant faction of the once-proud GOP is riddled with election deniers and candidates who are making it clear that they have no interest in the peaceful transition of power. In fact, many of them, like Doug Mastriano in Pennsylvania, have taken the Trumpian position that they can simply ignore the will of the people and commandeer elections if, God forbid, they find themselves in positions of power.

There have always been spirited, partisan debates at all levels. But there have always been statesmen and stateswomen who understood their oath of office and the need to rise above demagoguery—one such moment occurred following the terrorist attack on the U.S. Embassy in Beirut in 1983. Two hundred and forty Marines lost their lives in the bombing, and some wanted to exploit the debacle for political gain.

President Ronald Reagan called the Democratic Speaker of the House, Tip O'Neill, to ask about follow-up hearings. "I guess you're going to have a field day with this," said the president.

"Mr. President," replied Speaker O'Neill, "you didn't kill those boys."

There was one—and only one—follow-up hearing, and both sides moved on with the people's business.

It is hard to imagine how we can get back to that level of decency when a large percentage of one party refuses even to accept that Joe Biden is the duly-elected president of the United States. It may be that the only solution is for all of us to reject candidates who cannot separate themselves from the Big Lie. Folks cannot be pro-insurrection and pro-democracy. We need to vote as if democracy is on the line because it is.

With that in mind, let us take a moment to acknowledge that there is hope. Two of the fiercest political adversaries are the current president and the current governor of Florida. Governor Ron DeSantis has been particularly feisty of late with direct attacks on President Biden and political stunts like shipping migrants around the country. Still, when Hurricane Ian ripped through Florida last week, the two men did what real leaders do; they did their jobs. Both passed up the opportunity to grandstand or politicize the event. Both summoned their resources and focused on getting immediate help to the storm's victims.

A third participant, Democrat Charlie Crist, who is running to unseat DeSantis, also maintained political maturity. He pulled his advertising in those parts of Florida under duress and offered his full support to ameliorate the situation.

Depending on what happens next in the recovery phase of the disaster, DeSantis has an opportunity to burnish his credentials as a crisis manager. It is equally possible that things can go wrong and damage his political trajectory. For now, it is notable that stark differences between political actors can be set aside for the greater good. There is always room for legitimate debate on issues, but there are times that cry out for cooperation and understanding. Just as we brace each other for the worst that nature can dish out, we should be willing to stand together to put aside disastrous threats to our system of government.

The storm is upon us. We have no choice but to let the flood waters of division recede. Let us support candidates who want that to happen. Let us hope that the midterm elections bring us all back to safety.

CHARACTER MATTERS

SEPTEMBER 30, 2022

We are all caught in the crossfire of the Pennsylvania campaigns for governor and senator. The tone has become increasingly negative, and some ads are just plain offensive. At this point, they are hand grenades meant to do indiscriminate damage to their opponent and rattle voters who may still be on the fence. But let's take a moment and look at events that are unfolding in the state of Georgia. Let's look objectively at the disintegration of politics unfolding in the Senate race between incumbent Raphael Warnock and challenger Herschel Walker.

Walker, personally recruited by Donald Trump, has been plagued with his own miscues since entering the race. He claimed to have graduated from the University of Georgia and worked for the FBI; he didn't. He denied reports of spousal abuse, including holding a gun to a woman's head—until his son stepped forward to confirm it. He has four children out of wedlock and, according to his son, never raised one of them.

Now comes the clincher: it is alleged that Walker, who espouses a complete ban on abortion with no exceptions for rape or incest, paid one of his paramours for an abortion a few years ago. This could be dismissed as a late campaign attack, except that the woman involved has stepped forward with details, receipts of the procedure, and a handwritten "get well" note from Walker. Herschel Walker took to the microphones to say he didn't know the woman—a preposterous statement since she is the mother of one of his four children. He claims that the whole story is a "flat-out lie" despite substantial evidence.

So, given the blatant hypocrisy of his pro-life pronouncements and the flawed character of this man, is the Republican Party distancing itself from him? Not at all. The GOP leadership—McConnell, Cruz, Scott, Graham—reaffirmed their support. Dana Loesch, a spokesperson for the National Rifle Association, made it clear that they would continue to pour money into the Walker campaign because they didn't care about "one broad's abortion."

Former Speaker Newt Gingrich, hardly a paragon of virtue himself, had this baffling perspective: "Walker is the most important Senate candidate in the country because he'll do more to change the Senate by his deep commitment to Christ." Are we really seeing fundamentalist Christians ignoring everything they preach from their pulpits to align themselves with someone who breaks every tenet of their faith?

Why is this not a disturbing moment for the pro-life movement? By their standards, Walker is not only pro-choice but was likely actively pro-abortion at least once in his life. If Walker were not a Republican, pro-life candidates in this post-Dobbs era would not hesitate to call his alleged actions murder. Walker may be exposing the real position of the Far Right: We are against all abortions except for the father's convenience or for holding on to political power. The chasm of pure political hypocrisy in Georgia is also a telling picture of where the Republican Party is today. Their midterm election message couldn't be more precise: win at any cost.

This is a far cry from where our democratic principles started. In Book Six of *Nicomachean Ethics,* Aristotle set some parameters for political behavior four thousand years ago. "We become just by the practice of just actions, self-controlled by exercising self-control, and courageous by performing acts of courage [. . .]. Lawgivers make the citizens good by inculcating good habits in them, and this is the aim of every lawgiver."

The race in Georgia has taken a turn that goes well beyond partisan politics. It is a test of whether voters can discern for themselves what is just. Despite the influence of money and the self-interest of leaders, character still matters. In Georgia and every other state, it is time for voters to show they know the difference between right and wrong.

Back to Pennsylvania, let us hope that voters can wade through the muck of last-minute ads and realize that we will have to find our way on our own. It is up to us to separate fact from fiction. We need to seek out candidates who demonstrate character. Those are the ones who are worthy of our votes.

CANDIDATES MUST MEET BASIC OBLIGATIONS

OCTOBER 21, 2022

The Constitution of the United States requires that candidates for the House of Representatives be at least twenty-five years of age and a U.S. citizen for seven years. He or she must also be a resident of the state where he or she is running. Similarly, the Pennsylvania Constitution has some basic requirements for running for governor. Such candidates must be at least thirty years old and a citizen of Pennsylvania for seven years.

In addition, there are statutory requirements for both offices that must be complied with. Signatures on nomination petitions must be secured. Financial interest statements and candidate affidavits are required. Filing fees apply, and hard deadlines are in place for presenting credentials to the PA Department of State.

While most candidates understand and comply with these basic requirements, another obligation is implied by the oath of office that they will take should they win. Simply put, the oath of office for both the U.S. House and the governor requires the newly-minted elected officials to support and defend the Constitution. The governor, of course, also swears to "support, obey and defend" the constitution of the Commonwealth of Pennsylvania. There is no gray area about this. In fact, Congresspersons promise, with their hand on the Bible, that they will "well and faithfully discharge the duties of the office on which I am about to enter. So help me, God."

I have spoken out strongly against those candidates who refuse to acknowledge the election of our current president. One hundred and forty-seven House members voted against Joe Biden's election certification. Many continue to flout a key component of the Constitution that they promised to defend: the peaceful transition of power. In addition, recent surveys indicate that as many as 40 percent of Republican candidates are election deniers and will not commit to accepting election results if they lose.

In a recent editorial, *The Philadelphia Inquirer* stated, "The extremist wing of the GOP remains a threat to American democracy. The January 6th House Select Committee did its sworn duty. Now it is up to Democrats, independents, and any remaining patriotic Republicans to vote against election deniers and to push to hold Trump and his enablers accountable."

Tami Davis Biddle is an instructor at the U.S. Army War College in Carlisle. She recently called out two of her own: Doug Mastriano, running for governor, and Scott Perry running for the U.S. House of Representatives. Both candidates are military officers who studied at the War College and claimed the high distinction that that honorable institution bestows. But according to Dr. Biddle, Mastriano and Perry violated their oaths as officers and elected officials. "The officer corps is sworn to defend the Constitution rather than any person or president. None of its members is entitled to toy with insurrection, treat January 6 as legitimate protest, or follow election deniers who would undercut our most important political institutions."

She concludes, like *The Philadelphia Inquirer* did that our very democracy is at stake in this year's midterm elections. In her words, it's essential to "protect our crucial democratic institutions by voting against candidates who would undermine or eliminate them, and those include, I'm sad to say, Doug Mastriano and Scott Perry."

One more observation: Congress member Perry's campaign for reelection has taken a decidedly bizarre tone lately. In his recent television commercial, he equates deaths by fentanyl with an attack by ISIS fighters and blames Biden for both. He suggests that, somehow, Biden could press some button that would magically eliminate ISIS or drug lords. Perry claims that because terrorism and drug threats persist, Biden displays a "dereliction of duty."

Remember that this charge comes from a military officer about his Commander in Chief. It comes at a time when that commander has his hands full fighting a brutal Russian incursion into Ukraine and staring down a real threat of nuclear war. Let us also remember that Representative Perry figured prominently in the conspiracy to allow President Trump to cling to power. He was willing to shred the Constitution to appoint an acting attorney general who would rule in Trump's favor and overturn the will of the American voters. If Representative Perry wants to see a "dereliction of duty," he should look in the nearest mirror.

The Constitution and oath of office matter. Voters have a chance to restore democratic norms, and this November, that is what matters most.

CANDIDATES REVEAL THEMSELVES

OCTOBER 28, 2022

Much has been written about the Fetterman-Oz debate, and predictably, the pundits are split about its impact on the critical race for U.S. Senate. Far Right outlets are piling on about Fetterman's halting delivery and lingering after-effects of a stroke he suffered in May. Democrats are pointing out that, while their candidate may not have been as polished as Oz, Fetterman's clipped responses were direct and more in sync with Pennsylvania voters.

Fetterman addressed the elephant in the room up front and alerted an international audience that he might miss a step or two. For his part, Oz took full advantage of his years of training on television and made rehearsed, rapid-fire points that often spilled over his allotted time.

I had the advantage of watching the debate close by and spent some time with pundits in the media circus tent before and after the event. At Fetterman's opening statement, a memory from my childhood blazed into my mind. A beloved relative had suffered a massive stroke, and I pictured him sitting in his adjustable chair, unable to walk or feed himself. I also recalled vividly the terror and frustration in his eyes. He had his mental abilities but was unable to communicate in any way. This man was a professor who spoke four languages, led the choir in his church, raised a family, and would spend the last twenty years of his life alert but imprisoned in his own body. It was an act of courage for him just to wake up every day.

That's what I saw when John Fetterman began to speak: courage. His team could have chosen to skip the debate altogether. Other candidates in this cycle with far less justification have done just that. Instead, Fetterman faced his opponent and an unprecedented sea of media exposure and hoped his auditory skills were up to the task.

There were stumbles and awkward pauses. Fetterman was hard-pressed to fend off a barrage of attacks from the more polished Oz. While Oz did not dwell on Fetterman's recovery, he couldn't resist a snide comment on an education-related question. "Do you want me to help you understand the question?" said Oz in a shockingly insensitive and revealing jab.

Winston Churchill had an acute stroke much like Fetterman's in 1953. He convalesced at his country house for months with little or no criticism from a friend or foe. When Churchill gave his first public speech following the medical incident, biographers reported that he was concerned not only about slurring words but about being able to stand for any length of time. He recovered fully and took his rightful place in history.

Likewise, Franklin Roosevelt was struck by polio at age thirty-nine. For the rest of his career, he relied on his arm strength to hold himself steady behind the podium. His condition was a carefully guarded secret throughout his service as governor and president. In fact, there is a story about an eleven-year-old visitor to the White House who watched with wide eyes as FDR was wheeled into the room. She tugged on her father's sleeve and said, "Don't worry, I won't tell anyone."

Back to the Fetterman-Oz debate. A writer from *The New Yorker* had this observation: "Fetterman was speaking in a sort of enforced simplicity that might not have got across the nuance that he would have liked but did point up how much Oz sounded like a politician—how stylized everything was in the Republican's mouth." In fact, Oz talked too much and made the only real unforced error of the debate. He suggested that abortion decisions should be made by "women, doctors, and local political leaders." It revived the initial outrage about overturning *Roe v. Wade* and may have an impact in the closing days of the campaign.

The other revelation from Oz was this: "I would support Donald Trump if he decided to run for president." In that one statement, he signals that he will overlook the January 6 insurrection that Trump ignited. He aligns himself with election deniers and those who will not support the constitutionally enshrined concept of a peaceful transfer of power. He supports a man who faces nineteen separate investigations for wrongdoing and continues wreaking havoc on our democratic norms.

From a technical point of view, Oz won the debate. But reviewing what was said and how the candidates handled their strengths and weaknesses showed Fetterman to be the better man.

BIDEN SHINES A LIGHT ON POLITICAL THREATS

NOVEMBER 4, 2022

Richard Ringer is a candidate for an open legislative seat in Fayette County, Pennsylvania. His home has been vandalized, and he has reported several incidents of harassment to the local police. One week before the election, he was assaulted and knocked unconscious in his backyard.

On that same day, Paul Pelosi, the eighty-two-year-old husband of Speaker Nancy Pelosi, was bludgeoned by an intruder who admitted that his goal was to kidnap Speaker Pelosi to interrogate her. He intended to send her back to Congress with broken kneecaps if he wasn't satisfied with her answers.

Across the country, the Department of Homeland Security has issued bulletins identifying increased threats to political candidates and election officials. They have warned that public figures are now facing a heightened risk of violence.

In an unusually blunt address, President Biden called out political violence of any type. "We must, with an overwhelming voice, stand up against political violence and voter intimidation, period," he said. "Stand up and speak against it. We don't settle our differences in America with a riot, a mob, a bullet, or a hammer. We settle them peacefully at the ballot box." Biden went on to decry the deterioration of democracy and the rise of election deniers. Hundreds of candidates appearing on Tuesday's ballots not only embrace the Big Lie, but they have also made their disdain for a peaceful transition of power a plank in their personal platforms. Many have already declared that they will accept election results only if they win. This is what undermines democracy. This gives rise to violence at polling places and at candidates' residences.

You would think Americans would be united in opposing violence of any type. Surely, we all understand that adherence to the Constitution and the peaceful transition of power are guardrails that can prevent mayhem. Accepting defeat gracefully assures the republic can endure without partisan differences tumbling into bloodshed. However, Republican leaders are not on board. Kevin McCarthy, the Republican leader of the U.S. House of Representatives, quickly criticized the president's remarks. He accused Biden of attacking Republicans and shifting the focus of the campaign season for political advantage.

Biden did draw a direct line from today's violence to the cowardly and selfish actions of one man. The defeated former president fomented violence on January 6 and continues to pour gasoline on the fire every chance that he gets. Still, Biden carefully distinguished between MAGA Republicans and those who still value country above partisanship. He clarified that the MAGA Republicans who take their marching orders from Trump are not the norm but the misguided exceptions.

Unfortunately, Republican candidates across the country cannot bring themselves to disassociate from the destruction of Trump. They need MAGA votes to win. They may espouse lofty campaign themes but will not acknowledge that democracy is also on the ballot.

There was a moment in recent history that shone with the promise of a civil reconnection for all Americans. Senate Majority Leader Mitch McConnell and Leader McCarthy both took to the floor in the aftermath of the January 6 riots to condemn the violence. They also made it clear that it all could have been avoided if Trump had simply done what all other presidents in our history have done: to accept the people's will.

That moment was dashed on the rocks of pure political partisanship when McCarthy made a pilgrimage to Mar-a-Lago to profess the fealty of the Republicans to the former president. History will not be kind to McCarthy or others who chose groveling over governing.

Since then, Republican leaders have been willing to support Far-Right militants and to support even the most outrageous conspiracy theories if it meant that their political fortunes benefit. In the final weeks of the midterm elections, they aided and abetted dangerous candidates with millions of dollars from their Washington-based operations. Much of that money went straight to mass media through ads trafficking in distortion and fear.

And what is the predictable result of such an abdication of leadership? What happens when these dark elements are permitted to infect the normal discourse between parties that have kept this country balanced? Richard Ringer gets assaulted. Paul Pelosi gets his skull cracked. Election officials are afraid to show up for work.

Biden has it right: vote for those who stand on their convictions. Vote for those who can bring us out of the darkness of political violence and back to a republic of clear-thinking leaders and citizens.

A SIGH OF RELIEF

NOVEMBER 4, 2022

Looking through the mountain of news stories following the midterm elections, I came across a completely unrelated article from *The Guardian*. The article reports that archeologists have uncovered the oldest known sentence written in an actual alphabet. The sentence is engraved on an ivory comb with large teeth for untangling hair and smaller teeth for removing lice and insect eggs. The comb dated to 1700 BC and was found in Canaan, a part of the ancient kingdom of Judah. Scientists believe this is the oldest discovered sentence in Western civilization: "May this tusk root out the lice of the hair and the beard."

Historically, midterm elections go very badly for the president's party. Reagan, Clinton, and Obama all took a beating in the middle of their first terms. In 2022, Democrats were not only facing history, but they were also staring at record inflation levels and a well-orchestrated campaign to demonize their party as big spenders and soft on crime.

But something happened amid the endless clutter of television ads; voters concluded that democracy mattered. They made a statement about protecting fundamental rights and rejected the stream of falsehoods about the last election that resulted in violence at the Capitol which spread to the home of the Speaker of the House in California. Enough voters—Democrats, moderate Republicans, Independents, suburban women, minorities—used their vote to say emphatically, "Enough is enough."

For the first time in our history, we had a significant number of candidates on the ballot who challenged the validity of the last presidential election. Some of them flat-out refused to say that they would accept the will of the people of their race unless they won. Worse, these were folks seeking positions with a direct impact on voting. Twelve candidates for secretary of state and twenty-two governors bought into the Big Lie and threatened to derail future elections if they got a chance.

Fortunately, only four of those twelve candidates for secretary of state prevailed. And the most vocal election deniers among the governor candidates also lost. An exception to this might be Kari Lake in Arizona, where the election is still too close to call.

At the U.S. Senate level, nineteen candidates used "election fraud" as a rallying cry. Some were Trump acolytes willing to ignore the January 6 insurrection and sign on to the Trump bandwagon for 2024. The loudest of those disrupters were defeated by more mainstream candidates. Whatever happens in Arizona, Nevada, and Georgia in the next few weeks, the 2022 elections will bring a slightly more collegial group of leaders to Washington. The diminishment of Trumpism means that the president, Senator Mitch McConnell, and Senator Chuck Schumer can return to a more productive give-and-take between professionals who take governing seriously.

On the U.S. House side, the very narrow majority now held by the Republicans means that leadership will have their hands full keeping their troops in line. It also means that the likely new Speaker of the House, Kevin McCarthy, will have to reach across the aisle to deal with Democrats occasionally.

One way to look at the midterm elections of 2022 is that we all took a step back toward the middle. We recognized as a people that it is more practical to work together than to continue to demonize each other. This will not stop outrageous behavior from some boisterous actors. It will not stop the fringes from lobbing grenades at each other. But hopefully, it means that uncivil behavior will become the exception rather than the norm.

The more I think about it, the more I am convinced that elections are the ivory comb that allows us to free ourselves from infestations. Every election, we can root out distractions, deceptions, and infections that, left unchecked, could threaten our fragile democracy. The rejection of election deniers and self-serving candidates with blind allegiance to a malicious leader in exile shows that Democrats and Republicans can guard their political health.

There will continue to be partisan division. There will be spirited policy debates. But the sigh of relief you are hearing from all corners of the country is because we have begun to recover from an era of chaos driven by fear and hatred. Like the ancient Canaanites, we have used our ivory comb to get a specific scourge out of our hair. That kind of grooming affords all of us some hope for the future.

SLIM MAJORITIES CAN CAUSE MAYHEM

NOVEMBER 18, 2022

Control of the Pennsylvania House of Representatives came down to a single race decided by less than thirty votes. The battle for the 151st seat in Montgomery County saw Democratic challenger Melissa Cerrato unseat incumbent Republican Todd Stephens by sifting through provisional ballots to eke out the win. As of this writing, there are lingering legal challenges and possible follow-up actions by the courts or the county election officials. Still, the House Democrats have taken control of that body with the absolute bare minimum of 102 members.

But wait, there's more! One of the Democrats elected sadly died in October. Representative Tony DeLuca of Allegheny County passed away too late in the campaign to alter the ballots. In addition, state Representative Summer Lee of Allegheny County will be leaving the legislature, having won a seat in Congress. Finally, Representative Austin Davis will leave his post to assume the lieutenant governor's duties when he steps down on January 17.

The Democrats will likely win the special elections to fill these seats in the spring of 2023 and assert a majority for the remainder of the legislative session. In the meantime, though, we can expect some fireworks from the loyal opposition, who will have more votes in their caucus in January. Stay tuned to see if this means maneuvering for control, even if their majority is short-lived.

At the federal level, the House of Representatives was returned to Republican control with a similar tenuous majority. While the Democrats defied history and minimized their losses in the midterm elections, the fact is that the Republicans can now proceed with their agenda even if their numbers are at or near the bare majority of 218 votes.

This presents serious challenges for anybody seeking to herd the votes necessary for leaders to emerge and for moving forward on legislative initiatives. The first evidence of this was in the closed-door vote for Speaker. The Republican Caucus supported current Minority Leader Kevin McCarthy by a vote of 188-31.

Notably, McCarthy was challenged by Arizona Representative Andy Biggs, former leader of the Far Right Freedom Caucus. While few expected him to topple leader McCarthy, he made it clear that the party's right wing would demand some attention. In January, McCarthy will need a majority of the entire House—218 votes—if he is to ascend to the Speakership. This means he has two months to convince, cajole, or compromise with at least thirty-one members of his party for their vote. The speculation is that they will demand more consideration on committee assignments, scheduling of legislative initiatives, and a host of investigations that they have been itching to launch. The challenge for McCarthy is to appease his Far-Right flank without losing the moderates and others more concerned with governing than posturing.

On the U.S. Senate side, Majority Leader Chuck Schumer is also operating with the slimmest of a working majority. The current 50-49 make-up of the Senate means that he, too, must go hat-in-hand with each of his members who know they could be the deciding vote on any given issue. The situation may ease slightly in December if Senator Raphael Warnock (D-GA) holds off a challenge from Herschel Walker in a runoff election in Georgia.

Still, the slim margins in the Senate, the House, and the PA House mean that the tensions in our legislative bodies are growing. The passions that translated into campaign attacks on volatile issues like inflation, abortion, crime, and elections will likely spill over into hearings, legislation, and amendments that will put our sharp divisions on full display.

Amid the rancor, however, it is still possible to glimpse graciousness when true leaders take to the podium. After twenty years of leading the Democrats in Congress, Speaker Nancy Pelosi stepped down with a farewell speech filled with kindness and maturity. Despite being demonized by her opponents for decades and despite a maniacal attack on her husband sparked by the rhetoric of the Far Right, she demonstrated again why her style of leadership matters. She spoke of patriotism and the "better angels of our nature," to which Lincoln referred. She demonstrated how to step down with class as power transfers to a different party and a new generation. As new leaders step up to the challenges of divided government, they would do well to govern with that example in mind.

PROFILES IN COURAGE

DECEMBER 2, 2022

John F. Kennedy's Pulitzer Prize-winning *Profiles in Courage* remains one of the most important books about some historical figures who faced enormous pressures and still managed to lead with honor and grace. Many faced financial and physical ruin and still did the right thing. These acts of courage are rare, which is why one editor said that *Profiles in Courage* was such a slim edition. Kennedy said about his book, "The stories of past courage can define that ingredient—they can teach, they can offer hope, they can provide inspiration. But they cannot supply courage itself. For this, each man must look into his own soul."

Looking back on the recent elections, and perhaps, in the spirit of the holidays, here are three recent instances of courage that should be noted.

First, the American voters passed the test of courage when they rejected the voices of the fringe element and clearly voted candidates committed to governance and not grandstanding. In nearly all the competitive races for governor, U.S. senator, and down-ballot offices, voters rejected those election deniers who have yet to accept the results of 2020. Some of those Far-Right candidates have yet to accept the will of the people in their defeats this year.

Tensions rose in the midterms when Republican-leaning PACs inundated the airwaves to pin inflation and crime on Biden and the Democrats. Biden himself raised the stakes when he challenged the electorate to look beyond the soundbites and stand up for democracy. He warned voters about the chaos that could ensue if bad candidates flushed with dark money came into office. "Yes," the voters said, we feel the pain of inflation, and we are concerned about urban crime, but our country comes first. They chose to support reasonable candidates committed to emerging from the chaos, and the country breathed a sigh of relief.

Speaking of crime, the Pennsylvania House Republicans sharpened their rhetoric on crime in the campaign's waning days. They flocked together as geese in a "V" formation pointed directly at the district attorney of Philadelphia, Larry Krasner. It seems they believe that impeaching and convicting Krasner would solve crime in the big city. At least they hoped to present a poster boy for their messaging. While the House moved quickly to support articles of impeachment and the Senate dutifully began conducting an impeachment trial, at least one Republican stood up amid the cackling and spoke his truth. Representative Mike Puskaric (R-Union County) was the lone Republican to vote against the impeachment of Krasner. He said his leadership used the issue as a last-minute political campaign weapon. "They were attempting to make Krasner their villain for basically campaign or political purposes," said Puskaric. The impeachment trial goes on, but at least one Republican decided that his sense of duty and courage demanded that he speak out.

Another Pennsylvanian departing the political stage is retiring Republican U.S. Senator Pat Toomey. In an extraordinary series of exit interviews, Toomey reasserted his credentials as a fiscal conservative and pointed out many achievements that benefitted his state. He also invited the wrath of his party when he refused to back down from asserting his principles in support of the Constitution in the days following the January 6 assault on the Capitol. It became clear to Toomey that then-president Trump "intended to thwart the outcome of the election." Senator Toomey had taken an oath to protect and defend the Constitution against "all enemies foreign and domestic." It appalled him that the gravest domestic threat to the Constitution was a sulking president refusing to give up power after a convincing defeat at the polls.

Toomey voted to remove Trump from office in the impeachment trial following January 6 and said, "It was not a close call." To make the point clear, Toomey went on to say that trying to overrule the people's vote was "beyond outrageous" and an "egregious offense to the Constitution as I can think of." Toomey also sounded the alarm for a party stuck in the detritus of blind allegiance to the former president when he said, "We can't nominate candidates who are completely unable to expand beyond a narrow base. That's never been a good strategy politically."

Voters who listen to their consciences rather than incendiary campaign ads, state representatives who speak out against a wave of political posturing, and a U.S. senator who places the Constitution above his political interests are all acts of modern-day courage. I, for one, am grateful for them.

BIPARTISANSHIP

DECEMBER 16, 2022

The current imbroglio over who controls the Pennsylvania House of Representatives needs to be resolved. Democrats claim that they prevailed in the recent elections, and they are correct. Republicans point out that three vacancies in the Democratic ranks (one by death and two by members who moved on to new positions) mean that they have the current majority by 101-99, and they are correct. Leaders have been communicating by press conferences and staged swearing-in ceremonies on a largely vacant House floor when they should be talking directly to each other instead.

Partisanship has been with us since the days of the founders. But it is comforting to know that leaders have risen above even the most challenging quagmires when they put their country or state above factionalism or politics. A few clicks into the internet and you can easily find an organization called the Bipartisan Policy Center. They identify a history of compromises and bipartisan actions that changed our lives for the better. Here are just a few examples:

1. The Great Compromise of 1787: While leaders from populous states felt entitled to greater representation in Congress, smaller states believed they should have equal representation. The solution? Roger Sherman from Connecticut proposed the now famous compromise that provided for a proportional House of Representatives and a Senate with two senators from each state. While the founders first rejected the proposal out of hand, opponents eventually realized that the Constitution was dead in the waters without some compromise. Fortunately, statesmanship won out over factionalism, and the modern legislature was formed.

2. Lincoln's Team of Rivals: Governor Salmon P. Chase (R-OH), N.Y. Senator William Seward (R-NY) and Judge Edward Bates of Missouri ran against

Abraham Lincoln in the primaries. President Lincoln invited them all into his cabinet, anyway, saying he had no right to deprive the country of its strongest minds simply because they sometimes disagreed with him.

3. The Civil Rights Act of 1964: President Johnson and the Democrats needed Republican votes in the Senate to break the filibuster and move forward will the landmark Civil Rights Act. When Majority Leader Mike Mansfield (D-MO) asked Minority Leader Everett Dirksen (R-Il) for help, Dirksen stepped up. "We are confronted with a moral issue. Today let us not be found wanting." He rounded up twenty-seven Republican votes to join the Democrats and carried the day.

4. John McCain and Health Care: In 2017, Senator John McCain (R-AZ) was on the Senate floor shortly after hospitalization and was placed in the awkward position of deciding on the survival of the Affordable Care Act. With two other Republicans, McCain voted against repealing the law and saved health care coverage for millions of Americans. He said: "We've been spinning our wheels on too many important issues because we keep trying to find a way to win without help from across the aisle. Let's trust each other. Let's return to regular order."

5. Problem Solvers Caucus: Co-chaired by Josh Gottheimer (D-NJ) and Brian Fitzpatrick (R-PA), the House Problem Solvers Caucus has already won numerous victories in areas like infrastructure, immigration, criminal justice reform, and healthcare. The caucus's web page states, "We are all tired of the obstructionism in Washington. We are a bipartisan group of Members Congress organized to get to "yes" to help solve some of our country's most pressing problems."

The 2023-24 Pennsylvania legislative session looks like it is off to a contentious start. With control of the House hinging on the narrowest of majorities, it does not make sense for one party or the other to claim a mandate or force their opinions on their opposition. Just like the statesmen in our history or the current band of problem solvers in Congress who can see beyond political infighting and focus on the greater good, elected officials from any party and at every level of government are capable of similar honor.

The Democrats will likely prevail in the upcoming special elections, but that will still only give them a majority of 102-101. It is impossible to hold that majority on every issue. This means that the eventual Democratic leadership team will need to work with their colleagues across the aisle regularly.

How about starting now? It wouldn't hurt to see a demonstration of bipartisanship coming from the new leaders in the Pennsylvania House of

Representatives that address the current situation in a fair, adult way. Citizens count on both parties to move beyond current squabbles to real governing. Let's get to it.

CHRISTMAS GIFTS

DECEMBER 23, 2022

Most of us know the story of Benjamin Franklin's encounter with a Philadelphian after the final draft of the U.S. Constitution was made public. "What have you given us, Dr. Franklin?" was the question. The wise old statesman responded, "A republic if you can keep it." During this season of giving, it is worth remembering that Franklin and the other founders did give the world a great gift. The American experiment in representative democracy was the epitome of what great thinkers had in mind dating back to Plato himself. But like most things of great value, there is a price to pay for keeping our gift safe and effective.

The Constitution itself prescribes the oath of office for all who would take up the mantle of leadership in our system of government. It requires that the president "faithfully execute the office of President of the United States, and [. . .] to the best of my ability, preserve, protect and defend the Constitution of the United States." Likewise, senators and representatives swear they "will support and defend the Constitution of the United States against all enemies, foreign and domestic."

So, what happens when a domestic threat comes in the form of our chief executive who simply ignores his oath, his duty to the Constitution, and the cherished tradition of the peaceful transfer of power? The answer is in the original assertion of our freedom from the English throne. The Declaration of Independence says, "Governments are instituted among Men, deriving their just powers from the consent of the governed." In other words, the people govern and must step up when their republic is at stake. In that spirit, the January 6th Committee has presented its findings to the U.S. Department of Justice. They have said, on behalf of the people they represent, that no man is above the law and that the Constitution shall be protected. Whatever happens next, Americans should recognize the solemnity of the moment and the importance of "we the people" willing to protect the republic.

This year, another great gift bestowed on America was the affirmation that citizens could and will act to assure order and reason in even the most raucous political environments. The midterm elections showed voters could see through the posturing, even when driven by millions of dollars of dark money. The people themselves chose to reset America's focus to tamp down inflammatory demagoguery. It remains to be seen how newly elected officials will behave in the coming year, but they would do well to heed the clear call for compromise and effective bipartisan leadership once again.

This year, my Christmas reading list included Jon Meacham's extraordinary work on the brilliance and character of President Abraham Lincoln. In *And There Was Light*, Meacham explores the trials and triumphs of our sixteenth president and extracts vital lessons for our times. Lincoln emerges as an imperfect man able to overcome his challenges and shortcomings because of a moral compass that was steady and unshakable.

The stakes for Lincoln could not have been higher. The fate of the Union, the survival of democracy itself, and the future of slavery hung in the balance. Today's hyper-partisanship seems trivial to the righteous fury that both North and South brought to their causes. The Confederacy believed that history and God himself favored the South. Lincoln confronted the nation's sin of slavery and the fracturing of the country head-on. The conflict that ensued would take hundreds of thousands of lives and push the nation to the edge of oblivion.

Emerging from that conflagration, Lincoln could have taken a hard line against his opponents. He could have extended his battle-tested mandate to the halls of Congress and beyond. Instead, he welcomed all citizens to reconstruct the country together. In the most gracious words ever uttered by an American statesman, Lincoln said, "With malice toward none, with charity toward all [. . .] let us strive on to finish the work we are in; to bind up the nation's wounds, to care for him who shall have borne the battle [. . .] to achieve and cherish a just, and a lasting peace among ourselves and with all nations."

Lincoln brought light out of the darkness. We should all be grateful for that gift. We can only hope for that caliber of leadership from our current leaders.

A TALE OF TWO CONGRESS MEMBERS

DECEMBER 30, 2022

On January 13, 2021, the U.S. House of Representatives faced a decision regarding a rogue president who decided that he would ignore the will of the people and hold onto his office through any legal or illegal means available. This included pressuring state and local officials to find votes for him, asking the Department of Justice to proclaim the election corrupt, and inciting a mob of supporters to attack the Capitol to derail the count of presidential electors.

The House's decision in early 2021 was whether to impeach the president for these actions. Adam Kinzinger, an up-and-coming Republican from Illinois, considered the vote a "no-brainer." He was sure that the House would impeach on a bipartisan basis and send the matter to the Senate for trial. In interviews following the vote, Kinzinger confided that as many as two dozen of his Republican colleagues had indicated their outrage with the disgruntled president and rejected his Big Lie. When the roll was called, Kinzinger looked around and found only nine Republican colleagues who shared his outrage that the Constitution had been trampled upon.

The rest of them had a variety of reasons for their vote. Some thought it unnecessary to subject a president to an impeachment trial when he was going out the door anyway. Some admitted they feared retribution from MAGA extremists who would primary them in the next election.

Kinzinger was having none of it. He excoriated Republicans for bowing to Trump and his Big Lie. He joined the January 6th Committee in presenting real-time evidence of a wide-ranging plot to derail a presidential election. He never wavered from speaking his truth--knowing full well that it could cost him his political career.

Today, Kinzinger remains a rare example of political courage. He is trying to wean voters back from their hyper-partisan positions so that truth and progress can prevail again. The key to democracy, says Kinzinger, "is to recognize that the majority of people are in the nuanced middle." He has also said that allegiance to Donald Trump has cost the Republican Party its moral authority.

As Kinzinger departs the scene, Representative-elect George Santos (R-NY) is about to take the oath of office. Even before he is sworn in, Santos is under investigation by the U.S. Attorney's office in New York and Nassau County for possible crimes committed regarding his finances and false statements in his campaign and official disclosure documents. While the investigations are in their early stages, one spokesperson said Mr. Santos's fabrications are "nothing short of stunning."

Santos said that he worked at Citigroup and Goldman Sachs. He didn't. Santos claimed to have graduated from Baruch College. He didn't. Santos supposedly lent his campaign $700,000. It is unclear whether that money was his own or prohibited corporate funds. In fact, Santos has admitted that he never made enough money to afford to take that loan.

There have been a few voices raised to object to Santos's behavior. *The New York Times* reported that one of his former supporters said, "He cheated. He intentionally put out that information knowing that it would persuade voters like me to vote for him." Santos's local party chairman said he expected "more than just an apology."

But the Republican leadership in Washington appears ready to seat George Santos despite blatant lies and possible corruption on the campaign trail. This is because the road to the Speakership for Kevin McCarthy includes counting every single Republican in his corner. The extreme House Freedom Caucus has already demanded Committee chairmanships and other shared powers. Radical vitriol from Far Right characters like Marjorie Taylor Green (R-GA), Lauren Bobert (R-CO), Louie Gomert (R-TX), and Jim Jordan (R-OH) is not only tolerated; they are rewarded. Adding George Santos to their ranks may be a complete violation of the responsibility to uphold the standards of the U.S. House of Representatives, but it serves the purpose of attaining power for power's sake.

The tale of two Congress members in January 2023 should give us concern for the quality of leadership in Washington and for the effect that it may have on democracy itself. Adam Kinzinger sacrificed himself because of his personal ethics and his commitment to the truth. George Santos arrives in Washington under a cloud of falsehoods and no apparent moral guideposts.

In the end, "we the people" allow this leadership decay to occur. Better leaders require more informed voters. At the very least, we need to reward courage above partisanship and reject blatant opportunism when we see it.

PART FIVE

2023 ARTICLES

SPORTSMANSHIP AND STATESMANSHIP

JANUARY 6, 2023

At this writing, the U.S. House of Representatives is tied up in knots by a handful of Far-Right dissidents who have decided to hijack the Republican Party for their purposes. Even if the logjam is broken in favor of Kevin McCarthy, the new Speaker will find himself in a legislative straitjacket that will require constant groveling to a rebellious faction. If the new Republican majority cannot achieve consensus in its ranks, it is highly unlikely that there will be bipartisan consensus on anything in the next two years.

It is time for political leaders to take a lesson from contestants in a different arena. In every NFL game, warriors wage a battle that involves gritty combat in the trenches and dangerous feats of physical prowess at high speeds. After every one of these contests, the generals and soldiers meet on the field of battle to acknowledge the efforts of their opponents, battered and bruised as they are.

After attending a Rose Bowl viewing party with some die-hard Penn State fans, I settled in to catch the Bengals/Bills game. The scene was shocking. Both teams encircled a player in serious condition to allow some privacy as EMTs frantically applied CPR. An ambulance stood by to provide immediate attention to Buffalo Bills player Damar Hamlin who was whisked off to the hospital, where he was listed in critical condition.

What happened on the field and in the country next matters. Bengals coach Zac Taylor walked across the field to console the other team and to consult with Bills coach Sean McDermott. Coach McDermott said, "I need to be at the hospital with Damar, and I shouldn't be coaching this game." In short order, both coaches, their teams, the NFL, and 60,000 fans put one player's life above the game itself.

Another coach opened his weekly press conference fighting back tears. Mike Tomlin of the Pittsburgh Steelers noted that he has known Damar Hamlin "since he was about twelve years old." He noted that football matters a lot less when lives are at stake.

One columnist said, "All of this shows that humanity is often hidden under helmets."

In McKees Rocks, PA, the hometown of Damar Hamlin, "get well" banners hung from buildings, and hundreds of school children took time to send cards. A longtime family friend said: "It's not just football. He's a human being. He's one of us."

In his adopted town of Buffalo, NY, Hamlin created a special charity to provide toys for needy children and saw donations go from about $30,000 to over $5,000,000. And across the country, friends and fans joined together to express genuine concern that transcended the importance of any football game.

As Damar Hamlin fights for his life, he has the assurance that America is with him. It doesn't matter what his team affiliation was. It doesn't matter that he fought as hard as possible against opponents. The lesson of Damar Hamlin is that we are all on the field together. We should not need life-threatening incidents to remind us of this human fact.

This is why the nattering of some political actors is so disappointing. Those who cross their arms and give no consideration to others are violating the basic concepts of our form of government. They are players in an arena much more significant than Sunday football, yet they can't seem to muster the empathy that professional athletes have for one another.

Like football players, Congress members are expected to "leave it on the field." They slug it out on the campaign trail to win elections. They engage in a spirited debate on issues that matter to them and their constituents, and they try their best to advance the philosophies of their team.

The problem occurs when the game becomes more important than the people on the field or in the stands. The current cadre of dissidents in the U.S. House of Representatives is not advancing the cause of the Republican Party or the American people. Instead, they are plunging that chamber into gridlock unless they get to call the plays. It may have crippling consequences for any progress in the legislative session ahead.

Our professional athletes have shown that sportsmanship matters. Our political leaders, whose actions have profound consequences, need to show some statesmanship. *Now.*

JUSTICE FOR VICTIMS

JANUARY 13, 2023

The Pennsylvania Senate has voted to approve a constitutional amendment to open a two-year window for victims of child sexual abuse to file lawsuits that have been derailed by the state's current statute of limitations laws. Pennsylvania has been the epicenter of child sexual abuse since grand juries uncovered extensive criminal behavior in institutional settings more than twenty years ago. Since that time, victims have been silenced on the grounds that the time had simply run out for them to face their abusers in court. Over the years, there have been excruciating delays in addressing the statute of limitations, including political maneuverings, protection of the powerful interests involved, and a massive error by the PA Department of State that stopped a ballot initiative from getting before the voters two years ago.

The Senate action would put the issue on track for resolution by voters in the May primary election. Or would it?

In yet another paper cut inflicted on the SOL initiative, Senate Bill 1 lumped the language for the constitutional amendment in with two other completely unrelated ballot initiatives. In addition to SOL reform, Republicans are attempting to push through a voter identification requirement and restrict the governor's authority over certain regulations. The bill that is now before the House contains not one but three constitutional amendment questions that muddy the political waters in Harrisburg and will confuse voters in May.

Professor Marci Hamilton, CEO of ChildUSA, a national think tank for child protection, outlined the danger of including three constitutional amendments in one bill: "Under Pennsylvania law, a constitutional amendment is supposed to be passed with identical language twice in consecutive and separate sessions in both Houses. Senate Bill 1 raises the question [of] whether the same language was passed twice. The first time it was the window by itself. This time it's three sets of amendment language. That could be fatal to the window because the first time they voted, the bill was only the window language."

Also, Pennsylvania has a single-subject rule for legislation. Voter ID, governor veto, and window amendments are not remotely related. In fact, a case pending before the Commonwealth Court challenges any bundling of constitutional amendments on the grounds that it violates this rule. In short, the format could invalidate all the ballot questions and delay justice for hundreds of victims who have been waiting for twenty years for their day in court.

The solution is simple: individually vote on the constitutional amendments and send them to the voters as three distinct questions.

Things are not simple in Pennsylvania, however. Senate Republicans believe that their best chance of achieving forced voter identification and curtailing the governor's power is to latch on to the momentum of the child sexual abuse issue. This may be a clever political strategy, but it is highly dangerous and threatens twenty years of effort to revise the antiquated statutes of limitation on litigating child sexual abuse. It may provide the poison pill necessary to stop statutes of limitation reform altogether.

Representative Mark Rozzi (D-Berks) has been a strong proponent of SOL reform. He is also the Speaker of the House and has vowed that the first order of business will be the SOL constitutional language—unencumbered by other amendments. Representative Jim Gregory (R-Blair) was critical of his party and said, "What they're trying to do, in my opinion, is use victims as pawns in a political game, and I'm not going to pay that."

And now, here is yet another boulder on the tracks to justice for victims: the House is at a standstill. Republicans currently have a razor-thin majority (101-99), but, despite Rozzi maintaining that he will operate as an independent Speaker, Republicans are already suspicious that he will side with the Democrats on important items like House rules and chairmanships. This has resulted in confusion that may not be resolved until after special elections fill three vacant seats and resolve the question of House control.

It is unacceptable for internal politics or crafty legislating to delay justice for victims of sexual abuse by one more day. For the constitutional amendment to appear on the ballot in May, the legislature must act by the end of this month. The governor's special session could be the forum to get this done. If both parties are as concerned about victims' rights as they say they are, they will seize the moment and put their concerns aside for this critical moment. If not, victims will be victimized by the political process yet again.

THE DEBT CEILING AND WILLFUL IGNORANCE

JANUARY 20, 2023

In 1957, producers at the British Broadcasting Corporation decided to test the willful ignorance of their viewers. The idea was to see how quickly people would buy into pure fantasy if it were what they wanted to believe. On April Fool's Day, a respected broadcaster narrated footage of a family harvesting spaghetti from trees. The fictional family was trying to produce the perfect texture and length of pasta and, indeed, were suggesting that spaghetti could, literally, grow on trees. The next day, television stations across Great Britain were flooded with calls from viewers with questions about how to start cultivating their own spaghetti trees.

Shortly after the great swindling of pasta lovers, Isaac Asimov wrote, "There is a cult of ignorance in the United States, and there has always been. The strain of anti-intellectualism has been a constant thread in our political and cultural life, nurtured by the false notion that democracy means that 'my ignorance is just as good as your knowledge." In fact, willful ignorance is identified in courts and psychology as a bad-faith decision to avoid becoming informed about something.

Such is the current argument over the United States debt limit. When we hit our debt limit of $31.4 trillion this week, the new majority in the U.S. House of Representatives made it clear that they would oppose raising the limit and grind the federal government to a halt. This is supposed to signal to their base that they are fighting to reduce spending.

They know better.

They know that increasing the debt is not about reducing future spending but about paying the bills we have already incurred. They are leading with bad faith to send their citizens down an angry path of misinformation.

Increasing the debt ceiling, which has happened seventy-eight times since the 1960s, is simply America's way of acknowledging that it will pay its debts. To use a real example, every household in America that has borrowed money to buy a home knows that it can't simply walk away from making its monthly mortgage payments. The bank would take their house! Likewise, America has made spending commitments that it must honor or face serious consequences. Moody's Analytics released a report that said a default would immediately decline our Gross Domestic Product and wreak havoc on stocks and IRAs, leading to a $15 trillion loss in household wealth.

Just as spaghetti doesn't grow on trees, playing politics with the debt ceiling will not affect government spending in any way. Those who claim that, somehow, freezing the debt ceiling will somehow reduce spending are deliberately misleading us. The fact is that government spending programs are determined each year through the appropriations processes. The time for putting the brakes on spending is when Congress debates funding for defense, Social Security, Medicare, infrastructure, tax cuts, and other priorities that are on the table. We must pay our bills once the spending levels are approved, and the country's total debt is determined. There are those in Congress who proclaim that they will "rein in reckless spending" or cut government spending by messing with the debt ceiling. No, what they are really saying is they want to reduce our country to a deadbeat nation that doesn't pay its creditors or fund vital services that Congress has already approved.

The Treasury Department has already said that it will take accounting measures to buy some time for Congress to come to its senses, but it's clear that the full faith and credit of the United States is on the line as craven Congress members grandstand on the issue.

Let us remember that both Democrats and Republicans ran up the national debt. The Democrats have expanded spending programs while the Republicans have spent billions on tax cuts for the wealthy. Both parties pushed for large recovery packages after the 2008 financial crisis and the lingering pandemic. It would be appropriate for both parties to take a more cautious approach to spending in the years to come. But taking a wrecking ball to the world's economy by tampering with the nation's current obligations is deliberately stupid.

It is the responsibility of every elected official to act responsibly. Some are choosing to score political points with rhetoric that they know is deceptive because they believe in the willful ignorance of their voters. Most of us know that spaghetti doesn't grow on trees, however. Most of us expect better from our elected officials.

RISING ABOVE CYNICISM

FEBRUARY 27, 2023

Recent polls show that President Biden's favorability rating has risen to the highest level of his presidency. It is worth noting that the surveys were conducted after what most observers believed was a strong State of the Union message and a bold wartime visit to Ukraine. It is also noteworthy that Biden's numbers are higher than his immediate predecessor but lagging behind presidents of other eras.

While Biden hovers at around a 50 percent favorable rating, he is nowhere near the numbers achieved by presidents who faced similar foreign and domestic challenges. George W. Bush, for example, rode a wave of popular support post-9/11. In February of 2002, he stood at 80 percent in the polls. Similarly, George H.W. Bush had solid support when he led an international effort to free Kuwait from Iraq and Saddam Hussein. Going back a few years, Dwight Eisenhower enjoyed a long honeymoon with voters who remembered and rewarded his service as the commander who delivered us from Naziism in World War II. Even John Kennedy, who had endured a humiliating defeat at the Bay of Pigs, got a reprieve from the voters that put his numbers in the seventies.

Like wartime leaders before him, Joe Biden has taken on responsibilities that most of us cannot even imagine. The daily barrage of news from the Ukraine battlefields and the jaw-dropping barbarity of Vladimir Putin's war crimes would be enough to wear down any leader. Instead, Biden put himself in personal jeopardy to visit Kyiv and pledge America's unwavering support for preserving democracy. While visiting President Zelensky and securing support from every NATO colleague, he was also engaged with Latin American leaders to begin a meaningful dialog about real immigration reform. By the way, his administration has shown real progress in getting inflation under control and announced the best job numbers we have seen in fifty years. In fact, his infrastructure program has already begun to put millions of Americans back to work and is lifting us confidently out of the pandemic era.

So why are his numbers not soaring? When does he get his George W. Bush rally? Why does he not get credit for a string of victories that rival those of Lyndon Johnson and Franklin Roosevelt? Maybe a more basic question is why are Americans incapable of full-throated support for a wartime president who needs the country to have his back?

One need only look at the circus of hyper-partisanship in the U.S. Congress for the answer. Marjorie Taylor Greene is calling for states to secede from the Union. Newly minted Republican leaders are more interested in hearing about Hunter Biden's laptop than securing world peace. Speaker Kevin McCarthy seems bent on twisting the truth by releasing the entire video record of the January 6 investigation exclusively to Fox News. In other words, we live in an age more interested in political theater than in shouldering the burden of responsibility in a crushingly real theater of war.

Politics has always been a part of our system of governance. It is healthy for points of view to be raised and debated on the campaign trail and in the halls of Congress. But what has happened to that discourse lately is decidedly unhealthy. When party leaders ignore reality and choose their narratives instead, we are in trouble.

A country that features a party unwilling to accept election results is teetering on the edge of collapse. It becomes easy for voters to villainize the other side with absurd attacks tinged with racism, fear, and any other weapon that shallow politicians choose to wield. It seems to me that American citizens have a duty to reach beyond politics during wartime. When democracy is at stake, at home and abroad, the American experiment needs to shine, not falter.

I support the president's high-stakes effort to stare down Putin and authoritarianism. I believe that most Americans are fair, reasonable, and patriotic and will do the same.

If we want to call ourselves patriots, we owe it to ourselves to act like Americans.

OF LIONS AND LEMMINGS

MARCH 3, 2023

Some people Wordle. Some do Sudoku puzzles. I like to thumb through the thesaurus occasionally to find unusual synonyms or artful phrases. To me, one of the most interesting language diversions is the appreciation of collective nouns. The most poetic I have found is an "exaltation of larks." But there are a number of other definitions of animals that are equally beautiful. An "arc of doves," for example. Or a "memory of elephants," a "tuxedo of penguins."

There are less flattering nouns for more threatening animals. Consider a "pounce of cats;" or the common "murder of crows."

The annual convening of the Conservative Political Action Conference (CPAC) reminds us that there are humans who band together in a way that can send one to the reference books to find the right words to describe their collective actions. For some time now, the conference has been less about actual conservative values and more about showcasing a Far Right agenda. Just a few years ago, CPAC served as a springboard that helped launch the candidacies of thought leaders in the conservative movement. People like Ronald Regan, George H.W. Bush, and Jack Kemp brought thoughtful input to the proceedings. As one GOP observer said, "It was the place to be." The reality is that CPAC has become a noisy pep rally for Trumpism and for those candidates who will take to the podium to profess their MAGA credentials.

Yes, the keynote is reserved for Donald J. Trump, who will likely air all his grievances to an enthusiastic audience. We all know that he continues defying reality by claiming that the 2020 election was stolen and that he will somehow reclaim the White House escorted by his loyal skulk of foxes. A pretty good collective noun, no? There will be others who take the podium with their own brand of Trumpism. Look for Kari Lake to whine that she is the actual Governor of Arizona. Expect a series of speakers like Representative Matt Gaetz (R-FL), Senator Ted Cruz (R-FL), and Senator Josh Hawley (R-MO) to spin their versions of reality with a generous dose of vitriol aimed directly at Joe Biden.

One participant took an interesting turn en route to the annual shouting match. Representative Marjorie Taylor Greene (R-GA) let the country know that President Biden was personally responsible for the fentanyl death of two young men from California. It did not seem to matter that they died in early 2020—during Donald Trump's presidency. Greene has become a fountain of misinformation and dangerous rhetoric. She is the first member of Congress since the Civil War to openly suggest secession—splitting the country into red and blue states. Expect that level of absurdity from the CPAC podium throughout the conference.

Still, there is a glimmer of hope that things could be a little different this year. Many possible presidential candidates are not attending. For example, former Vice President Mike Pence is heading to an exclusive fundraiser sponsored by the Club for Growth. Governor Glenn Youngkin of Virginia and Governor Kristi Noem of South Dakota have tried to distance themselves from the dogma of Trumpism. They are also distancing themselves from CPAC this year.

At this writing, neither Speaker Kevin McCarthy nor any Republican governors will be addressing the group. Former Governor Nikki Haley (R-SC) is the only other credible presidential candidate who will be speaking.

Make no mistake; the event has been transformed from an exchange of ideas into a pep rally for Trump and Trumpism. That's why the MAGA faithful will hear from the likes of "pillow man" Mike Lindell and conspiracy theorist Representative Lauren Boebert (R-CO). It is also why a good percentage of reasonable Republicans are tuning out.

Strategists are beginning to take a hard look at the numbers. If nothing else, the midterm election vote demonstrated Trump fatigue among many Republicans. The emergence of moderates and the surprising showing of Democrats in key battleground states should make it clear that the route to the White House involves a reasonable platform of issues that resonate with voters—not the mechanical adherence to a dogma that could well lead them off a political cliff. Interestingly, one linguist has coined a collective noun that might apply here: a suicide of lemmings. The Republican Party needs to find its footing beyond the CPAC pep rally. Both parties should be willing to enter the fray of the coming presidential election cycle like a pride of lions.

THIS JUST IN: BEETHOVEN'S HAIR

MARCH 24, 2023

What do you do if you're facing three grand jury investigations and a Department of Justice probe by a Special Prosecutor? If you're Donald Trump, you tell your supporters that you are about to be arrested and that you expect them to be at his beck and call once again. It turns out that the prediction of his demise was premature, but once again, the con job worked. Trump dominated the news cycles for an entire week and raised millions from the MAGA world.

This column is not about Trump; it's about Ludwig van Beethoven—a man who will be remembered for his positive contributions to mankind.

Beethoven is my go-to guy when I think about achievements, and widely considered the greatest composer of all time. He is a crucial transitional figure in the development of Western music. Beethoven's body of musical compositions stands with Shakespeare's plays at the extreme limits of human accomplishment. In the early 1800s, he composed an opera, six symphonies, four solo concerti, five string quartets, six string sonatas, seven piano sonatas, five sets of piano variations, four overtures, four trios, two sextets, and seventy-two songs. Beethoven composed most of these extraordinary works while going deaf. In fact, he was functionally deaf by the time he reached forty-five years old. This is an unparalleled feat of creative genius, perhaps only comparable to John Milton's *Paradise Lost* (Milton wrote this while blind).

Some quick notes about the impact of his work: In 1918, German prisoners of war bolstered morale by singing Beethoven's "Ode to Joy." Their Japanese captors were impressed and called the music "*Daiku,*" meaning "the great song." Years later, the European Union declared the song its official anthem, and years after that, NASA included Beethoven's Fifth Symphony on the

Golden Record that was launched into space on Voyager One. If humans were to present their finest art to any new species, it might as well come from the genius of Beethoven.

This week, Beethoven was still making news. A study published in *Current Biology* noted a host of other ailments that beset the composer based on DNA obtained from samples of his hair. After two hundred years, scientists complied with Beethoven's request that his health challenges—including hearing loss—be investigated and shared with the public. While the study about Beethoven's hearing is inconclusive, it released some interesting findings: the maestro had liver disease and severe Hepatitis B. This condition was exacerbated by heavy alcohol consumption. After analyzing chromosomes from living descendants, scientists determined that they do not match those of Beethoven. Sometime before Beethoven's birth, there was what scientists call an "extra pair paternity event." In other words, someone had an affair that resulted in an illegitimate child—maybe Beethoven himself, an interesting tidbit that might someday shed light on where his extraordinary gifts really came from.

Beethoven died at the age of fifty-six. Even the folklore about his final hours is compelling. It seems that a flash of lightning shook the dying man out of a two-day coma. As though conducting for the last time, Beethoven lifted his right arm to the percussion of the thunderstorm. When the drums subsided, he fell back and died.

Most historians believe Beethoven's last recorded words were, "Pity, pity, too late!" Some have suggested that he was talking about a late inspiration that came to him before he could translate it into music. Others believe he was lamenting that medical care was too little and too late to save him, or he longed for the vice that may have compromised his health since his manager had sent twelve bottles of his favorite wine, and Beethoven would not have the time to enjoy them.

After two hundred years, the world still trembles at the power of Beethoven's genius. The fact that the simple analysis of his hair can make news today demonstrates that humans can produce and admire greatness through the generations. It also gives some of us a pleasant respite from the obsession with lesser men. For those as tired as I am of the non-stop babble of certain self-absorbed charlatans, it's time to tune them out and listen to the truth of Beethoven's "Symphony No. 9." The "Ode to Joy" matters and will remain significant long after the froth of today's politics.

DO SOMETHING

MARCH 31, 2023

There is a good chance that nearly half of you will not finish reading this article. Poll after poll says that citizens have become numb to the horror of classroom killings. If there ever was any outrage, it is being replaced by the cold reality that our leaders just don't care. In fact, the response to the murder of more children and teachers at the Covenant School in Tennessee was shockingly cavalier from some Republicans. "Congress can't do anything about it," said one particularly craven weasel. Many of the people we elected to office at the federal and state level are cowards. They continue to put gun ownership rights over our children's safety, and the worst part is that citizens accept their rhetoric and continue to elect them.

If you are still with me, thank you. I would like to reward you with an idea or two to do something about gun violence in schools. First, understand the urgency of this cause. *The Associated Press* did a grim roll call of the students whose lives ended in what they thought was their safe place, their place of learning. There have been 175 kids killed in classrooms since Columbine. We have suffered through thirteen mass shootings in classrooms since the beginning of this year. That's one massacre per week. Another sickening reality is that gunfire has become the leading cause of death among children. Not cancer, not car crashes—guns.

Roy S. Johnson of the *Alabama Media Group* said, "We love our guns more than we love our children [. . .]. Oh, we feel. We hurt. Our stomachs go weak. Our hearts skip when we learn of yet another godawful killing spree [. . .]. Yet we don't care."

More to the point, our elected representatives don't care. Representative Andy Ogles (R-TN) represents the Nashville district where Covenant School is located. He let us know that he was "utterly heartbroken" and offered his "thoughts and prayers." He has also steadfastly opposed any effort to enact background checks or to keep assault weapons out of the hands of potential murderers. In fact, he and his family have posed for their Christmas card wielding automatic weapons. Nothing says "Merry Christmas" like glorifying the tools of death.

Now, put yourself in the shoes of that parent who waited for their nine-year-old son or daughter to come home from school only to be told that an AR-15 assault weapon ripped through his or her tiny body. Parents have a right to their outrage. We all have a responsibility to join them in their grief and efforts to make our kids safe.

There are now more guns in America than people. It is also true that many gun owners twist the 2nd Amendment into a blanket justification for them to gather as wide a variety of guns as they can stuff into their display cases. They would not take kindly to any effort to take those weapons away. Politicians are not about to change their pro-gun positions. They rely on generous funding from the gun lobby when campaign time comes around. Clearly, the only way to counteract the gun lobby is to be direct with every candidate seeking our vote. Ask them, "Do you support common-sense gun safety legislation?" Do not vote for anyone who cannot answer that question with a simple "Yes."

And what are some of those common-sense ideas? First, universal background checks. It should be a given that anyone purchasing a gun should be vetted for any prior criminal record and for any impairments that could make them dangerous. Second, aggressive red-flag laws in every state. These allow citizens to alert authorities if they believe a current gun owner has shown violent tendencies. Most killers have tipped their hands on social media platforms or in other settings and should be reported to the courts or law enforcement before they gun down children. Third, raise the age to purchase guns to at least eighteen. Kids should not be anywhere near firearms until they demonstrate the maturity to handle a deadly weapon. Age limits aren't imperfect, but they are a start. Finally, proper weapons storage and appropriate gun safety training should be mandatory.

The next time your Congress member or state senator tries to hide behind the 2nd Amendment, tell them that these are some common-sense actions they can take immediately. When they talk about thoughts and prayers for our dead children, tell them to do something about it, for God's sake.

THE POLITICAL FALLOUT FROM A FLAILING PRESIDENT

APRIL 7, 2023

In a story that appeared in *The Wall Street Journal* last week, Joe Wolf, a key operative for the Arizona Democratic Party, was asked which candidate he would prefer to run against in the 2024 election. "Donald Trump, hands down," said Wolf. "He's combustible. He's undisciplined—he's been beaten before. I think the country is over him."

Another Democrat agreed, saying, "If I had a choice, I'd say I'd rather have a sane candidate running who [upholds] the Constitution, doesn't perpetuate the Big Lie, didn't participate in the insurrection." It's not just Democrats rejecting Trump and his antics; a recent CNN poll showed that 62 percent of independent voters—a key demographic in any presidential race—approve of the indictment brought by the New York district attorney.

Of course, the Republicans continue to put on a brave face. The Republican National Committee spokesperson said, "The eventual Republican nominee will beat Biden, full stop." Really? We already know that the critical, independent vote leans heavily toward President Biden in any match with prospective GOP candidates. We also know that the country has taken a decided turn away from the Far-Right doctrine in recent elections.

Then take a look at Kansas, where citizens in August of last year overwhelmingly rejected a referendum to outlaw abortion rights. Kansas was the first state to vote on abortion rights since the U.S. Supreme Court handed down its ruling in Dobbs, and the state's voters made their voices heard.

The Republican Party has talked a big game about individual liberty and freedom, but Kansas showed that it is the Democrats who can seize that mantle.

This includes not only women's rights but the freedom to vote without hysterical losers claiming fraud.

In other words, Kansas set the tone for the midterm elections, where right wing Trump zealots abounded on the Republican side. Sure enough, 2022 saw a wholesale rejection of those candidates and confirmed what began in Kansas. It was a return to logic and moderation.

Just last week in Wisconsin, the progressive candidate for the state Supreme Court won decisively over a right-winger who spouted the company line on Dobbs. He also represented a continuation of Republican control over the critical redistricting issue. The voters knew that he would enable the GOP to run roughshod over Democrats in coming elections, and they rejected him.

This brings us up to date on the ongoing circus surrounding an indicted ex-president.

Watching the parade of Republican candidates scurrying to coddle Trump is bewildering. We have seen Senator Lindsey Graham (R-SC) sobbing on the cable networks and begging the MAGA world to support a legal defense fund (never mind that the ex-president brags about his net worth and flies to and from his indictments on his jet). We have seen craven politicians like George Santos (R-NY) and Matt Goetz (R-FL) attest to the character of a man accused of paying off a porn star to hide his misdeeds from voters just weeks before a presidential election. We have heard from Marjorie Taylor Greene (R-GA), who had the audacity to compare the indicted ex-president to Jesus Christ. Collectively, these antics range from outrageous to blasphemous.

Note also the recent proposals put forth by Republican leaders to defund the police. That's right, to derail the criminal justice system, some would be willing to cripple the FBI and the Department of Justice. Even that would not stop prosecutors from doing their jobs. The continued painstaking review of Trump's activities relating to January 6, the presidential documents, and his potential meddling in the Georgia vote count prove that America still believes we remain a nation of laws.

The never-ending saga of chaos in Trump's world is wearing thin on the electorate. Sure, the hard-core right wing will rally behind a wounded and howling leader. This will likely bump up his poll numbers in the short-term, but it will turn off the swing voters he would need in November 2024. Indeed, a Quinnipiac poll taken before Mr. Trump's indictment found that 57 percent of Americans thought Mr. Trump should be disqualified from running again.

The legal problems of the ex-president will soon get much worse. The reaction from even his most loyal supporters must surely turn into Trump fatigue. The larger universe of all American voters—the people who will elect the new president in 2024—has already moved on.

TRUTH MATTERS

APRIL 7, 2023

A Scottish writer named Charles MacKay wrote a bestseller in the 1840s titled *Extraordinary Popular Delusions and the Madness of Crowds.* The book points out that sometimes reality is just a trend that sweeps over the population. It's not based on truth; it's based on whichever leader or faction has the loudest megaphone at the time.

Two quick examples: Europeans thought of the tomato as a poison apple. In the late 1700s, there were some unexplained deaths among the aristocracy after consuming tomatoes, so the entire society stopped eating them. It turns out that the acidity of tomatoes absorbed the high lead content of the pewter plates then in use, and these well-to-do diners were actually dying of lead poisoning. Fortunately, this discovery was made just in time for the invention of pizza in Italy.

In terms of fashion, King Louis XIV began wearing a cravat around his neck in the mid-seventeenth century. This started a fashion craze that has evolved into the less complicated but equally irrelevant tie that businessmen wear today. Ties have no purpose whatsoever. We wear them just because everybody does it.

The madness of crowds takes a serious turn when we are fed a diet of lies and begin to accept them as truth. There is an actual term for it called the illusory truth effect. This is when we hear the same false information (tomatoes are poison, ties are required) repeated so often that we come to believe it is true. Even when we know better, political campaigns, the internet, and commercial advertising seep into our brains as truth. This phenomenon is so toxic that it blurs our common sense. Some of us become so caught up in the fantasy that we cannot accept the truth even when it stares us in the face.

As we work through the never-ending saga of an ex-president with unprecedented legal woes, we should all be interested in ferreting out the truth. It does us no good to hide behind misguided loyalties or accept the notion that the whole criminal justice system is corrupt. This would be like attacking umpires every time our team loses a baseball game.

Yes, Donald Trump is entitled to the presumption of innocence. But he is not entitled to stir up an angry mob or to tell all of us, "Look away. There's nothing to see here." In the coming months, Trump will likely face serious charges in four separate jurisdictions. Our legal system is fair and strong enough to separate facts from fiction. Attacking district attorneys, judges, and anyone else seeking the truth undermines a critical component of our American way of life. What's worse is that a component of the population has shown itself willing to resort to violence to tilt the scales of justice in their favor. The district attorney in New York is getting suspicious packages in the mail. The judge and his family continue to get death threats.

Trump himself has ignored the judge's directive to avoid stirring up his followers. Instead, he revels in the indictment. He raises money from it. He continues his stream of invective against his accusers and is doing his best to inflict his opinions on folks who might end up as jurors in his case. Worse, he has already shown that he can energize an unruly mob, whether it means storming the Capitol building or fighting indictments brought by legitimate grand juries and authorities. The judge in New York has taken great pains to avoid infringing on an ex-president's right to free speech. It is unclear if the continuing diatribe from Trump's social media postings and other ramblings will result in some gag order so that the proceedings can move forward in an orderly fashion that is fair to the accused and the accusers. In other words, the judge may need to step in to ensure that the madness of crowds does not drown out the truth.

As for the rest of us, critical thinking and fact-checking have never been more important. Neil deGrasse Tyson, a leading authority on astrophysics and human nature, said, "The good thing about science is that it's true whether or not you believe in it." He also said that "Ignorance is a virus. Once it starts spreading, it can only be cured by reason. For the sake of humanity, we must be that cure."

We can all benefit from that perspective, whether or not we eat tomatoes or wear ties.

A VISIT TO COAL TOWNSHIP

MAY, 26, 2023

Coal Township is located deep in the hills of Northumberland County, Pennsylvania. It takes it name from the once thriving anthracite industry that built the hard-scrabble community and others like it in the north central part of the state. Today, it is tucked away between green mountains in a beautiful setting that can have a calming effect on travelers. That sense of tranquility is shattered the moment that you see the double fencing of barbed wire surrounding the perimeter of the State Correctional Institution at Coal Township.

The population at the facility includes 50 inmates currently serving life sentences without the possibility of parole. In an extraordinary effort to share their stories with policy makers, the lifers organized a seminar on criminal justice and invited key leaders to join them for a day. Led by Robert Pezzeca and Derrick Stevens, two inmates who are serving maximum sentences for capital crimes, the seminar presented an opportunity for legislators and state officials to hear directly from prisoners about the impact of Pennsylvania's severe sentencing laws and the need for some measure of compassion in our pardons' process.

Key figures like Lieutenant Governor Austin Davis, Secretary of Corrections Designee Laurel Harry, State Senator Sharif Street (D-3), State Senator Camera Bartolotta (R-46), State Senator Nikil Saval (D-1), and former Speaker of the House William DeWeese made the trip to Coal Township and each made poignant remarks about the need for compassion and mercy as we mete out justice in our state.

It was an honor to join this group especially since I am something of a footnote in the history of commutations for life prisoners in Pennsylvania. As Lieutenant Governor, I chaired the Board of Pardons. During the period of

1991-1993, there were 2,600 lifers in our prisons. The Board of Pardons determined that 55 of them had rehabilitated to the point that they were worthy of a second chance in society. Of those 55, the Governor commuted the sentences of only 8. The Commonwealth decided to extend the mercy of freedom to a mere eight out of 2,600 lifers at that time.

One of those eight, Reginald McFadden, was charged with the rape of a New York woman and the murder of another from Long Island. The crimes occurred one month ahead of the 1994 Gubernatorial election in which I had a comfortable lead. My opponent went into full attack mode. After a brutal series of ads that all but charged me with the murders, I saw my campaign and my political career disintegrate.

In 2022 the New York University Law School Center on the Administration of Criminal Law did an extensive review of the history of Pennsylvania's record of granting clemency to prisoners serving life sentences in our jails before and after the McFadden incident. "The Demise of Clemency for Lifers in Pennsylvania" documents the dramatic fall off in commutations. "For a time, the State's harsh sentencing policies were tempered by a practice of commuting several dozen life sentences each year. That changed around 1980, when commutations in Pennsylvania fell off dramatically. The study also says bluntly that the 1994 "crime spree of Reginald McFadden completely derailed the State's clemency system."

The Commonwealth overreacted to the McFadden incidents by choking off commutations. In a special session on crime, the legislature changed the procedures for any lifers to get to a commutation. Specifically, a recommendation to the Governor for commutation now requires a unanimous vote from all five members of the Pardons Board. This has had the effect of making any application a nearly futile exercise.

The numbers bear this out. Governor Shapp commuted 251 lifers between 1971 and 1978. Governor Thornburgh commuted 7 in eight years. Casey commuted 27. Ridge did not commute a single life sentence post-McFadden.

The Senate Judiciary Committee is considering a number of criminal justice reform proposals. SB 197 would restore the four-to-one majority for a recommendation to the Governor. Another bill would allow automatic consideration of a lifer's petition after 25 years of misconduct-free behavior. Other initiatives would address how we deal with terminally ill inmates and abuse victims who have been separated from their families because of harsh mandatory minimum sentences.

I support these initiatives not because I am weak on crime but because I am strong on compassion. For me, mercy and compassion are the antidotes to the fear and hatred that permeates our public discourse today. I know better than most that providing second chances to known criminals is risky. But I prefer that to a society that looks with indifference at those who have turned their lives around and still languish in our overcrowded prisons.

RETHINKING THE DEATH PENALTY

JUNE 1, 2023

Scholars and theologians have been debating capital punishment for years. The modern-day discourse emanates from the U.S. Supreme Court case *Furman v. Georgia* (1972) which declared that the death penalty violated the 8th Amendment that prohibited cruel and unusual punishment. That ruling would be short-lived.

Looking back at that period in our history, and considering capital punishment as public policy, it is hard to overstate the impact that U.S. Supreme Court Justice John Paul Stevens had on the discourse. Stevens was appointed by President Gerald R. Ford in 1975 and began his service with all of the earmarks of a traditional conservative. Early in his career on the bench, the U.S. Supreme Court considered five cases involving capital punishment. Justice Stevens supported the constitutionality of the death penalty in all five decisions. In fact, he provided the decisive fifth vote in *Gregg v. Georgia*, a case that effectively reinstated the death penalty and reversed the *Furman* decision.

At the end of his career, Justice Stevens changed his mind. In 2008, he wrote that "the imposition of the death penalty represents the pointless and needless extinction of life with only marginal contributions to any discernible social or public purposes." He went on to say that capital punishment is a "patently excessive and cruel and unusual punishment violative of the Eighth Amendment." (See Death Penalty Information Center posting on July 17, 2019).

In nationally broadcast interviews, Justice Stevens expressed his personal regret for his vote on *Gregg v. Georgia* and specifically named a death row inmate named Carlos DeLuna as an example of one who was executed even though he was, in Stevens's words, "unquestionably innocent of murder."

Two other public officials weighed in on the death penalty recently. According to the May 23, 2023, Washington Post, former Governors Robert Bentley (R-AL) and Don Sigelman (D-AL) have reflected on their service as Alabama's Chief Executive and both now oppose the death penalty. They point to ongoing prosecutorial misconduct, mistakes in the preparation and presentation of capital cases, and the imbalance of death sentences handed out along racial lines as reasons for their change of hearts.

According to the Washington Post article, the Governors put it directly: "We missed our chance to confront the death penalty and have lived to regret it, but it is not too late for today's elected officials to do the morally right thing."

The U.S. Supreme Court ruled in 2020 that a unanimous verdict is required to sentence someone to death. Despite that, politicians seeking to enhance their "tough on crime" credentials are heading in the opposite direction. Florida Gov. Ron DeSantis (R), is launching his campaign for President after signing a bill that allows juries to recommend death with only an 8-4 vote. On the other side of the spectrum, Governor Josh Shapiro (D-PA) has said that he will not sign a death warrant while he holds the office.

My own wrestling with the morality of capital punishment goes back to my days as Lieutenant Governor of Pennsylvania. In that role, I chaired the Board of Pardons and saw a steady stream of prisoners petitioning for mercy. It was not until I served as Acting Governor that the gravity of imposing a death sentence hit home. There was a of list of prisoners on death row in various stages of litigation. The one that had exhausted all appeals and was recommended to me was the case of Fredric Jacob Jermyn.

His crime was heinous. On December 31, 1985, Jermyn had beaten his own mother into unconsciousness then set her mattress on fire. She died of smoke inhalation. The courts had imposed the death penalty and the Department of Corrections and legal counsel were united in recommending that I sign the death warrant. It is a rare occurrence for any Governor to take pen in hand to end a person's life, but I did so and set a date for his execution at the end of 1993.

Shortly thereafter, Jermyn said in an interview that the execution order was null and void because the Acting Governor had died of complications related to syphilis. These and other pronouncements, including some bizarre poetry that professed he was an agent of God raised the specter that I had imposed the ultimate penalty on someone who was detached from reality.

The Atlantic Center for Capital Representation monitored developments in Jermyn's case and kept in touch with his lawyers. They were able to get a stay of execution and continued to file petitions relating to Jermyn's competence and the effectiveness of his original defense lawyer. After the Pennsylvania courts denied relief, the federal court's Third Circuit stepped in to point out deficiencies in the evidence presented in the original case and in the sentencing procedures. In its findings published on Sept. 21, 2001, the court ruled that "the testimony would have provided the jury with an entirely different view of Jermyn's life and childhood which would have both aided in understanding the seriousness and origin of his mental illness." The Third Circuit ruled that Frederic Jacob Jermyn's sentence should be commuted to life without parole. This was a full eight years after I signed his death warrant.

In the years following my public service, I have come to realize that every capital punishment case is bursting with complexities. The finality of a death sentence ignores those twists and turns and gives society a callous solution—one human is simply eliminated.

I believe that Governor Shapiro and other leaders like Justice John Paul Stevens and Governors Bentley and Sigelman have it right: capital punishment is cruel and unusual and should not be a used as a remedy in civilized society. To those politicians who think that being tough on crime should include putting people to death, I say: think again. I was wrong to sign a death warrant and I regret it to this day.

UKRAINE'S D-DAY

JUNE 9, 2023

Seventy-nine years after D-Day, Ukraine launched its own counteroffensive to push back on the merciless invasion of their country by Russia. Like the original D-Day, the stakes could not be higher. If successful, Ukraine can reclaim at least portions of the territories seized by Putin's forces. It could also expose continued disarray among the invading troops and force Russia to rethink its ruthless aggression. The Ukrainians have shown that they will fight tirelessly for their country. This means that if the current counteroffensive fails, the war will drag on and thousands more will die.

The landings on the Normandy beaches in 1944 stopped Hitler's aggression. Thousands of allied troops not only changed the direction of the war but they ensured a rejection of Naziism and the threat that it posed to our own country and to freedom around the world. The stakes of the battle now raging in Ukraine are identical.

The United States and its allies are heavily invested in Ukraine for a reason. We understand the consequences when a brutal authoritarian seeks unlimited power and conquest. It is in our interest to defend democracy as heroically as the troops did in 1944. It is critical that Ukraine's counteroffensive succeeds.

David Ignatius of the *Washington Post* wrote this about the fight: "If Ukraine can drive back an already shaky Russian army, it stands a chance of forcing Moscow to bargain for an end of its failed invasion. But if Ukraine fails, it would be a bitter blow to the country's weary population and could endanger continued support from some restless NATO members." The whole world is watching. This includes powerful interests in China and elsewhere who may place their bets on Russia if the counteroffensive stalls.

The terrain in this fight is daunting. Russia seems willing and capable of reducing roads, bridges, and dams to rubble in an effort to thwart the opposition. They are heartless enough to sacrifice thousands of their own troops and innocent Ukrainian citizens who are caught in the crossfire.

The barrage of missile attacks and endless bombings of hospitals and schools should be appalling to any rational observer. This past week featured an explosion that wiped out a dam that provided water to hundreds of thousands of families. It also flooded towns and supply routes that were essential to Ukraine's battle strategy. The clear message is that there is no empathy coming from the Kremlin. From the start Putin's invasion has been brutal and relentless. Ukraine is making a bold statement that they have had enough.

We might not know the results of the counteroffensive immediately but there are already signs of progress. Ukrainian forces have returned to pummeled areas along the eastern front and are reclaiming them inch by inch. Reports from the field say that the Russians are losing their tenuous grip on Bakhmut and other towns.

On the home front, there are indications that some political leaders' support for Ukraine is less than robust. With the conclusion of a bipartisan deal on the debt ceiling, some House members are retreating to their ideological corners and balking at new support for the war effort. While the U.S. Senate is proceeding with a supplemental funding bill to aid Ukraine at this critical turning point, budget hawks and far-right members of the House are hesitant.

Speaker McCarthy says that Ukraine support and the entire Defense Budget is locked in by the debt ceiling deal. His position is buttressed by a handful of far-right activists who would cripple the war effort and, in the process, endanger world peace. In a remarkable tale of two houses, the U.S. Senate has found strong, bipartisan support for the Ukrainian cause. The House, on the other hand, is pinned down by ideologues who would rather score political points than face up to the realities of war. Ironically, the loudest anti-funding voices are coming from a faction that calls itself the Freedom Caucus.

As the Ukrainians fight on, we salute their courage. We also remember the sacrifices that they, like the soldiers who came before them, endured. Says David Ignatius: "Any visitor to Omaha Beach in Normandy will recall the steep cliffs at Pointe du Hoc that American Rangers had to scale to dislodge German forces. The grave markers for the soldiers who died on D-Day seem to stretch almost to the horizon. But they won the battle — and the war."

REDEMPTION FOR BLACK SHEEP

JUNE 23, 2023

Hunter Biden is no choir boy. He has admitted to his struggle with drugs. His early years were rocked by the death of his mother and sister in a car accident. His brother died at an early age due to brain cancer and he bore the brunt of constant attacks on him and his family that contributed to reckless behaviors that made the news on a regular basis. He failed to pay taxes in 2017 and 2018 and he obtained a gun permit without disclosing that he was a habitual drug user. Even though he has long since paid those taxes, and even though he is continuing an intensive personal rehabilitation regimen, Hunter Biden has plead guilty to misdemeanor tax offenses and possession of a firearm as a drug user.

He has admitted his guilt and has cooperated fully with authorities. As a result, the U.S. Department of Justice has wrapped up its investigation and recommendation with a recommendation for a two-year probation and continued rehabilitation for Hunter Biden.

But the Republican echo chamber is showing no empathy. "If you are the President's son, you get a sweetheart deal," said Speaker Kevin McCarthy. Candidates Trump and DeSantis were quick to pile on as well. They know better. Failure to pay taxes rarely results in criminal charges. Typically, taxes, fines, and interest arrangements are made with the IRS even in cases that go back many years. One need only look at the latitude that certain businessmen are given. Reporting huge losses and not paying taxes at all seems to be acceptable if you happen to be a Republican standard-bearer.

Possession of a firearm while fighting the demons of drug abuse is troubling. But it is an unfortunate fact that a large percentage of the 340 million guns that exist in this country are in the hands of people who should not own weapons of any kind. An incomplete application for a gun permit is an offense that is not nearly as consequential as, say, stealing and hiding classified documents. The ongoing demonization of Hunter Biden is simply the right-wing clinging to any conspiracy theory that maligns the current President and his family.

What is even more troubling than the blatant partisanship of these attacks is the heartlessness that it exposes. Almost every family I know has a troubled son or daughter who is coping with demons that can be overwhelming. Public families do not have the luxury of dealing with those challenges in private.

When former U.S. Rep. Patrick Kennedy (D-NH) arrived in Congress at the age of 21, he was a rising star with a magic name. A DUI led to revelations about substance abuse and a lifelong struggle with bipolar disorder. Patti Davis, the daughter of President Ronald Reagan, admitted to a drug addiction and publicly opposed many of her father's policies. In both cases, the Kennedys and the Reagans comforted their children and eventually reconciled with them. There was some salacious reporting during their tumultuous years but there was little or no political exploitation of the torment that beset the black sheep. The political rules of engagement included a hands-off policy when it came to troubled family members of either party.

Today's Republican Party doesn't play by those rules. Hunter Biden's misdemeanors are being blown out of proportion by the feverish far right who have sunk their teeth into the matter like dogs with a bone. Next up is Hunter Biden's purported involvement with foreign governments when his father was Vice President. It doesn't matter that no illegalities have been found to date. Even if the inquisition comes up empty, the attackers will have fired an arsenal of weapons in the process.

This is not good government. This is heartless victimization of people who can't fight back. It is also an attempt to draw false comparisons between minor indiscretions and major disruptions in our system of law and order. Hunter Biden admitted his guilt. He repaid all of his taxes and fines and he cooperated fully with investigators and officials. If he is receiving leniency, it is because he did not run and hide from the law.

This is a far cry from those who stand on much larger stages and think they are above the law. Hunter Biden showed that the path to redemption involves humility. This is a quality that seems to be lost on the former President who denies, deludes, and derides anyone who challenges him. The reckoning is coming.

MCCARTHY AND REPUBLICANS NEED TO TAKE A STAND

JUNE 30, 2023

Schuyler Colfax, a cofounder of the Republican Party, served in the House of Representatives during the Civil War. He rose to the position of Speaker and led efforts to support Abraham Lincoln and his policies. His last meeting with Lincoln was on the subject of Reconstruction just hours before the President was assassinated.

By most accounts, Colfax was effective in uniting factions in Congress and winning support for the critical issues of the day. When the 13th amendment, which banned slavery, passed the House on January 31, 1865, House rules did not require that he, as Speaker, needed to vote. Colfax stared down the opposition in Congress and in his own state and insisted on casting his vote for all posterity to see.

In a similar show of spine, Rep. Kevin McCarthy (R-CA), then Minority Leader of the House, took to the floor to condemn the actions of the outgoing President and the mayhem that occurred at the Capitol on January 6, 2021. He forcefully noted that Trump bore responsibility for the attack and signaled that his party would choose law and order over the chaos that Trump caused before, during and after January 6. Unlike the principled Colfax, McCarthy caved within weeks and made a personal pilgrimage to Mar-a-Lago to reestablish his fealty to the ex-President.

In his first term as Speaker of the House, Kevin McCarthy has shown nothing but blind allegiance to the cult including establishing alliances with the most radical members of his party who continue to fly the Trump banner. This past week brought another example of his weakness. The New York Times reported that McCarthy made a casual comment to an interviewer about Trump's chances in the 2024 Presidential election. "Can he win that election?

Yeah, he can win that election," Mr. McCarthy said. "The question is, is he the strongest to win the election; I don't know that answer."

Even that simple declaration was unacceptable to Team Trump. Within hours, McCarthy was all over right-wing news outlets walking back the comment with the affirmation that Trump was still the "strongest possible candidate" and that he was "stronger today than he was in 2016." McCarthy also called Trump to apologize for any misunderstanding about his devotion.

What Speaker McCarthy and his slim majority in the House of Representatives do not seem to grasp is that Donald Trump is the bombastic captain of a sinking ship. Put aside the drama of his presidency and the constant anxiety of investigations, impeachments, and chaos that he caused. Trump's current legal entanglements and the new indictments that are likely to come, mean that the Republican Party could be saddled with a leader who spends more time in court than on the campaign trail next year.

Judge J. Michael Luttig a conservative jurist appointed by President George W. Bush who served on the United States Court of Appeals Fourth Circuit for 15 years wrote a recent essay entitled: *It's Not too Late for the GOP.*

"Building the Republican campaign around the newly indicted front-runner is a colossal political miscalculation," writes Judge Luttig. "No assemblage of politicians except the Republicans would ever conceive of running for the American presidency by running *against* the Constitution and the rule of law. But that's exactly what they're planning."

The Republican leadership may be groveling to Trumpism but Judge Luttig is not. Here is his unequivocal assessment of the coming election: "There is no path to the White House for Republicans with Mr. Trump. He would need every single Republican and independent vote, and there are untold numbers of Republicans and independents who will never vote for him, if for no other perfectly legitimate reason than that he has corrupted America's democracy and is now attempting to corrupt the country's rule of law."

Still, politicians are willing to put principles aside and ignore their own oaths to defend the constitution because they fear the wrath of a petulant candidate and his minions. Trump remains the front runner because very few Republicans have the courage to call him out.

Unless more of them stand up for the Constitution and the rule of law, the Republicans will fall under the weight of a self-serving candidate with slim prospects of putting together a winning majority in the fall of 2024. In the past, there have been shining examples of leaders who put the country over party even when it involved great personal and political risk. The country is searching for those statesmen today.

BALD-FACED LIES

JULY 7, 2023

It used to be a stinging rebuke to accuse someone of uttering a bald-faced lie. The phrase goes back to the 16th century when men wore whiskers and masks and were rarely seen with a "bald face." The visage of a shaved man could be read more easily than one who was hiding behind a beard or a mask. Today, someone caught in a bald-faced lie knows that his words are obviously false. This does not stop him from lying to us anyway.

Journalists have raised fact-checking to an art form. They parse the statements of candidates on a scale that ranges from misleading to "pants-on-fire." It is no secret that the former President set new records in making pronouncements that were demonstrably false. The New York Times chronicled 30,000 such statements over the course of Donald Trump's Presidency. Those comments were dangerous because it caused our allies to question the stability of America itself. They were even more impactful to his base of supporters who bought into the notion that a Presidential election had been rigged. Motivated by a leader spouting bald-faced lies, they stormed the U.S. Capitol in an attempt to impede the election of the new President.

The Republic survived the attack and our judicial system is slowly meting out justice to the people who lied shamelessly to all of us. The followers who swallowed those lies and acted on them are going to jail in the hundreds. You would think that America has learned to avoid the snake-oil of self-serving salesmen. Not so.

The fundraising arm of Trump's presidential campaign reports that it has raised more than $35 million in the three months since the first indictment of the ex-President on charges of fraud related to hush money paid to a porn star.

In that time, a second indictment relating to mishandling of documents has raised concerns about national security. These developments are in addition to a guilty verdict returned on charges of defamation relating to sexual abuse in New York.

But the pitch team Trump keeps making to its mailing list is that the entire judicial system is corrupt and that none of the charges or the actual conviction are legitimate. What's more, the match that lights the fire under MAGA donors is still that the 2020 election was rigged. Notwithstanding a 7 million vote defeat and rejection of challenges in courtrooms across the country, MAGA contributors continue to fork over money in solidarity with the big lie.

To those of us not involved with the cult, it is bewildering. It is inconceivable that the entire MAGA movement is willfully swallowing the fantasy about a stolen election. It is equally shocking that far right Republicans pander to a candidate who is lying about the 71 felony charges he is facing. Surely the GOP can do better than to nominate a candidate who exploits indictments for serious crimes and uses them to shake the money tree even harder.

In 1976, a candidate emerged with a unique message for Americans weary from the Watergate nightmare. Jimmy Carter rose to the presidency with a simple slogan but an important promise: "I will never lie to you." His administration suffered from an extended oil crisis, an Iranian hostage situation and a general economic malaise for which he took responsibility. Carter was not effective with the inside baseball of Washington politics. He eventually succumbed to the communication skills of his successor, Ronald Reagan. But Carter left office with the knowledge that he had lived up to his own standards and that he had restored the integrity of truth to the nation's political discourse.

It is noteworthy that several declared GOP candidates have begun to distance themselves from Trump. Former Governor Asa Hutchinson (R-AR), said recently of Trump: "I do not believe he's the right one to lead our country, and we're going to have a massive loss if he is our nominee." Will Hurd, a self-described common sense Republican from Texas, has taken issue with most of Trump's antics. Former Governor Chris Christie (R-NJ) may be the loudest voice for a return to reason in this early election fight. The home page of his website proclaims: "The truth matters. Chris Christie believes in it, champions it, and isn't afraid to tell it like it is."

Whether truth prevails over bald-faced lies remains to be seen. It is worth the fight.

GOOD AND EVIL

JULY 28, 2023

The drama of new indictments for the former President and the implosion of the Hunter Biden plea agreement are keeping most pundits on overdrive at the moment. Much of what makes the news is the worst possible versions of current events coming from increasingly hostile corners. It is hard to ferret out the truth when political combatants are more interested in inflicting pain on each other.

Sometimes reality seeps in at unusual moments. A Republican friend of mine posed a thoughtful question when we were on the golf course recently: What happened to us? When did we get to be so mean to each other? It only took a post-round beer for two grown-ups with different political perspectives to reach the same conclusion: It doesn't have to be this way.

It turns out that this is not a frivolous matter. The current issue of National Geographic has a feature article entitled: "Is the World in an Empathy Deficit?" The article discusses the origin and prevalence of what the Germans call *schadenfreude*—the feeling of pleasure at other people's misfortune. It goes on to suggest that the barrage of nastiness from social media posts is more assaultive than illuminating. It also suggests that the pandemic drove us further into the bias of our personal shells.

Whatever the cause, one does not need to look far to see examples of evil working its way into the public discourse. On a cable network show, one talking head suggested that there were positive aspects to the Holocaust. The shocking comment was a continuation of a discussion about slavery and the absurd notion that the enslaved might have actually benefitted from their bondage. In fact, a new denialism about the horrors of humans owning other humans is creeping into classrooms in the south. According to the anti-woke crowd, slaves should have been grateful that they learned a trade even though it may have been beaten in to them.

So, the question on the talk show was: do you believe there were any benefits to the Holocaust? Maybe, responded one of the cretins. He suggested that prisoners learned to survive in a concentration camp by being useful. The reaction from the Auschwitz Memorial, was immediate: "Being skilled or useful did not spare Jewish people from the horrors of the gas chambers." The White House press office weighed in on both topics: "There was nothing good about slavery; there was nothing good about the Holocaust. Full stop."

Sometimes political leaders go beyond hurtful rhetoric. In Texas, Governor Greg Abbott is deploying buoys in the Rio Grande River to deter migrants from swimming across the border. This, says the U.S. Department of Justice, is in violation of the Rivers and Harbors Act that requires federal permission for building any structures in U.S. waters. What's worse is that the barriers pose threats to navigation and to the safety of border guards who must maneuver around the buoys to do their jobs.

But the truly evil aspect of the Abbott buoys is that they are designed to cause physical harm to anyone who comes in contact with them. These are barrels wrapped in razor sharp wire that menaces people who are already desperate. For the most part, these are women and children who have already risked everything to seek new lives. Whether they are eligible for asylum or not, more than a few of these human beings will challenge the buoys and be sliced up by the floating barrier—a made-for-television moment devised by a petty Governor. Surely, we are capable of developing an immigration policy that doesn't use women and children as pawns in a mean-spirited game.

We may be losing our capacity to discern good from evil. It may be necessary for all of us to relearn the lessons from our childhoods about right and wrong. It is not good enough to shake our heads and criticize the atrocities of the day. We need to do better as Americans and understand that thinking clearly and kindly is a way to bridge the gaps between us.

Sometimes we can make progress over a round of golf and a beer.

SOMETIMES CONTRIBUTORS SHOULD JUST SAY NO

AUGUST 17, 2023

In this era of social media, candidates have learned how to blanket voters with a constant stream of fundraising requests. Anyone who has ever donated to a political campaign can count on an increasing barrage of requests from contenders for office who may not be from their own state or from their own party for that matter. This is because candidates share lists with each other and cross pollinate their campaigns with small donors who respond to their urgent internet pleas.

The lifeblood of any campaign is money. As a believer in a robust two-party system, I continue to urge all citizens to vote, volunteer, and contribute generously to the candidates of their choice. It seems to me that doling out small checks to every candidate who manages to find your e-mail address is not the best way to participate. Look for opportunities to attend a few events for those candidates whose positions have earned your personal and financial support. If possible, meet the candidate or his staff to assure that you are betting on the right horse.

The reality is that the small dollar, internet driven fundraising is a fraction of what candidates need to run for office. Congressional campaigns that once cost $500,000 to $1 million are now approaching $15 million and up. Governors and U.S. Senate Candidates are now facing $100 million campaigns. Much of this money is solicited by and routed through PAC committees that support campaigns but, supposedly, operate independently from the candidate. The U.S. Supreme Court decision in the Citizens United case allowed unlimited amounts of corporate cash to be provided by PACS unbridled by the limits placed on individual contributions in federal elections.

This has pushed modern campaign seasons into multibillion enterprises that drown us all in non-stop advertising. This has already begun for the 2024 Presidential season.

To all donors, here is a timeless admonition: "Caveat emptor." Let the buyer beware. The New York Times did an expose that concluded that the former president is using money from small donors to defend himself legally. His Save America PAC has spent tens of millions of dollars over the past two years defending Trump. With new indictments came new legal fees and the Times notes that Save America spent $16 million in 2022 and has already shelled out $27 million this year.

FEC regulations require that campaign dollars cannot be used for personal expenses. The campaign skirts the issue by saying that all of the charges were related to actions related to Trump's former official duties. While this may be technically true, the question that remains: Is it ethical? Or is it an abuse of campaign donors?

With this background, the Philadelphia Inquirer reports that Trump's Save America PAC is hosting a high dollar fundraiser in Philadelphia next month. It is reported that tickets for the event run as high as $23,200 per couple which includes a VIP reception and a photo with the former President. Here's a suggestion to all of those who received the on-line invitation: Just say no.

Campaign operatives around the country know that there are big donors in both parties in Philadelphia. These are businesspeople, lawyers, bankers, other highly successful professionals who know how to influence campaigns and to establish relationships with political leaders. They are also well aware of the odds of their candidate winning and the way in which their money will be spent in that effort. That is why candidates view Philadelphia contributors as "smart money."

There are two specific reasons for those contributors to beware of bolstering the Trump bank. First, Trump is a flawed candidate who is facing litigation in four different jurisdictions. The most jarring of the 91 charges that he faces is the accusation that Trump and his cronies willingly and knowingly joined in a criminal operation to unlawfully overturn the results of the Presidential election. At best, Donald Trump will be spending most of the primary season in courtrooms. At worst, he could be the only Presidential candidate to run a campaign from a prison cell.

Secondly, your money may not be advancing any political or policy agenda at all. The unwillingness of Donald Trump to shoulder his own legal fees and the ability to tap into campaign contributions means that he will continue to exploit small and large donors who are blindly tossing money at a man who defies the U.S. Constitution and the rule of law.

Just say no.

THE POLITICS OF RAGE

AUGUST 24, 2023

It took Florida Governor Ron DeSantis all of fifteen seconds to toss out the opening snarkiness in the GOP Presidential debate. "Let's send Biden back to his basement." The line was received well by an excitable audience who reacted noisily to similar canned lines throughout the evening. For the most part, the debate seemed more like a MAGA pep rally than a serious discussion about the issues.

One clear shortcoming of the debate format was the disruptive nature of the studio audience. They hooted their approval of extreme positions on climate change, education, and immigration, and they made sure that the candidates knuckled under to their preferred front runner. Playing to that audience and the far-right wing of their party, six of the contenders failed the test of leadership when they meekly acknowledged that they would support Trump—even if he was convicted of the felonies that he now faces in four jurisdictions.

Governor Asa Hutchinson of Arkansas and Governor Chris Christie had the temerity to call out the former President and their own party. Hutchinson said that he would not support a felon for President; Christie said that Trump's behavior was beneath the dignity of the Presidency. Both were loudly booed for their statements.

At the outset of the 2024 campaign, the Republican Party is careening toward nominating a man who may contend for the Presidency from a jail cell. At the very least, Trump will be dividing his time between the campaign trail and four different court proceedings next year. The federal and Fulton County indictments paint a damning picture of a desperate man who appears to have willfully violated the Constitution and broken countless laws just to hold onto power. Yet, given the choice between supporting our fundamental belief in the rule of law or groveling to a dangerously flawed megalomaniac, the party faithful continue to grovel.

What's worse is that they do so with rage. Watching the audience at the debate jump to their feet to cheer on a candidate who didn't even bother to show up was telling. There was no way for any other contender to score debate points when all the audience wanted was their red meat. Border walls, book bans, election fraud—all of the far-right grievances crowded out any real chance to actually address issues.

Vivek Ramaswamy, the upstart entrepreneur from Ohio added gasoline to the fire by providing a long list of ideas attached to no reality except the roar of the crowd. He called climate change a hoax in the midst of a summer of unprecedented natural disasters. He would curtail election rights and women's rights because that is what the beast demands.

Ramaswamy may have stepped too far when it came to foreign policy. When he opposed further aid to Ukraine, it was former Governor Nikki Haley who reacted with her own rage. Haley, who served as Ambassador to the United Nations, pointed out the existential crisis for democracy in Ukraine and the global implications of the conflict. She showed her credentials as a thoughtful leader and demolished the vapid position of Ramaswamy. "You have no foreign policy experience," she said, "and it shows."

Haley also broke out of the morass of Trumpism when she took on deficit spending by both parties. She challenged GOP assertions of fiscal restraint when she noted the $8 trillion deficit incurred in the Trump administration. She also searched for consensus on what may be the thorniest issue facing Republican candidates throughout the country—abortion rights. While the other candidates locked themselves into untenable positions that were guaranteed to alienate women voters, Haley broke through with a proposal to reach across ideological lines to find common ground. A rare glimmer of statesmanship in the darkness that hung over the debate for most of the evening.

Other pundits have weighed in on the numbers and other questions. Who won? Who lost? Who will have the courage to rise up against the tide of anger that blinds some voters to the reality of the moment? With the possible exception of Nikki Haley's clarity and Chris Christie's direct challenge to the front runner, little has changed. The party faithful continues to snub any candidacy that presents a real challenge to Donald Trump. The mug shot has become a rallying cry for defiance. It makes his base even more angry.

There is hope, however. Yes, a majority of Republicans continue to toe the line behind their flawed candidate. But the general election calculus remains the same. Democrats, moderate Republicans, Independents, women, minorities, and rational Americans know that the politics of division is unsustainable. Even if Trump survives his legal challenges, he will face a more thoughtful electorate in the fall. Americans have proven that they are good stewards of the Republic notwithstanding the occasional flare up of misguided rage.

SELECTED BIBLIOGRAPHY

PART ONE: EARLY OP-EDS

Ambrose, Steven, *D-Day: June 6, 1944: The Climactic Battle of World War* (Simon and Schuster, 1994)

"John Adams to John Quincy Adams, 18 May 1781," *Founders Online,* National Archives, https://founders.archives.gov/documents/Adams/04-04-02-0082. [Original source: *The Adams Papers*, Adams Family Correspondence, vol. 4, *October 1780–September 1782*, ed. L.H Butterfield and Marc Friedlaender. Cambridge, MA: Harvard University Press, 1973, pp. 117–118.]

Bush, George H.W., University of California, Santa Barbara, February, 1989, https://www.presidency.ucsb.edu/documents/address-administration-goals-before-joint-session-congress

———. D-day statement to soldiers, sailors, and airmen of the Allied Expeditionary Force, 6/44, Collection DDE-EPRE: Eisenhower, Dwight D: Papers, Pre-Presidential, 1916-1952; Dwight D. Eisenhower Library; National Archives and Records Administration.

Herbert Hoover, Foreign Policy Association, https://foreignpolicyblogs.com/2007/08/10/%E2%80%9Colder-men-declare-war-but-it-is-youth-that-must-fight-and-die-and-it-is-youth-who-must-inherit-the-tribulation-the-sorrow-and-the-triumphs-that-are-the-aftermath-of-war%E2%80%9D-herbert-hoove/. [Original Source: Speech to Republican National Convention, June 1944]

———. "Immigration Fact Check: Undocumented Immigrants Already Paying Billions in State/Local Taxes," Keystone Research Center and PA Budget and Policy Center, February 26, 2016, https://krc-pbpc.org/research_publication/immigration-fact-check-undocumented-immigrants-already-paying-billions-in-state-local-taxes/

Kennedy, John F., JFK Presidential Library and Museum, March 1958, https://www.jfklibrary.org/archives/other-resources/john-f-kennedy-speeches/des-moines-ia-19580322

Kessler, Glen, "A history of Trump's promises that Mexico would pay for the wall, which it refuses to do," Washington Post, January 8, 2019, https://www.washingtonpost.com/politics/2019/live-updates/trump-white-house/live-fact-checking-and-analysis-of-president-trumps-immigration-speech/a-history-of-trumps-promises-that-mexico-would-pay-for-the-wall-which-it-refuses-to-do/

Zach Klitzman, "Lincoln and Immigration," President Lincoln's Cottage, July 1, 2019, https://www.lincolncottage.org/lincoln-and-immigration/

Charlie Savage, Adam Goldman, and Katie Benner, "Barr Pressed Durham to Find Flaws in the Russia Inquiry Unraveled," New York Times, January 26, 2023, https://www.nytimes.com/2023/01/26/us/politics/durham-trump-russia-barr.html

"The Sacrifices Made By the Declaration Signers," Michael W. Smith, July 4, 2015, https://michaelwsmith.com/the-sacrifices-made-by-the-declaration-signers/#news

———. "What is Your Life's Blueprint?" The Seattle Times, 2017, "https://projects.seattletimes.com/mlk/words-blueprint.html

Pete Williams and Phil Helsel, "DOJ partially discloses memo on why Trump wasn't charged with obstruction," May 2021, https://www.nbcnews.com/politics/justice-department/doj-partially-discloses-memo-barr-used-clear-trump-obstruction-russia-n1268445

Michelle Ye Hee Lee, "Donald Trump's false comments connecting Mexican immigrants and crime," Washington Post, July 8, 2015, https://www.washingtonpost.com/news/fact-checker/wp/2015/07/08/donald-trumps-false-comments-connecting-mexican-immigrants-and-crime/

PART TWO: 2020 OP-EDS

Nikki Carvajal and Maegan Vazquez, "Trump said he takes no responsibility for any spike in people using disinfectants improperly," CNN, April 27, 2020, https://www.cnn.com/2020/04/27/politics/donald-trump-disinfectants-coronavirus/index.html

Sheldon Drobny, Huff Post, May 25, 2011

David Allan Coe, "You Never Even Called Me by My Name," Lyrics.com, https://www.lyrics.com/lyric/1307803/David+Allan+Coe/You+Never+Even+Called+Me+by+My+Name

Stephen Collinson, "Obama issues a dire warning about American democracy in stunning rebuke of Trump," CNN, August 20, 2020, https://www.cnn.

SELECTED BIBLIOGRAPHY

com/2020/08/20/politics/barack-obama-dnc-speech-donald-trump-joe-biden/index.html

Ralph Waldo Emerson, "Concord Hymn," Poetry Foundation, https://www.poetryfoundation.org/poems/45870/concord-hymn

Faber, Michael, *Book of Strange New Things* (Hogarth, 2014)

Jamie Gangel, Jeremy Herb, and Elizabeth Stuart, "'Play it down': Trump admits to concealing the true threat of coronavirus in new Woodward book," CNN, September 9, 2020, https://www.cnn.com/2020/09/09/politics/bob-woodward-rage-book-trump-coronavirus/index.html

Robin Givhan, "Rudy Giuliani is a Mess," Washington Post, November 18, 2020, https://www.washingtonpost.com/nation/2020/11/18/rudy-giuliani-is-mess/

David Leonhardt, "Trump's Refusal to Concede," The New York Times, November 12, 2020, https://www.nytimes.com/2020/11/12/briefing/ron-klain-jeffrey-toobin-tropical-storm-eta.html

Kennedy, John F., *Profiles in Courage* (Harper Collins, 1955)

Hannah Knowles, "Trump defiant, some 2024 GOP rivals supportive as he faces DOJ charges," Washington Post, June 8, 2023, https://www.washingtonpost.com/politics/2023/06/08/trump-charges-reaction-2024/

Marquez, Gabriel Garcia, *Love in the Time of Cholera* (Editorial Oveja Negra, 1985), 224.

Claire McCaskill, *Deadline Whitehouse with Nicole Wallace*, MSNBC___ National Archives, "President Outlines Pandemic Influenza Preparations and Response," November 1, 2005, https://georgewbush-whitehouse.archives.gov/news/releases/2005/11/20051101-1.html

Grayson Pope, "What to Do When Work is taking Over Your Life" *Relevant Magazine*

Toluse Olorunnipa, Josh Dawsey, Rosalind S. Helderman, and Emma Brown, "Trump Assembles a Ragtag Crew of Conspiracy-Minded Allies in Flailing Bid to Reverse Election Loss," Washington Post, December 21, 2020, https://www.washingtonpost.com/politics/trump-assembles-a-ragtag-crew-of-conspiracy-minded-allies-in-flailing-bid-to-reverse-election-loss/2020/12/21/d7674cd2-43b2-11eb-b0e4-0f182923a025_story.html

Joseph Powers, "Why Joe Biden might be the Warren Harding we need right now," Pennsylvania Capital-Star," August 5, 2020, https://www.penncapital-star.com/commentary/why-joe-biden-might-be-the-warren-harding-we-need-right-now-joseph-r-powers/

Robert Reich, "Trump's Presidency is All But Over," The Day, June 1, 2020, https://www.theday.com/columnists/20200601/trumps-presidency-is-all-but-over/?print

Tom Ridge, "Selfish Protests Against Stay-at-Home Orders Dishonor America's Veterans," USA Today, April 29, 2020, https://www.usatoday.com/story/opinion/2020/04/29/coronavirus-stay-at-home-protests-dishonor-veterans-column/3038871001/

Karl Rove, "This Election Result Won't Be Overturned," Wall Street Journal, November 11, 2020, https://www.wsj.com/articles/this-election-result-wont-be-overturned-11605134335?mod=e2fb

Paul Simon, "Mrs. Robinson," Lyrics.com, https://www.lyrics.com/lyric/26356912/Simon+%26+Garfunkel/Mrs+Robinson

Jeanine Santucci, "Ruth Bader Ginsburg's last wish: 'I will not be replaced until a new president is installed'," USA Today, September 18, 2020, https://www.usatoday.com/story/news/politics/2020/09/18/ruth-bader-ginsburgs-last-wish-replaced-different-president/5832544002/

William Shakespeare, "Hamlet" (1603), 183.

Maegan Vazquez, "Trump now says he wasn't kidding when he told officials to slow down coronavirus testing, contradicting staff," CNN, June 23, 2020, https://www.cnn.com/2020/06/22/politics/donald-trump-testing-slow-down-response/index.html

PART THREE: 2021 OP-EDS

"Aristotle: Politics," Internet Encyclopedia of Philosophy, https://iep.utm.edu/aristotle-politics/

Jeremy Barr, "Fox News Hosts Urged Meadows to Have Trump Stop Jan. 6 Violence, Texts Show," Washington Post, December 13, 2021, https://www.washingtonpost.com/media/2021/12/13/fox-ingraham-hannity-kilmeade-jan-6-trump-texts/

———. The White House, "Remarks by President Biden in Address to a Joint Session of Congress," April 29, 2021, https://www.whitehouse.gov/briefing-room/speeches-remarks/2021/04/29/remarks-by-president-biden-in-address-to-a-joint-session-of-congress/

Clinton, Bill and James Patterson, *The President's Daughter* (Little, Brown, 2021)

Amanda Gorman, "The Hill We Climb," CNBC, January 2021, https://www.cnbc.com/2021/01/20/amanda-gormans-inaugural-poem-the-hill-we-climb-full-text.html

David Leonhardt, "The Future of Voting Rights," The New York Times, March 2, 2021, https://www.nytimes.com/2021/03/02/briefing/andrew-cuomo-myanmar-nigeria-students-kidnapped.html

Ornstein, Norman, *It's Even Worse Than It Looks* (Basic Books, 2016)

Paine, Thomas, *The Age of Reason*, (1794)

Aimee Picchi, "U.S. Debt Default Could Wipe Out 6 Million Jobs and $15 Trillion in Wealth, Moody's Says," CBS News, September 22, 2021, https://www.cbsnews.com/news/debt-ceiling-default-6-million-jobs-15-trillion-wealth/

———. "Republicans – even Mitt Romney – will crash the economy just to make Democrats look bad, Editorial Board writes," The Salt Lake Tribune, September 29, 2021, https://www.sltrib.com/opinion/editorial/2021/09/29/republicans-even-mitt/

Jennifer Rubin, "Biden's Address to Congress Proves We Have an Adult Back in the Presidency," Washington Post, April 28, 2021, https://www.washingtonpost.com/opinions/2021/04/28/bidens-address-congress-proves-we-have-an-adult-back-presidency/

Lydia Saad, "Gallup Vault: Cuba Embargo Popular After Bay of Pigs Fiasco," Gallup Vault, April 14, 2016, https://news.gallup.com/vault/190772/gallup-vault-cuba-embargo-popular-bay-pigs-fiasco.aspx

Schlesinger, Arthur, *Cycles of American History* (Mariner Books, 1986)

Shakespeare, William, *Hamlet* (1599)

Maanvi Singh, "'Study Newsom's Playbook': What Democrats – and Republicans – Can Learn from California's Recall," The Guardian, September 15, 2021, https://www.theguardian.com/us-news/2021/sep/15/california-recall-election-national-us-politics

Van Den Bossche, Edmond, "The Message for Today in Orwell's '1984'," The New York Times, January 1, 1984, https://www.nytimes.com/1984/01/01/nyregion/the-message-for-today-in-orwell-s-1984.html

PART FOUR: 2022 ARTICLES

Tim Alberta, "The Revenge of the Normal Republicans," The Atlantic, March 28, 2022, https://www.theatlantic.com/ideas/archive/2022/03/will-hurd-2024-book/629398/

W.H. Auden, "Musee des Beaux Arts," Emory University, 1940, http://english.emory.edu/classes/paintings&poems/auden.html

W.H. Auden, "September 1, 1939," October 18, 1939, https://poets.org/poem/september-1-1939

Danielle Campoamor, "Uvalde's only pediatrician shares the horror of treating school shooting victims," NBC News, May 29, 2022, https://www.nbcnews.com/news/us-news/uvaldes-only-pediatrician-shares-horror-treating-school-shooting-victi-rcna31045

———. "Carpetbaggers," New World Encyclopedia, https://www.newworldencyclopedia.org/entry/Carpetbaggers

Robert Costa, "Former federal Judge Michael Luttig has stark message for Jan. 6 committee," CBS News, June 15, 2022, https://www.cbsnews.com/news/january-6-committee-michael-luttig-trump/

Emily Dickinson, "Tell All the Truth But Tell it Slant," Poetry Foundation, 1858-1865, https://www.poetryfoundation.org/poems/56824/tell-all-the-truth-but-tell-it-slant-1263

Bob Dylan, "Shelter From the Storm," 1974, https://www.lyrics.com/lyric/824288/Bob+Dylan/Shelter+from+the+Storm

David Frum, "Kevin McCarthy, Have You No Sense of Decency?" *The Atlantic*, June 28, 2022, https://www.theatlantic.com/ideas/archive/2022/06/january-6-hearings-liz-cheney-trump-cover-up/661421/

Michael Gold, Ed Shanahan, Brittany Kreigstein, and Rebecca Davis O'Brien, "George Santos Faces Federal and Local Investigations, and Public Dismay," The New York Times, December 28, 2022, https://www.nytimes.com/2022/12/28/nyregion/george-santos-long-island-investigation.html

John F. Kennedy, Commencement Address at Yale University, June 11, 1962

———. "The Education of an American Politician," JFK Library, https://www.jfklibrary.org/archives/other-resources/john-f-kennedy-speeches/atlantic-city-nj-19570219

Kennedy, John F., *Profiles in Courage* (HarperCollins, 1955)

———. "Abraham Lincoln's Second Inaugural Address," Bill of Rights Institute, https://billofrightsinstitute.org/activities/handout-a-abraham-lincolns-second-inaugural-address

Meacham, Jon, *And There Was Light,* (Random House, 2022)

Dana Milbank, "As One Joe Builds, Another Joe Destroys," Washington Post, January 19, 2022, https://www.washingtonpost.com/opinions/2022/01/19/joe-biden-faces-off-with-joe-manchin/

Sergio Pecanha, "Stop for a Minute. These Space Images are Worth Your Time," Washington Post, July 12, 2022, https://www.washingtonpost.com/opinions/2022/07/12/james-webb-space-telescope-photos-explanation/

Ken Silverstein, "The Bipartisan Lobbying Center: How a Washington Think Tank Advocates for Political Unity - and its Top Donors," Harvard University, July 9, 2013, https://ethics.harvard.edu/blog/bipartisan-lobbying-center

Paul Simon, "El Condor Pasa," 1913, https://www.lyrics.com/lyric/350681/El+Condor+Pasa+%28If+I+Could%29

Paul Simon, "So Long, Frank Lloyd Wright," Lyrics.com, https://www.lyrics.com/lyric/23294691/So+Long+Frank+Lloyd+Wright

———. "As Election Day Nears, Jan. 6 Committee Hearing Serves As a Reminder That Democracy is on the Ballot," The Philadelphia Inquirer, October 19, 2022, https://www.inquirer.com/opinion/editorials/jan-6-committee-hearing-election-denial-20221019.html

———. "Trump Proven Unfit for Power Again," Washington Examiner, June 29, 2022, https://www.washingtonexaminer.com/opinion/editorials/trump-proven-unfit-for-power-again

Benjamin Wallace-Wells, "What to Make of John Fetterman's Struggles at the Pennsylvania Senate Debate," The New Yorker, October 26, 2022

PART FIVE: 2023 ARTICLES

David Darby, "How Much Ignorance Can We Survive?" Daily Montanan, July 10, 2022, https://dailymontanan.com/2022/07/10/how-much-ignorance-can-we-survive/

———. *Harrisburg Patriot News,* January 10, 2023

Claudia Lopez Lloreda, "What Killed Beethoven? DNA From Hair Provides Clues," Science.org, March 23, 2023, https://www.science.org/content/article/what-killed-beethoven-dna-hair-provides-clues#:~:text=Fragments%20of%20hepatitis%20B%20DNA,disease%20and%20ultimately%20his%20demise.

Roy S. Johnson, "Face it America, We Love Our Guns More Than We Love Our Children," AL.com, March 28, 2023, https://www.al.com/opinion/2023/03/roy-s-johnson-face-it-america-we-love-our-guns-more-than-our-children.html

MacKay, Charles, *Extraordinary Popular Delusions and the Madness of Crowds,* (Broadway Books, 1995)

Jessica Orwig, "Neil DeGrasse Tyson's Best Quotes Will Make You Fall in Love With Science All Over Again," Science Alert, November 24, 2015, https://www.sciencealert.com/neil-degrasse-tyson-s-best-quotes-may-make-you-fall-in-love-with-science-all-over-again

Brian Stelter, "'Ignorance is a virus:' How local news outlets are reporting on Covid-19 vaccine rejection," CNN, August 10, 2021, https://www.cnn.com/2021/08/10/media/covid-19-vaccine-rejection-news-coverage-reliable-sources/index.html

ABOUT THE AUTHOR

MARK SINGEL worked as a contract lobbyist and a consultant from 1995 through 2021. From 1987 through 1995, Singel was Lieutenant Governor and, for a period of time, Acting Governor of the Commonwealth. The only person in Pennsylvania history to serve an extended period as Acting Governor, Singel received high marks for his stewardship. He led the state by enacting the first modern workers' compensation reform package, refinanced the state's park system through the "Key 93" program, and helped launch the high-tech era with landmark telecommunications legislation. He was also instrumental in reducing state and local taxes, the implementation of a statewide 911 emergency phone system, and the creation of thousands of new jobs in recycling and environmental technologies. He was the original author of the state's mortgage assistance bill that has saved 50,000 Pennsylvania homes.

Prior to his terms as Lieutenant Governor, Singel served six years in the Pennsylvania State Senate and was chief of staff to two members of the U.S. Congress.

Singel ran for U.S. Senate in 1992 and for Governor in 1994. He served as Chairman of the Pennsylvania Democratic Party from 1995-1998 and was the President of Pennsylvania's Electoral College in January 1997.

Upon leaving public service, he founded Singel Associates and later established The Winter Group which developed into one of the most effective and prestigious government relations firms in the state.

Singel served as chairman of Governor Ed Rendell's Transition Executive Committee and maintains strong personal and political ties with leaders at all levels today. Singel maintains collegial relationships with key members of the House and Senate on both sides of the aisle and is a known Harrisburg "insider" with a reputation for getting results.

ABOUT THE AUTHOR

A magna cum laude graduate of Penn State, Singel has served on the Boards of Penn State and St. Francis Universities. He holds several honorary doctorate degrees and currently serves as the Chairman of the Board of Trustees of Harrisburg University of Science and Technology. He is the author of a book about his service as Acting Governor entitled: "A Year of Change and Consequences," and a book about the life and times of Thaddeus Stevens.

Singel is considered a key operative at the state level and is a regular commentator on local and statewide political broadcast programs. He is a sought-after speaker at both political and academic events and is active in numerous community and philanthropic activities.

Singel has been married to Jacqueline for 47 years and has three children and six grandchildren.

www.ingramcontent.com/pod-product-compliance
Lightning Source LLC
Chambersburg PA
CBHW011949150426
43194CB00019B/2853